MORE WITNESSES TO THE BAPTIST HERITAGE

More Witnesses to the Baptist Heritage retells the Baptist story from the perspective of those too often consigned to the margins of history. But as the collection reveals, these characters were more than witnesses. Pivotal players, they shaped and influenced Baptists in new and progressive ways, particularly in the realms of racial, economic, and gender justice. As a result, the volume's incisive reflections testify to a Baptist identity that is bold, innovative, and liberative, a proclamation for Baptists today as they look to the future.

—Elizabeth H. Flowers, associate professor of American Religion, Baylor University

Professor Williams has done it again! This follow-up companion to *Witnesses to the Baptist Heritage* provides twenty-four additional informative biographical articles on a variety of Baptists, a valuable resource for Baptists and non-Baptists alike. In a time when denominationalism is being disparaged by many, these inspiring brief biographies by top-notch historians show how Baptist Christians have made a difference. This volume expands the number of women and African Americans included and hints at a volume to come that will focus on Baptists around the world. Thank you, Michael Williams and Mercer University Press, for providing a distinctive, must-have resource!

—William M. Pinson, Jr., executive director emeritus, Baptist General Convention of Texas; director, Texas Baptist Heritage Center; and distinguished university professor, Dallas Baptist University

What has mattered to the Baptist people since their seventeenth century beginning? Read these brief biographies by these diverse historians and you will surely know. Thanks to Michael Williams for believing that biography is a tasty way to teach the Baptist tradition.

—Walter B. Shurden, minister at large, Mercer University

Religious history can be written from top down or bottom up, from the perspective of pulpit or pew. Baptists have often preferred a third option because their loose polity clears space for charismatic, plodding, non-conforming, even quietly subversive individuals who leave their mark on an otherwise turgid institutional church. This excellent volume continues that fascinating exploration.

— Wayne Flynt, distinguished university professor emeritus, Auburn University

The James N. Griffith Series in Baptist Studies

This series on Baptist life and thought explores and investigates Baptist history, offers analyses of Baptist theologies, provides studies in hymnody, and examines the role of Baptists in societies and cultures around the world. The series also includes classics of Baptist literature, letters, diaries, and other writings. For a complete list of titles in the series, visit www.mupress.org and visit the series page.

—C. Douglas Weaver, Series Editor

More Witnesses to the Baptist Heritage

Twenty-Four More Baptists Every Christian Should Know

Edited by Michael E. Williams, Sr.

MERCER UNIVERSITY PRESS
Macon, Georgia

MUP/ P632

Published by Mercer University Press
1501 Mercer University Drive
Macon, Georgia 31207

25 24 23 22 21 5 4 3 2 1

Books published by Mercer University Press are printed on acid-free paper that meets the requirements of the American National Standard for Information Sciences—Permanence of Paper for Printed Library Materials.

Printed and bound in the United States.

This book is set in Adobe Caslon Pro.

Cover/jacket design by Burt&Burt.

ISBN 978-0-88146-806-9
Cataloging-in-Publication Data is available from the Library of Congress

Contents

Dedicated in honor of Teresa Yarbrough and Stephanie Joyner,
my great sisters-in-law;

To the memory of Brenda Bradley, friend, saint, poet,
and witness to the Baptist heritage;

And to honor Robbie, my always.

MERCER UNIVERSITY

MERCER UNIVERSITY PRESS

Endowed by

TOM WATSON BROWN

and

THE WATSON-BROWN FOUNDATION, INC.

Acknowledgments

As always, I am grateful to Mercer University Press for their continued publication of books on Baptist history. I thank my colleagues and students at Dallas Baptist University, especially those who have heard these stories, for their encouragement. Of course, major thanks goes to all the contributors to this volume, especially those who wrote for my first volume, *Witnesses to the Baptist Heritage.* A special thank-you goes to one of the contributors, Brian Franklin, who read many of the chapters and made helpful suggestions and proofreading corrections. I am also thankful to our dean of the Dallas Baptist University College of Humanities and Social Sciences, Rob Sullivan; to our history department chair, Greg Kelm; to former secretaries/administrative assistants, Tina Bourgeois and Erin Smith; and especially to the current administrative assistant in Humanities and Social Sciences and graduate student in history, Taylor Gee, for her technical assistance with merging the manuscript, and with the index. I am very thankful to Provost Norma Hedin and DBU President Adam Wright for their support and for the sabbatical they granted me in 2019. It was used in part to work on this manuscript as well as other research and writing and in part to give family care to my parents and brother. A special thanks goes to my friends, Randall Bradley, Jan Kennamer Hart, and Wanda Allen for their steadfast encouragement of all my writing and editing. As always, I am thankful for the love and support of my wife, Robbie, our three sons, Michael, Josh, and Carey, and our daughters-in-law, Allison and Morgan, and our soon-to-be daughter-in-law Shelby. In this season, I am especially grateful for the joy that our grandsons Jackson and Luke bring to our lives. This book is dedicated to my great Christian sisters-in-law Teresa and Stephanie. It is also dedicated to the memory of my good friend, Brenda Bradley, saint, poet, encourager, friend, and witness to the Baptist heritage. Finally, it is dedicated, as are all of my books whether they say so or not, to Robbie always.

Contributors

LARRY ASHLOCK, President of the Baptist Center for Global Concerns in Arlington, Texas

KAREN O'DELL BULLOCK, Distinguished Professor of Christian Heritage and Director of the PhD Program, B. H. Carroll Theological Institute, Irving, Texas

PAMELA R. DURSO, President of Central Baptist Theological Seminary, Shawnee, Kansas

JOHN INSCORE ESSICK, Associate Professor of Church History and Director of the Rural Ministry Program, Baptist Seminary of Kentucky, Georgetown, Kentucky

BRIAN FRANKLIN, Associate Director of SMU Center for Presidential History and Adjunct Lecturer in the Clements Department of History, Southern Methodist University, Dallas, Texas

JACK GOODYEAR, Dean of Gary Cook Graduate School of Leadership and Professor of Political Science, Dallas Baptist University, Dallas, Texas

MICHELLE HENRY, Department Chair and Professor of English, Dallas Baptist University, Dallas, Texas

DAVID HOLCOMB, Professor of History and Political Science and Director of the Honors Program, University of Mary Hardin-Baylor, Belton, Texas

LAURA RODGERS LEVIN, Assistant Professor of Christian Missions, Baptist Seminary of Kentucky, Georgetown, Kentucky

MELODY MAXWELL, Associate Professor of Church History and Director of Acadia Centre for Baptist and Anabaptist Studies, Acadia Divinity College, Wolfville, Nova Scotia, Canada

MANDY MCMICHAEL, Associate Director and J. David Slover Assistant Professor of Ministry Guidance, Baylor University Religion Department, Waco, Texas

PHILIP IRVING MITCHELL, Director of the University Honors Program and Associate Professor of English, Dallas Baptist University, Dallas, Texas

DAVID W. MUSIC, Professor Emeritus of Academic Studies in the School of Music, Baylor University, Waco, Texas

COURTNEY PACE, Prathia Hall Scholar in Residence in Social Justice History, Equity for Women in the Church, Memphis, Tennessee

KELLY D. PIGOTT, Professor of Church History, Hardin-Simmons University, Abilene, Texas

T. LAINE SCALES, Professor, Garland School of Social Work, Baylor University, Waco, Texas

C. DELANE TEW, Professor of History, Samford University, Birmingham, Alabama

MICHAEL E. (MIKE) WILLIAMS, SR., Professor of History, Dallas Baptist University, Dallas, Texas

Introduction

Michael E. Williams, Sr.

"Why another collection of Baptist biographies?" you might ask. As I suggested in the introduction to *Witnesses to the Baptist Heritage: Thirty Baptists Every Christian Should Know*,[1] biography is a great way to tell a story, especially when interwoven with the context out of which the story grows. At a seminar on gender history in 2007, Susan Ware, author of *Why They Marched* and editor of *Notable American Women*, reflected that good biography could open a "window" into "a larger world as well as put a human face on broad historical trends." Further, Ware offered that to write a good biography "was to do good history." As James Friguglietti reported, "She also advised her audience that lives of unfamiliar individuals would prove as valuable as those of more familiar ones." In concluding, Ware urged her listeners, whatever their choice of subjects, to "just do it." Given these words of encouragement from respected historians, my students' heightened interest in biography when I taught Baptist history and used *Witnesses to the Baptist Heritage* for the first time, and the success that the previous volume had in other classrooms, I decided to "just do it" and follow with this second work.[2]

Much of my desire comes from the same passions about Baptist history and biography that generated *Witnesses*, and I wrote about these in its introduction. Part of my motivation also comes from the fact that upon completion of *Witnesses*, I had a list of more Baptists whose stories I believed deserved to be told. I wanted to publish an additional volume to highlight some of these Baptist Christians who dominated the denominational landscape of their eras but have largely been forgotten by Christians today. I also wanted to elevate the stories of many Baptist women and African American Baptists who served as often unsung heroes during

---

[1] *Witnesses to the Baptist Heritage: Thirty Baptists Every Christian Should Know* (Macon, GA: Mercer University Press, 2016).

[2] James Friguglietti, "Writing Past Lives: Biography as History," *Perspectives on History*, November 2007, https://www.historians.org/publications-and-directories/perspectives-on-history/november-2007/writing-past-lives-biography-as-history.

those same periods. In speaking to churches and students about the first volume, I often found that they were most fascinated by the stories of people like Anne Dutton, Nannie Helen Burroughs, Lott Carey, and other forgotten giants of the past.

Like *Witnesses to the Baptist Heritage*, *More Witnesses to the Baptist Heritage* is designed to be a collection of introductory Baptist biographies, longer than dictionary or encyclopedia articles but far shorter than full-length biographies. Also like *Witnesses*, each chapter focuses on one Baptist and why Christians should know more about her or him. The chapters are not exhaustive, and some writers have focused primarily on one aspect of their subjects' lives and ministries. They are written so that students, pastors, and laypeople gain basic knowledge and are inspired to learn more. At the same time, they are written so that a professional historian or scholar might also pick up the book and gain insight from it. To aid the beginning student, most chapters utilize limited annotation but still provide information for further research for more scholarly tasks.

Once again, I have chosen authors for the chapters based on their specific area of interest or their expertise on a particular time period. Many of them contributed chapters to *Witnesses*, while others are individuals I have come to know since editing the first volume four years ago. They are all people I knew I could trust to meet deadlines and do quality work. Once again, I also wanted to utilize young—at least younger than me—Baptist historians and scholars to write many of the chapters while sprinkling in some seasoned writers. As a result of a greater spotlight on Baptist women and African American Baptists, many of these biographies tell the story of Baptists who are more recently deceased or, in some cases, have not previously been recognized for their contributions to Baptist life. I am often reluctant to utilize biographies of more recent figures because, for some, the verdict may be still out as to their significance for Baptist and Christian history. Despite this reluctance, the reader will find more Baptists who have died in recent years in this volume than in the first book. Some readers may question the inclusion of these selections to the exclusion of others, but hopefully readers will judge these biographies on their own merit.

Likewise, I hope the reader will remember those biographies in the first volume and recognize the slight difference in the approach for this one. As I said in the introduction to *Witnesses*, of course there will be some readers who will wonder why I left out their favorite Baptist again, or why either the editor or the author has categorized a Baptist known for multiple contributions or achievements in one way or another. For those questions, I refer the reader to the introduction to *Witnesses*. I hope that the quality of the following chapters will outweigh any perceived shortcomings that I may have created in my attempts to categorize them. The fact that some key Baptists are included while others are left out demonstrates once again the rich heritage of witnesses that Baptist life and thought have generated over the past four centuries. I also hope that this contribution, like *Witnesses*, may cause historians to widen their gaze and identify more international Baptists and lesser-known Baptists who do not appear in this volume and "just do it" regarding their own future projects. As the subtitle for both volumes suggests, one of my greatest hopes is that the broader Christian community will learn more about this strange people called "Baptists" and recognize how much Baptists have contributed to Christian history, to history in general, and to the world at large.

Obadiah Holmes (1610–1682), *Freedom's Warrior*

Religious Liberty

Karen O'Dell Bullock

The year was 1638. The sturdy glassmaker stoked the fire with fresh billets and stirred the cauldrons on the furnace wings as he pondered: Would the decision to journey to "Ye Wilderness" be the right one for himself and his family? The answer to his question would set in motion a life whose legacy cannot be forgotten to this day. A New England settler, a persecuted Baptist minister, and a legend in his own lifetime, Obadiah Holmes has a story that inspires the spirit, challenges the heart, and is worthy of passing down to the generations.

Early Years in England

In early March 1610, Obadiah Holmes was born into a glassmaker's family at Reddish, near the village of Didsbury close to Manchester in Lancastershire, England.[1] He was baptized at the parish church as a babe on March 18, one of six sons and daughters of Robert Hulme and Katherine Johnson. While he and his brothers attended Brasenose College at Oxford, Holmes admitted later to having a "turbulent youth, full of wild rebellion" and hot-tempered restlessness. He wrote of this time, "from a child I minded nothing but folly, and vanity…. I was not only rebellious against my parents but against the Lord…continuing in such a course for four or five years…."[2] His behavior grieved his devout parents, who never ceased to love and care for him and to pray for his soul's transformation.

---

[1] Louis Franklin Asher, *John Clarke (1609–1676): Pioneer in American Medicine, Democratic Ideals, and Champion of Religious Liberty* (Pittsburgh, PA: Dorrance Publishing Company, 1997), 2–4; and George Andrews Moriarty, "Additions and Corrections to Austin's Genealogical Dictionary of Rhode Island," in *The American Genealogist* 19 (1942–1943): 221–29. Holmes's birthdate is still debated by historians, who place it between 1606 and 1610. His name was also variously spelled until early in the eighteenth century, when it settled into the spelling now known as "Holmes." These spelling variations are partly to blame for the confusion about his birth year.

[2] James T. Holmes, *The American Family of Rev. Obadiah Holmes* (Columbus, OH: private, 1915), 12. This is a document containing several hundred original

At about age twenty, three important things happened that changed the course of his life. The first was the illness of his mother and his certainty, upon her deathbed, that his rebellion had contributed to her demise. They reconciled before she died, for which he was ever grateful to God. He then experienced a "spiritual awakening." He began to read his Bible, spent much time in prayer, and committed his heart and life wholly to Jesus Christ. He felt called to preach the Bible and to speak of Christ with whomever would listen. The last of the life-changing events was his marriage to Catherine Hyde (1608–1682) at Collegiate Church in Manchester on November 20, 1630. Three years later, they became parents of baby John, who died as an infant and was buried at Stockport in the family plot.

A yearning to move to "Ye Wilderness" began to tug at their imaginations. England was convulsing on the brink of civil war, and daily routines became almost impossible as skirmishes broke out between the King's men, the Loyalists, and those who called for more popular freedoms—the Parliamentarians, with whom Obadiah's family identified. The glasshouse business came to a halt as violence spewed across the land. The dream to flee became a reality in 1638 when Obadiah and Catherine, with their new young son Jonathan, packed their belongings and set sail from Preston, northwest of Manchester. They landed six weeks later in Boston and made their way some thirty miles up the seaboard to Salem, a village in the Massachusetts Bay Colony.[3] They soon learned that life in the New World was not all that they had expected.

Settling In and Out of Salem

In Salem, Obadiah and Catherine Holmes were greeted warmly and granted two acres of land by the village. Holmes and two others set up a glass-making factory there, the first of its kind in the colony, specializing in windowpanes. In March 1639 they became members of the Puritan

---

sources, including letters, court documents, wills, bills of sale, family records, genealogical research, published eyewitness accounts, and other materials copied into the volume. It also includes three series of documents written by Obadiah in 1675, each written to a different group: church members and friends; his children; and his beloved wife, Catherine, who died a few days after Obadiah in 1682. A digital copy is available at https://archive.org/stream/americanfamilyof00holm/americanfamilyof00holm_djvu.txt.

[3] John Osborne Austin, *Genealogical Dictionary of Rhode Island* (Albany, NY: J. Munsell's Sons, 1887), 104.

church in Salem, which seemed almost immediately to be a poor fit. Under laws compelling attendance, almsgiving, and behavioral strictures, Obadiah considered the Puritanism practiced there to be more rigid than they had ever known. He had long questioned whether civil authorities should dictate matters of conscience and faith, and his questions about the validity of infant baptism and restrictive church practices put him at odds with Salem's civil and church leaders. Commanded to keep silent, Holmes refused. By 1644, the immigrants were no longer welcome at Salem. They determined to move away from Massachusetts Bay, which was gaining a reputation for persecuting those who dissented from the established church.

Rehoboth and Resistance

After selling his Salem acreage, Holmes purchased property in a newly created settlement called Rehoboth, known then as Seekonk, some forty miles south of Boston in the Plymouth Colony. Obadiah moved his family there in 1646. By this time, he was thirty-six, the father of five children, and in his prime. He had also been labeled "perverted in faith and excommunicated therefore" when he received word that the Salem church had cast them out. His brush with the Puritan establishment's opinion of him followed the couple to their new home.

The Holmes family became part of the Puritan church in Rehoboth, pastored by Dr. Samuel Newman, who staunchly favored state-supported Puritanism. Obadiah soon earned the respect of many among Rehoboth's congregation who were also exploring the biblical teachings about baptism, communion, ordination, and the role of the state in matters of individual faith. Holmes was convinced that the state should have no jurisdiction over the human heart in matters of belief and conscience. He taught and preached, usually in homes during the week, basing his views about church practice, doctrine, and order on the New Testament church model, where there was no ecclesial hierarchy and no state interference. Instead, he taught that the Holy Spirit gifted each believer in Jesus Christ to do the work of God, that baptism existed only for those who followed Christ voluntarily, and that believers had no need of a priest to stand as mediator between the believer and God.[4]

By 1649, Reverend Newman and Rehoboth's leaders had found Obadiah's teachings intolerable. Obadiah and Catherine, together with

[4] Holmes, *American Family*, 18.

several other men and women, had been baptized as believers in Christ by Baptist missionary church planter Dr. John Clarke. Together with others, they had become Baptists and met in homes on Sundays. Obadiah served as their pastor. The matter came to a head in June when the Puritan church in Rehoboth excommunicated Obadiah and his small group. Following this indictment, four months later Obadiah went to court to clear his name from false charges leveled by his former pastor. As a result of the proceedings, Reverend Newman confessed to perjury, having slandered Holmes without facts or evidence.[5] However, the court ruling in Obadiah's favor only intensified the hostility. In early October 1650, the small group was arraigned in court to answer for their dissent and for holding meetings "on the Lord's Day from house to house, contrary to the order of the court." Governor William Bradford, Captain Miles Standish, and John Alden, "gentlemen," declared them guilty and subsequently banished them from the colony. Holmes and fourteen other men and women were left without recourse but to move yet again.

Newport a Safe Haven

Eight miles away a new colony existed, founded in 1636 by Roger Williams. The land had been purchased from his friends, the Narragansett Indians, and was intended to be a refuge, offering "liberty of conscience." Known as Providence Plantations, later Rhode Island, Williams based it on the tenets of religious freedom, separation of church and state, and fair treatment of the Native Americans, both Narragansett and Massasoit, who occupied the region. From the beginning, a majority vote of the heads of households governed the new settlement, but only in civil matters. Newcomers could also be admitted to full citizenship by a majority vote.[6] Here Williams and friends had settled the first place in modern history where citizenship and religion were separate, combined with the principle of majoritarian democracy. Williams also strongly defended the abolition movement, free speech, and believer's baptism, and he is called the Father

[5] Ibid.

[6] In August 1637, the settlers again voted to restrict the government to civil matters. In 1640, thirty-nine freemen, who had full citizenship and voting rights, signed yet another agreement that declared their determination "still to hold forth liberty of conscience." See also Edwin Gaustad, *Liberty of Conscience: Roger Williams in America* (King of Prussia, PA: Judson Press, 1999), 28.

of Baptists in America for establishing the first Baptist church in the New World in 1638/1639.

This new colony's neighbors, however, considered it a threat to the established order and viewed its foundational declarations as "heretical" and "infectious." For the next three decades, Massachusetts, Connecticut, and Plymouth exerted pressure to destroy both Rhode Island and the Narragansetts. In 1643, the neighboring colonies formed a military alliance, called the United Colonies, which pointedly excluded the villages around Narragansett Bay. In response, Williams traveled to London to obtain a charter for the Providence Plantations and returned the following year with the document, signed by King Charles I, in hand.

For Obadiah Holmes and the small band who had been banished from Rehoboth in 1650, Providence Plantations seemed to be a fine prospect, full of like-minded neighbors. The Holmes group met with Williams, who soon became a close friend. Holmes traveled through Providence, heading for the village called Newport, located thirty miles farther on the southwest tip of Aquidneck Island. This settlement had been founded in 1639 by eight men from Portsmouth and was already a thriving port with many businesses and storefronts. Its Baptist church was pastored by one of the original founders, John Clarke, the brother who had baptized the Holmeses. Holmes and his friends quickly became part of the community. They bought land, built houses, and began businesses and farms. They also joined the Baptist congregation at Newport. Obadiah was invited to preach often and was well received, helping John Clarke with the work of pastoring. While they remained inside the Providence colony, they were safe. If they ventured into neighboring territories, however, they knew they would be subject to seizure and arraignment. Obadiah soon experienced these consequences personally.

Persecution in Boston

In July 1651, John Clarke, John Crandall, and Obadiah Holmes, all leaders of the Baptist church, planned a trip up through Providence and then into Massachusetts between Boston and Salem, concerned about former neighbors and the welfare of the fledgling Baptist groups to the north. While passing through the village of Lynn, Massachusetts, they stopped to visit with an elderly friend, William Witter, and his family, who had been members of the church in Newport. Neighbors had heard of the visitors' arrival and on Sunday, July 20, came to attend the house worship service where John Clarke was to preach. As he was reading and expounding Scripture, two constables with warrants broke into the service and arrested the three visitors.

The magistrate, Robert Bridges, charged the three with "conducting services with non-conformity with the statutes" and with worshipping God "according to the dictates of their own consciences" and "not in the places and in the prescriptions and forms of the established civil law regulating worship in the established church." They were also declaring doctrines on the subject of baptism that were described as "heretical in the high degree."[7] Bridges then took Clarke, Crandall, and Holmes from Witter's house to the Puritan church in Lynn, which was holding services at the time and which the civil law required each person to attend. They were hauled before the pastor, and when they did not quickly remove their hats, Bridges knocked them off their heads. John and Obadiah asked that they might be heard "concerning the questions about which they disagreed," but they were denied the privilege. Obadiah was insistent that they be allowed to answer the charges, and for this he was later punished more harshly.[8]

Holmes tells what happened to him, Clarke, and Crandall at this point. The authorities released them for two days, during which they held a preaching service and Obadiah baptized three new converts in the nearby creek. On July 22, they were taken to Boston, about twelve miles south, and held in the common jail to await their trial by the General Court. On July 31, the officers gathered. Governor John Endicott and his Deputy Thomas Dudley, along with Richard Bellingham, William Hibbins, and Increase Nowell, judges of the church, sat in judgment of their case. When the trial commenced, it was called in the broadside of that day a "howling farce," since the prisoners were predetermined to be guilty, no witnesses stood to accuse them, and they were allowed no defense or rebuttal of the charges.[9] Governor Endicott declared that the three men "deserved death, and he would not have such trash brought into his jurisdiction."[10] To make things worse, bystanders cursed and delivered blows to them while they

[7] Holmes, *American Family*, 19.

[8] James Holmes's account of this confrontation at the Lynn church is taken from original sources (*American Family*, 19).

[9] Holmes, *American Family*, 19. Among those who hurled charges was the elderly Reverend John Cotton, a staunchly Puritan leader who died a year later in 1652.

[10] Holmes, *American Family*, 20.

were standing in custody, with no rebuke from the court. Finally, the court handed down sentences.

For having conducted a service outside the jurisdiction of the established Puritan church, for having denied infant baptism, and for preaching and taking communion while under the edict of "excommunication," they fined Obadiah Holmes 30 pounds, John Clarke 20 pounds, and John Crandall 5 pounds. They were to be held in jail until the fines were paid or be "well-whipped." As Holmes was being led away, he spoke to the bar: "I bless God I am counted worthy to suffer for the name of Jesus." At this, the Boston Puritan minister, the Reverend John Wilson, delivered a blow to Obadiah's head, screaming, "The curse of God or Jesus go with thee!"[11]

The three were not without sympathy or supporters, however. Friends quickly raised the funds for Clarke and Crandall and paid them. The two were released. When Holmes found that the money for his fine was also being raised, he refused to accept this intervention. He was firmly convinced that no human authority had the jurisdiction to decide whether or where he could preach. This was a matter of conscience. He denied the right of any civil power to thrust its "hand or mace" between man and his Maker. For Holmes, a higher law was at stake. He said he was responsible to, and governed by, the "Creator and Governor of the Universe."[12] He intended to take the matter further with the General Court. For five weeks he remained in jail. All pleas to appeal his case were denied.

On September 5, 1651, Obadiah Holmes was taken from jail to the whipping post near the market.[13] Increase Nowell attended, but, while the crowds and officers awaited the Governor's arrival, he did not come. Finally, an elder in the Puritan church, Mr. Flint, spoke to the executioner and said, "Fellow, do thine office, for this fellow would make a long speech to delude the people." Nowell signaled to begin. Holmes was bound to the post and stripped to the waist, all the while imploring Nowell for an

[11] Ibid.

[12] See Holmes's statements from his "Last Will and Testament" in Edwin Gaustad, *Baptist Piety: Last Will and Testament of Obadiah Holmes* (Grand Rapids, MI: Arno Press, 1980), 22–29.

[13] The site of the 1650s whipping post today is near the circular cobblestone monument in the street that marks the place where the Boston Massacre of 1770 occurred in front of the Old State House in historic Boston. The Old State House was built in 1712–1713 on the site of an older Town House, constructed in 1657. When Obadiah was taken from jail and whipped at the post erected in this place, none of these events or sites remembered today had occurred yet.

opportunity to speak, which was his right by law. "I am to suffer for...the Word of God and testimony of Jesus Christ," he pled, but his entreaties fell on deaf ears. The thirty lashes began, one for each pound Obadiah owed. The executioner, with two hands gripping the stock of his three-corded whip, slowly delivered each of the strokes—equaling ninety lashes in all due to the three cords. They were intended not merely to fulfill the law but to inflict great suffering in doing so. In this, the executioner was successful. The severe beating ripped every inch of flesh from Obadiah's back, neck to waist. Holmes never uttered a sound.[14]

When the cruel scourging stopped and he was cut free from the post, Holmes stood upright, the blood streaming down his body. He leaned toward the executioner and spoke so that all could hear: "You have whipped me as with roses." Dr. Clarke wrote later "that in many days, if not some weeks, he could take no rest, but as he lay upon his knees and elbows, not being able to suffer any part of his body to touch the bed whereon he lay."[15] Much later, Rhode Island's governor, Joseph Jenckes, wrote, "Those who have seen the scars on Mr. Holmes' back (which the old man was wont to call the marks of the Lord Jesus), have expressed a wonder that he should live."[16] It was many weeks before Holmes could be moved. In the interim, family and friends ministered to him, including John Hazel of Rehoboth, an old Baptist neighbor. Hazel had heard of his imprisonment and public whipping and traveled to sit with him as he recovered. While in Boston, Puritan authorities also arrested, fined, imprisoned, and whipped Hazel, even thought he was sixty years old, for sharing sympathy with his friend Holmes.[17]

The day Obadiah Holmes walked out of jail, as an indication of the depth of malice against him, the authorities issued a new warrant to re-arrest him to face a second whipping, but his friends "defeated the purpose," he later recalled. They "spirited him away" back to Newport, where a great crowd of church members and loved ones met him four miles outside of town and escorted him home. Holmes's friend, Roger Williams, wrote a letter to Governor Endicott, pleading for toleration in matters of conscience and religion, but it found no hearing.

---

[14] Holmes, *American Family*, 22–23.

[15] In Thomas Williams Bicknell, *The Story of Dr. John Clarke* (Little Rock, AR: The Baptist Standard Bearer, Inc., 2005), 48.

[16] In Henry Sweetser Burrage, *A History of the Baptists in New England* (Philadelphia, PA: American Baptist Publication Society, 1984), 37.

[17] Holmes, *American Family*, 26.

In reaction to the whipping, John Clarke left Newport for London in October 1651, where he took up the causes of the colony and pled for religious liberty in the New World. He wrote *Ill News of New England*, which gave an account of Obadiah's persecution, to stir up the English Parliament for freedom of conscience. He remained in London for more than a decade until King Charles II took the throne in 1660 and stamped his seal upon the *Rhode Island Royal Charter* three years later. This document, written by Clarke, granted unprecedented freedom and religious liberty to Rhode Islanders.[18] Holmes became pastor of the Baptist church while Clarke was away and co-pastored with Clarke upon his return in 1664 following his success at procuring the charter. Clarke continued to stay active in civil affairs there until his death in 1676.

Meanwhile, Obadiah continued to pastor, farm, and conduct trade in Newport. He became highly revered as a wise statesman and was one of sixteen representatives requested to advise the colony during the King Philip's War of 1676. Obadiah and Catherine had nine children, eight of whom lived to adulthood and all of whom served Christ faithfully. Their son married a granddaughter of Roger Williams, and sons, grandsons, and great-grandsons became pastors, speaker of the house, general treasurer, governors, and chief justices of Rhode Island. Perhaps the greatest freedom-fighting descendent of all was their sixth-generation grandson, Abraham Lincoln (1809–1865), sixteenth president of the United States,[19] for whom freedom, like his grandfather long before him, was a most precious gift.

On April 9, 1682, Obadiah wrote *The Last Will and Testament of Obadiah Holmes*, in which he bequeathed his material possessions to his family and friends. Of more importance, perhaps, was the testimony he

---

[18] The charter contains unique provisions that make it significantly different from the charters granted to the other colonies. It gave the colonists freedom to elect their own governor and write their own laws, within very broad guidelines, and also stipulated that no person residing in Rhode Island could be "molested, punished, disquieted, or called in question for any differences in opinion in matters of religion." The *Rhode Island Royal Charter* remained in effect for 180 years until 1843, making it the longest-lasting constitutional charter in history. Those liberties were replaced by a new charter, extending rights to all adult males. See "Charter of Rhode Island and Providence Plantations: The Laws of Nature and Nature's God," in Samuel Greene Arnold, *History of the State of Rhode Island and Providence Plantations* 1 (New York: D. Appleton & Company, 1859), 290–369.

[19] Gary Boyd Roberts, *Ancestors of American Presidents* (Boston, MA: New England Historic Genealogical Society, 2009), 49–52.

included about his devotion to Christ and what his unbending stance for his convictions had cost him. This he wrote in order that his family, for generations to come, would know the importance of the principle of religious liberty. When he died six months later on October 15, he was buried in his own field in the family plot, where his grave marker still stands today as a reminder of the courage of the Baptist who was freedom's warrior.[20]

Suggested Reading

Edwin Gaustad, *Baptist Piety: Last Will and Testament of Obadiah Holmes* (Grand Rapids, MI: Arno Press, 1980).

James T. Holmes, *The American Family of Rev. Obadiah Holmes* (Columbus, OH: private, 1915). A digital copy is available at https://archive.org/stream/americanfamilyof00holm/americanfamilyof00holm_djvu.txt.

[20] Originally located in Newport, what was once the old Holmes family farm is now within the township of Middletown, Rhode Island, near the eastern edge of the island. Today, the tiny family burial plot, enclosed within its original stone wall, is called the Reverend Obadiah Holmes Cemetery and is located just off Summerfield Lane near the intersections of Vaucluse and Green End avenues.

Thomas Grantham (c. 1633/1634–1692), Apostolic Messenger and Baptist Defender

Theology

John Inscore Essick

Thomas Grantham's family and friends inscribed his legacy as Baptist luminary even as they laid his body to rest in 1692.[1] An epitaph affectionately summed up the lasting impact of the most important General Baptist leader of the later seventeenth century:

> Within this Tomb, here Lies inclosed a guest
> which was with universall Love possest
> Its famous grantham, whoe is dearly mist
> A preacher, Bishop and Evangelist.
> Of his great worth can none but Angells
> Hasten to him, and them, and soe farewell.

These words convey how beloved and esteemed Thomas Grantham was during his lifetime and underscore the nature of his multifaceted leadership among General Baptists in England. Was there, one may ask, such a thing as a Baptist "Bishop"? This article delves into that question below. After a brief biographical sketch of Grantham's life, we will examine two ministerial roles he capably fulfilled as a witness to the Baptist heritage: messenger and apologist.

Biographical Sketch of Thomas Grantham

The life of "dearly mist" Thomas Grantham began in the large, rural area of Lincolnshire, England. Baptists had been present in the county since at least the 1620s. Grantham was born in 1633/34 to a humble family that

[1] Portions of this chapter have been adapted with permission from the author's book, *Thomas Grantham: God's Messenger from Lincolnshire* (Macon, GA: Mercer University Press, 2013).

supported itself through tailoring and farming, though the larger Grantham family tree was of reputable and "ancient" lineage. Grantham was a self-taught scholar. He may have lacked formal, university education, but evidence exists that he read broadly and developed some facility with Hebrew, Greek, and Latin.

Grantham experienced a conversion in his teenage years, much to his father's chagrin, which eventually led to his 1652 baptismal immersion into the Baptist congregation in Boston (a city in Lincolnshire). Throughout the 1650s he continued to relate to the Boston congregation. In 1656 he took on the responsibility of pastoring a Baptist church in the south marsh area of Lincolnshire, a post he would hold for the next thirty years. In 1666 his fellow Baptists in Lincolnshire ordained Grantham to the office of "Messenger." The office of messenger will be described in more detail below, but it should be noted here that in the mid-seventeenth century messengers constituted a variably understood third group of General Baptist leaders in addition to pastors/elders and deacons. Grantham was the most capable defender of the office of messenger as a distinct third office of church leadership among the Baptists of his day.

When Charles II (1630–1685) returned from the continent to take the English throne in 1660, Grantham's ministry took on a more public and confrontational tone as persecution of Baptists and other radicals increased. Practically speaking, Grantham and other Baptists saw in Charles II a potential guardian against animus directed at religious dissenters. Grantham petitioned King Charles II on behalf of the persecuted General Baptists in Lincolnshire in 1660, 1661, and 1672. In July 1660, for example, Grantham was among several General Baptist leaders to write, sign, and send a *Narrative and Complaint* to Charles II protesting their ill treatment at the hands of local magistrates. Baptists found relief elusive, however, as authorities jailed Grantham and Baptist leaders in the city of Lincoln and otherwise harassed and persecuted them throughout the 1660s and beyond. Grantham did not languish in prison as long or as often as some other Baptists, but the experience of seeing his fellow Baptists spend years in prison or have their corpses dishonorably dug up shaped and sharpened his commitment to defending the Baptist cause. Grantham faced resistance on account of his Baptist beliefs throughout his life and even in death.

Baptists could work with the crown, too, as was the case with government-issued licenses. When Charles II offered to issue licenses to religious dissenters under a "Declaration of Indulgence" in 1672, dissenting groups of all stripes faced a dilemma. Some feared that such an expansive indulgence would open the door for a revival of Roman Catholicism, while others wondered whether accepting a government-issued license amounted to tacit affirmation of the government's right to permit or restrict religious expression as it saw fit. Quakers largely refused to apply for a license. Presbyterians, though divided on the question of licenses, accounted for more licenses than any other group. Baptists did not respond uniformly, either.

Thomas Grantham was among approximately 200 Baptists who registered as a "Teacher" or "Preacher." Charles II's indulgent experiment was short-lived, however, and those dissenters it was designed to protect were soon exposed yet again to the vulnerabilities they had long known. In Norfolk, Grantham instructed Baptists to take a similar path in 1689 and register a meeting place for worship according to the Toleration Act. Such positions and advice were not without controversy, but in all of this Grantham steadily guided the General Baptists in Lincolnshire and Norfolk to work with the civil authorities, whenever possible, in pursuit of peace and order.

Like many Baptists of the period, Grantham stood ready to cooperate with civil authorities as much as possible. In *The Loyal Baptist* (1674) and *Christianismus Primitivus* (1678), Grantham insisted that Baptists sought to be loyal and peaceful citizens. In these documents he unequivocally instructed his readers to avoid revolution or sedition. Instead, he encouraged them to obey laws enacted by civil rulers and uphold the common good. Grantham allowed that Christians could hold government positions and serve as soldiers. He argued that because General Baptists, like other citizens, paid taxes for poor relief and the upkeep of cemeteries, they should share in equal access to governmental benefits. In a time when the government and the established church in England refused to recognize marriages between dissenting Christians, Grantham published a sample marriage certificate for Baptists to use when they conducted their own marriages! Grantham's positions on these issues reflect the degree to which many of the Baptists with whom he associated were—or sought to be—integrated into English civil life. Far from desiring to overturn society, Grantham argued that the baptized believers supported the welfare of England and its people. He did, however, specify that Baptist loyalty was limited by the degree to which laws established by earthly magistrates were consistent with God's decrees.

A prolific writer of more than twenty tracts, pamphlets, and books, Grantham is known for his most famous publication, *Christianismus Primitivus* (published in 1678), a composite work of more than 600 pages. In *Christianismus Primitivus* Grantham made the case for primitive Christianity, a return to what he considered New Testament Christianity. Working from a robust commitment to *sola scriptura* and selective reliance on tradition, Grantham addressed a vast range of issues from across the theological and ecclesiastical spectrum. He wrote at length about Scripture, translation, the divine attributes, Christology, eschatology, angelology, worship, baptism, the Lord's Supper, church polity, Christian discipline, sabbatarianism, the Christian's relationship with civil authorities, the question of whether Christians may hold civil offices, the roles of women in the church, marriage and familial roles, and the proper understanding of the Jewish people. The first systematic theology ever published by a Baptist, *Christianismus Primitivus* established Grantham as an important figure who bequeathed to the Baptist evolutionary process "a set of factors that qualified [it] as a maturing evangelical Protestant tradition."[2]

Sometime between 1686 and 1690, Grantham departed Lincolnshire and headed west to Norwich, the major city in Norfolk. After thirty years of ministry in and around Lincolnshire, the late-in-life departure is somewhat surprising. Though the exact circumstances of Grantham's removal to Norwich remain unclear, upon arrival he immediately set about to preach and persuade others to embrace the Baptist position. His evangelistic efforts met with immediate success and hostility. Fellow Baptists in London sent an assistant, Thomas Long, in 1690, and the General Assembly of General Baptists sent a second assistant in 1691.

Grantham as "Messenger": The Complexities of Inter-Congregational Authority

Thomas Grantham served as perhaps the greatest and most articulate Baptist messenger of the seventeenth century. Convinced that a correct read-

[2] William H. Brackney, "Thomas Grantham, Systematic Theology, and the Baptist Tradition," in *From Biblical Criticism to Biblical Faith: Essays in Honor of Lee Martin McDonald*, ed. William H. Brackney and Craig A. Evans (Macon, GA: Mercer University Press, 2007), 199–216. See also Clint C. Bass, *Thomas Grantham (1633–1692) and General Baptist Theology* (Oxford, UK: Regent's Park College, 2013), 30–31.

ing of the New Testament called for a third ordained office, that of "messenger," in addition to deacons and pastors/elders, Grantham labored extensively to restore the apostolic office among the General Baptists of his day. He argued that Baptist messengers were successors of the original twelve apostles even as he insisted that Baptist messengers did not inherit all aspects of the ministry entrusted to the original twelve. The tasks they did share, Grantham argued, included itinerant elements such as preaching the gospel in all places, founding new churches, and defending the gospel.

Grantham contributed in several ways to the establishment of the office of messenger among many General Baptist congregations between 1660 and 1700. His published defenses of the messenger's office between 1671 and 1692 constitute perhaps the greatest source of information pertaining to the office of messenger and its place among the sectarian General Baptists of the post-Restoration decades. His most detailed treatment of the subject was *A Defence of the Offices of Apostles* (originally published in 1671; published again in 1674 and 1678 with similar titles). Grantham's writing and ministry solidified the peripatetic office to which he had been ordained in 1666.

The congregations with which Grantham worked had a distinct process for electing and ordaining messengers. Ordained messengers served under the authority of their own local congregations, yet their ordination service reflected an inter-congregational cooperation as it consisted of a gathering of elders and other messengers. Ideally, according to Grantham, General Baptists assigned messengers a region and had them work in conjunction with local congregations—especially those they planted—to preach, baptize, celebrate the Lord's Supper, ordain, arbitrate, and defend the faith. Due in large part to Grantham's tenacious commitment to his role as a messenger, by the end of the seventeenth century General Baptists enjoyed a strong presence in Lincolnshire and were pioneering a permanent presence in the county of Norfolk.

Questions and concerns about the nature and extent of a messenger's authority persisted, however, so students of this period should be prepared to live with a variety of Baptist positions on the subject. Particular Baptists messengers typically carried out a specific task on behalf of a congregation and were not usually made a messenger for life. Not all General Baptists agreed with Grantham on the legitimacy and necessity of messengers. General Baptists maintained relationships with other congregations through local associations and a national body known as the General

Assembly. By the end of Grantham's life, the General Assembly seems to have gotten more involved in ordaining and funding messengers, a situation that may have introduced some degree of ambiguity and possibly tension between the decisions made by a centralizing, national General Baptist body and the ongoing responsibilities of local congregations to ordain their own messengers. Regardless, Grantham contributed greatly to the establishment of an "apostolic" office of messenger that would continue after his death.

With rare exception, Baptists have not had bishops.[3] General Baptist Francis Stanley had already introduced the idea that messengers served as bishops insofar as they were overseers, but exactly how far a messenger's authority extended remained an open question for Grantham and his fellow Baptists. Grantham, like several other Baptists of his day, could use the terms "bishop," messenger," and "apostle" interchangeably. They usually preferred the title "messenger." "Bishop" may seem out of place in the Baptist lexicon, but the epitaph included above demonstrates that some Baptists considered Grantham a Baptist "Bishop" extraordinaire. Grantham's legacy pushes Baptists to reconsider whether apostolic "messengers" are still necessary and, if so, what their presence and authority within a congregational framework might look like.[4]

Grantham as Apologist: Debating and Befriending Opponents

Debating Opponents. Thomas Grantham expended considerable energy as an ordained messenger fulfilling a primary role of the office: that of defending Baptist theology and practice. He developed a reputation as a capable defender of the baptized believers, and Baptists called upon him to contend with other Christian groups by means of public debates and correspondence. In the cases of William Fort (Anglican) and an unnamed Roman Catholic, Baptists encouraged Grantham to respond on behalf of the baptized believers in Lincolnshire. As his correspondence with the

[3] An example of Baptist bishops can be found in the Evangelical Baptist Church of Georgia, which includes elements of the Orthodox tradition. For more information on this Baptist denomination, see Malkhaz Songulashvili, *Evangelical Christian Baptists of Georgia: The History and Transformation of a Free Church Tradition* (Waco, TX: Baylor University Press, 2015).

[4] See John Inscore Essick, "A word about…Baptist apostles," *Review & Expositor* 111, no. 2 (May 2014): 103–04.

Presbyterian John Collinges of Norwich in 1690 shows, Grantham could also engage in extensive letter writing to address the ever-popular theological question concerning God's sovereignty and humanity's free will.

Knowledge of Grantham's debates and interactions with non-Baptist opponents may be primarily derived from his own publications, though his adversaries recorded much helpful information. Ever willing to engage opponents in apologetic dialogue, he published transcripts or summaries of the exchanges, especially when he felt he was the victor. As one might expect, Grantham's presentation of the disputes portrayed the Baptist position in a favorable light. Grantham's account of his 1673 debate with the Anglican William Fort suggests that Grantham had acquired considerable expertise in formal public debate. When recounting his 1672 debate with the Quaker John Whitehead on the subject of Christ's earthly body, Grantham described his own debate demeanor as calm and collected, quite the opposite of the short-tempered Whitehead. Grantham continued to debate the merits of predestination when he removed to Norwich, and those exchanges remained tense and testy.

Befriending Opponents. Frosty interactions with some did not preclude more courteous relations with others. One particular effort to explain and defend the Baptist position culminated in an unlikely friendship between Grantham and John Connould, the vicar of St. Stephen's Church in Norwich. Baptist meetings organized by Grantham attracted some of Connould's own flock, so the vicar wrote to Grantham in April 1691 seeking information about his ordination and his rejection of infant baptism. In the following months, Grantham and Connould exchanged sixty letters in which they discussed a range of theological questions and disagreements. The two also forged a close friendship despite their persistent difference of theological opinion. Connould granted Grantham access to Connould's personal library, where, among other writings, he may have read Michael Servetus's *Restitution of Christianity* (1553).[5] So close was their bond in life that Connould had Grantham's corpse reinterred inside St. Stephen's nave to protect it from desecration. When Connould died in 1708, he requested that he be laid to rest next to his Baptist friend, Thomas Grantham.

[5] Michael Servetus (d. 1553) was a brilliant scientist and controversial theologian who was condemned by Catholics and Protestants alike for his heretical views. Servetus was burned alive for his beliefs in Geneva during John Calvin's tenure as a reformer and minister in the city. Grantham had referenced Servetus in previous debates in order to undermine predestinarian appeals to John Calvin.

Grantham made sure that his General Baptists were involved in the most important debates of the day. Taken together, his many disputes and the documents describing them underscore the public nature of Baptists' disagreements with other dissenters and the established Church of England. His final years were filled with conflict and friendship, both stemming from a deep commitment to spreading and defending the Baptist witness.

Conclusion

Grantham's witness to the Baptist heritage is one of a teenager being asked to pastor a congregation. His is a story of bearing witness before kings and in prison. His is a story of leadership during tumultuous and uncertain times. His is a story of telling others there is a better way. His is a story of Baptist witness in the face of Quakers, Presbyterians, and the Church of England. Regardless of whether one considers him a bishop, apostle, or messenger, Grantham's legacy witnesses to an early Baptist desire for a robust third office of leadership among Baptist churches. Grantham thought that Baptists still need apostles and apostolic leadership. Such a precedent calls attention to how complex and elastic Baptist ideas of "authority" have been, especially the group of voluntarily associated General Baptist churches to which Grantham belonged in the seventeenth century. Granted, he did not represent *all* General Baptists, but Grantham did represent *some* General Baptists. And for a lot of Baptists, the past example of *some* is more than enough to inform future Baptist witness.

Suggested Reading

Clint C. Bass, *Thomas Grantham (1633–1692) and General Baptist Theology* (Oxford, UK: Regent's Park College, 2013), for a theological introduction.

John Inscore Essick, *Thomas Grantham: God's Messenger from Lincolnshire* (Macon, GA: Mercer University Press, 2013), for a historical introduction.

Anne Steele (1717–1778), *Pioneer Hymn Writer*

Worship

David W. Music

The eighteenth century is often called the "Golden Age of English Hymnody." Prior to that time, the congregational singing of English-speaking churches consisted mainly of metrical psalmody. This involved the arrangement of texts from the book of Psalms into meter and rhyme so they could be sung to strophic tunes, that is, melodies that could be repeated for each stanza of text. Metrical psalmody was particularly characteristic of the followers of John Calvin, who believed that the best material for people to sing to God was the very words God himself had given for that purpose, the Psalms. It was also another way to put the scriptural text into the mouths, hearts, and minds of believers. By 1700, metrical psalmody had been the common practice in English-speaking churches for 150 years.

As the eighteenth century dawned, however, many Protestants began to question the use of exclusive psalmody. Particularly influential in this questioning was the Congregationalist minister Isaac Watts, who observed that some of the psalms are "foreign to the State of the New-Testament" and are "widely different from the present Circumstances of Christians."[1] While Watts noted that it was far from his thoughts "to lay aside the Psalms of *David* in public Worship," he acknowledged that "there are a thousand Lines in it which were not made for a Saint in our Day to assume as his own."[2] He argued further that congregational singing should represent the *response of the people* to God's revelation—"our Love, our Fear, our Hope, our Desire, our Sorrow, our Wonder, and our Joy, all refin'd into Devotion"[3]—rather than merely parroting back to God the words of Scripture. Watts provided a model for hymns that expressed the sense of

---

[1] Isaac Watts, *Hymns and Spiritual Songs* (London: J. Humfreys for John Lawrence, 1707), iv.

[2] Ibid., vi.

[3] Ibid., vii.

the gospel by publishing a collection of *Hymns and Spiritual Songs* (1707) and one of *The Psalms of David Imitated in the Language of the New Testament* (1719), from which come his "When I Survey the Wondrous Cross" and "Joy to the World," respectively.

Many later writers in the eighteenth century, most prominently Charles Wesley ("O For a Thousand Tongues to Sing"), John Newton ("Amazing Grace"), and William Cowper ("There Is a Fountain Filled with Blood"), took up Watts's example. Among the important writers who followed in Watts's footsteps was the Particular Baptist Anne Steele.

Anne Steele was born in 1717 (the specific month and day are not known) in Broughton, Hampshire, England, the second child of a well-to-do timber merchant. Anne's mother, after whom she was named, died when she was three years old, and her father remarried when she was six. Her stepmother, also named Anne, maintained a diary that records young Anne's conversion and baptism in 1732. At the time of Anne's conversion, her great-uncle Henry Steele was volunteer pastor of the Broughton Baptist Church, a position he held for forty years. When Henry died in 1739, Anne's father William Steele, who had served as Henry's assistant in the timber business, took over both the trade and the pastorate of the church.

Part of Anne's education came from attendance at boarding schools in Trowbridge and Salisbury, but much of her learning seems to have been acquired by personal reading and contact with prominent Baptist ministers and a large circle of correspondents. When her stepmother died in 1760, Anne (who by then was in her forties) looked after her father's household until he passed away in 1769. She then went to live with her older brother (also in Broughton) until her own death on November 11, 1778, after having been confined to her room by illness for several years.

Anne was in poor health during much of her life. She suffered from "ague" (malaria) beginning at an early age and experienced frequent stomach "indisposition" and toothache (probably an abscess), as well as other physical ailments.[4] She never married, though there is evidence that she may have received at least three proposals, one of which was from a fellow Baptist hymn writer, Benjamin Beddome.[5] Of one proposal, she remarked

[4] See Michael F. Dixon and Hugh F. Steele-Smith, "Anne Steele's Health: A Modern Diagnosis," *The Baptist Quarterly* 32, no. 7 (July 1988): 351–56.

[5] See J. R. Watson and Nancy Cho, "Anne Steele's Drowned Fiancé," *Bulletin* of the Hymn Society of Great Britain and Ireland 251, vol. 17, no. 8 (October 2004): 198–202. The first proposal—if indeed there was one—was from a young man who

in a letter to her sister Mary that "I looked over [the stile of marriage] and saw no flowers, but observ'd a great many thorns, and I suppose there are more hid under the leaves."[6] The picture that is often drawn of her is of a "reclusive, melancholic, and extremely pious woman," but she was well educated for a woman of her time and was "a member of a prominent, wealthy, and remarkably literary family."[7] While there is no doubt that she experienced ill health, injuries (including falls from horses), deaths in the immediate family, and disappointments, she also "possessed a native cheerfulness of disposition, which not even the uncommon and agonizing pains she endured in the latter part of her life could deprive her of."[8] It is apparent that it was simply her preference to lead the quiet life of a single woman in a rural village, though she also had a wide circle of friends and acquaintances with whom she carried on stimulating conversations and correspondence.

Even in her childhood and adolescence, Anne discovered "her love of the muses." Although some of her hymns had been used successfully in worship at her own church, as the advertisement of her work read, it was only with "extreme reluctance" that "she was prevailed on to submit any of them to the public eye."[9] While such claims have often been made by authors who leave the impression that they have to be dragged kicking and screaming into publication, this testimony is probably largely true since it is from a second party who was in a position to know the facts. Also, it was unusual at that time for women to publish works of any kind, especially ones dealing with religion, and her work would probably be compared (or contrasted) with Isaac Watts, Charles Wesley, Philip Doddridge, and other established hymn writers, as well as contemporary non-hymnic religious poets such as Alexander Pope, Edward Young, and James Thompson. Steele's diffidence is undoubtedly reflected in the fact that when her works were issued in two volumes in 1760 as *Poems on*

---

was drowned sometime before the wedding, but the evidence of Anne's betrothal to him is uncertain.

[6] Quoted in Sharon James, "Anne Steele (1717–1778)," in *In Trouble and In Joy: Four Women Who Lived for God* (Faverdale North, Darlington, Eng.: Evangelical Press, 2003), 158.

[7] Cynthia Aalders, *To Express the Ineffable: The Hymns and Spirituality of Anne Steele* (Milton Keynes, UK, 2008), 28.

[8] Caleb Evans, "Advertisement," in "Theodosia," *Miscellaneous Pieces, in Verse and Prose* (Bristol: W. Pine, 1780), ix.

[9] Ibid., vii.

Subjects Chiefly Devotional, they appeared under the pseudonym "Theodosia" (God's gift).

The first volume of *Poems on Subjects Chiefly Devotional* is divided into two sections, the first consisting of "Hymns on Various Subjects" and the second of "Poems on Several Occasions." The "hymns" were apparently designed primarily for singing—they all deal with sacred subjects and use traditional hymnic meters[10]—while the "poems" were intended for reading, as can be seen by their secular topics, length, and other factors. The second volume is likewise in two parts, the first continuing the "occasional poems" and the second providing "Some Parts of the Book of Psalms, Attempted in Verse." Some of the latter are stanzaic in structure and could certainly be sung, but others are not so formatted (e.g., Psalm 16). It is likely that all the psalm versions were also meant primarily for reading rather than congregational singing.

Each of the 105 hymns in the first volume contains a title giving the general subject matter of the text—for example, "Thirsting After God," "A Rural Hymn," or "The Presence of Christ the Joy of His People." Many also list a Scripture reference that serves as a background to the hymn. Some of the texts are quite long; one of them, "Come Heavenly Love, Inspire My Song" ("Redeeming Love," p. 7 in *Poems*) contains thirty-nine stanzas, while the others range from four to sixteen stanzas.

Steele's hymns are characterized by "themes of language and suffering," as one biographer writes, with an unusual (for that era) introspection and tentativeness.[11] In terms of language, "She expresses considerable doubt regarding her personal ability to articulate praise while at the same time doubting the capacity of language itself to convey meaning when God is the subject."[12] Her questioning of "why the godly suffer" (theodicy) is at least as old as the book of Job but has seldom been addressed in hymnody either before Anne's time or since. "For the first time," according to Richard Arnold, "hymns appear which portray, and do not resolve, doubt and struggle, and which portray a writer acknowledging a form of defeat rather

[10] Hymnic meter refers to the number of lines in a stanza and the number of syllables in each line. Steele's hymns are exclusively in Common Meter (8686), Long Meter (8888), and Short Meter (6686), except for a single instance of 66664444.

[11] Aalders, *To Express the Ineffable*, 172.

[12] Ibid., 66.

than celebrating a form of victory."[13] Her answer to the questions of both language and theodicy is found in the incarnation of Christ.

Despite the fact that Steele's hymns stand somewhat apart from those of other eighteenth-century writers because of their introspective nature, she wrote on many of the same subjects as other hymnists, including the glory of God in creation and the hope of eternal salvation and heaven.[14] Thus it is not surprising to find in her hymns echoes of individual lines or stanzas by her predecessors and contemporaries, especially Isaac Watts, whose texts were widely used among Dissenters, including Baptists. Resemblances (as well as differences) between Watts's "When I Survey the Wondrous Cross" and Steele's "Stretch'd On the Cross the Saviour Dies" have been pointed out,[15] and individual stanzas from two other Steele hymns seem to reflect knowledge of another Watts hymn, "Salvation! O the Joyful Sound."[16]

STEELEWATTS
Sin throws in vain its pointed dart,Salvation! O the joyful sound!
For here a sovereign cure is found;'Tis pleasure to our ears;
A cordial for the fainting heart,A sov'reign balm for ev'ry wound,
A balm for every painful wound.A cordial for our fears.

Wrap'd in the gloom of dark despair,Buried in sorrow and in sin,
We helpless, hopeless lay:At hell's dark door we lay;
But sovereign mercy reach'd us there,But we arise by grace Divine
And smil'd despair away.To see a heav'nly day.

---

[13] Richard Arnold, "A 'Veil of Interposing Night': The Hymns of Anne Steele (1717–1778)," *Christian Scholars Review* 18, no. 4 (June 1989): 379.

[14] Priscilla Wong, *Anne Steele and Her Spiritual Vision: Seeing God in the Peaks, Valleys, and Plateaus of Life* (Grand Rapids: Reformation Heritage Books, 2012), 9.

[15] Cynthia Y. Aalders, "'In Melting Grief and Ardent Love': Anne Steele's Contribution to Eighteenth-Century Hymnody," *The Hymn* 60, no. 3 (Summer 2009): 18–20. Aalder's article also compares the two hymns to Charles Wesley's "Where Shall My Wandering Soul Begin" and suggests that Wesley's and Steele's texts were written in imitation of Watts's.

[16] The two Steele hymns are "Deep Are the Wounds Which Sin Hath Made" (st. 6) and "Come Heavenly Love, Inspire My Song" (st. 6). The term "sovereign balm" also appears in stanza 3 of "Deep Are the Wounds." The line "Wrap'd in the gloom of dark despair" is reminiscent of the first line of another text by Watts, "Plunged in a Gulf of Dark Despair." Other minor similarities to Watts's hymns can be found throughout Steele's works.

In turn, Steele's hymns perhaps influenced other hymnists, as can be seen in the following comparison of two lines of hers with two by fellow Baptist Samuel Medley, who would surely have been acquainted with Steele's work (Medley's hymn was first published in 1775, fifteen years after Steele's).

STEELEMEDLEY
He lives, the great Redeemer lives,I know that my Redeemer lives,
(What joy the blest assurance gives!)What comfort this assurance gives!

Of course, such likenesses may simply be a result of two authors working from the same scriptural passage or on the same topic or were perhaps subconscious; the surrounding material is often quite different in subject matter and language. Such interchanges of material—if that is indeed what they are—were common in the eighteenth century, and what is ultimately important is what an author did with them.[17] In Steele's case, her distinctive "voice" gave passages such as these a meaning and flavor that differed considerably from her putative models.

The influence of Steele's hymns was enormous during the late eighteenth and nineteenth centuries. Nine years after the publication of her *Poems on Subjects Chiefly Devotional*, two Baptists, John Ash and Caleb Evans, included sixty-one of her texts (some of which she revised for their book) in their eclectic *A Collection of Hymns Adapted to Public Worship* (1769), usually called the "Bristol Collection" after its place of publication. Two years after her death, publishers reprinted the two volumes of *Poems on Subjects Chiefly Devotional* (1780). They added a third volume of previously unpublished poems edited by Caleb Evans, who also provided a biographical "Advertisement" of the author. In 1787, John Rippon's *A Selection of Hymns from the Best Authors* (1787), the most important British Baptist hymnal of the eighteenth century, reprinted forty-five Steele texts,

[17] Indeed, Watts himself is known to have borrowed heavily from earlier authors in putting together his *Psalms of David Imitated in the Language of the New Testament*. See David W. Music, "Isaac Watts' Sources for *The Psalms of David Imitated* (1719)," *Bulletin* of the Hymn Society of Great Britain and Ireland 302, vol. 22, no. 9 (Winter 2020): 371–85.

adding seven more in subsequent editions.[18] A reprint of her works appeared in London in 1863 under the title *Hymns, Psalms and Poems, by Anne Steele.*

Steele influenced more than just English Baptists. In 1808, the three volumes of Steele's works were reissued in Boston as *The Works of Miss Anne Steele*. Baron Stow and Samuel F. Smith's *The Psalmist* (1843), the most popular hymnal among Northern Baptists in the United States during the mid-nineteenth century, contained fifty-four of her texts. A "southern supplement" published four years later added another four. In 1876 the "new and enlarged edition" of S. L. Caldwell and A. J. Gordon's *The Service of Song for Baptist Churches* attributed thirty-six hymn texts to Steele. The first "official" Southern Baptist hymnal (official in the sense of having the imprimatur of the Southern Baptist Convention), Basil Manly and Basil Manly, Jr's. *The Baptist Psalmody* (1850), included fifty-one Steele texts. The British and American Baptist hymnal compilers probably found Steele's hymns to be useful because they dealt distinctly with the four principal elements of a "historical Baptist theology of worship": sincere devotion of the heart, the primacy of Scripture, the community of believers, and the kingdom of God.[19]

Nor was use of Steele's hymns confined to Baptists. In 1795, Jeremy Belknap, a Boston Unitarian, issued *Sacred Poetry*, which included no fewer than sixty-five texts by Steele (plus several that were partly hers) as well as extracts from Caleb Evans's biographical sketch. Belknap's book served as the principal source for another Boston collection, *Hymns, Selected From the Most Approved Authors, for the Use of Trinity [Episcopal] Church, Boston* (1808), the preface of which observed that "if we have extracted more copiously from Mrs. Steele, than from any other writer, we

---

[18] Joseph Van Carmichael, "The Hymns of Anne Steele in John Rippon's *Selection of Hymns*: A Theological Analysis in the Context of the English Particular Baptist Revival" (PhD diss., Southern Baptist Theological Seminary, 2012), 9.

[19] Holly M. Farrow, "A Baptist Theology of Worship and the Hymnody of Anne Steele," *The Hymn* 70, no. 4 (Autumn 2019): 25–34. Farrow's analysis follows Christopher J. Ellis's analysis of Free Church worship in *Gathering: A Theology and Spirituality of Worship in Free Church Tradition* (London: SCM, 2004). Ellis's listing is similar in some regards to David Bebbington's quadrilateral of the conversionism, biblicism, activism, and crucicentrism of Baptists in his *Evangelicalism in Modern Britain: A History from the 1730s to the 1980s* (London: Routledge, 1989), but Ellis's work is specifically about worship whereas Bebbington's deals more generally with Baptist beliefs. See also Jacob Porter, "Songs of Suffering and Sanctification: The Hymnody of Anne Steele," *Puritan Reformed Journal* 5, no. 2 (2013): 169–90.

have done no more, than what we thought due to her poetical superiority, and to the ardent spirit of devotion, which breathes in her composition." The fact that an Episcopal church found her texts to be so useful is remarkable. Even as late as 1892, the official U. S. Episcopal hymnal still contained five Steele texts.[20]

The website www.hymnary.org, which incorporates the Hymn Society in the United States and Canada's Dictionary of North American Hymnology, catalogs publications of hymns in American hymnals from the Bay Psalm Book (1640) to the present. The website lists 22 Anne Steele hymns that were published at least 150 times in North American collections. The most widely used of these hymns, "Father, Whate'er of Earthly Bliss" and "Father of Mercies, in Thy Word," received 820 and 732 printings, respectively.[21]

However, the website and other research also reveal a pattern of decline in the use of Steele's texts during the late nineteenth and the twentieth centuries. Whereas, as seen above, the two most important British Baptist hymnals of the eighteenth century contained dozens of Steele hymns, by the time of the Baptist Union of Great Britain and Ireland's *Baptist Praise and Worship* (1991), her contribution had declined to a single text, "Father of Mercies, in Thy Word."[22] The more than fifty Steele texts in the Manlys' *Baptist Psalmody* have been abandoned by Baptists in the South to the extent that not one appeared in any of the five most recent hymnals published for the churches of that American denomination.[23]

While Steele's hymns have largely disappeared from present-day congregational singing, there has been a resurgence of interest in her life and work. The "retuned hymns" movement, which seeks to set historic texts to contemporary music, has made particular use of her texts.[24] As can

[20] *The Hymnal Revised and Enlarged as Adopted by the General Convention of the Protestant Episcopal Church in the United States of America* (New York: Henry Frowde, 1892).

[21] See https://hymnary.org/text/father_whateer_of_earthly_bliss; https://hymnary.org/text/father_of_mercies_in_thy_word.

[22] Ruth Bottoms, "Contemporary Baptist Congregational Singing and the Hymnody of Anne Steele (1717–1778)," *Baptist Quarterly* 48, no. 4 (October 2017): 150, 152.

[23] The hymnals are the 1956, 1975, 1991, and 2008 editions of *Baptist Hymnal* and the 2010 *Celebrating Grace*.

[24] Indelible Grace Music has been a leader in the retuned hymns movement and the use of texts by Anne Steele. See http://www.igracemusic.com/.

been seen in the suggested readings and notes to this article, her life, work, and influence have recently received considerable attention from scholars.

Such attention is well deserved, for Steele was not only the best Baptist hymn writer of the eighteenth century but was also the first important English-language woman hymn writer of any denomination. In her hymns and poetry she left a unique legacy of spirituality that reflects honest questioning and doubt but also faith and trust in her Lord and Savior.[25] Certainly, as one analysis of Steele's hymns has shown, Anne Steele's "spirituality of exploration, uncertainty and questioning, together with an honest bringing before God of all of life's experiences, has something to teach contemporary Baptist congregational singing that will enable worshippers to give a right attention to Scripture, enable a devotional response to God, be inclusive of everyone present and be concerned about the kingdom of God."[26]

It is fitting to close with one of Steele's hymns, "The Heavenly Shepherd," based on Psalm 23:1-3. The text demonstrates some of her typical themes of faithfulness to the Scriptures, personal unworthiness, and trust in God's guidance and provision.[27]

While my Redeemer's near,
My shepherd and my guide,
I bid farewell to anxious fear,
My wants are all supply'd.

To ever-fragrant meads,
Where rich abundance grows,
His gracious hand indulgent leads,
And guards my sweet repose.

---

[25] See J. R. Broome, *A Bruised Reed: The Life and Times of Anne Steele* (Harpenden: Gospel Standard Trust Publications, 2007), 173.

[26] Bottoms, "Contemporary Baptist Congregational Singing and the Hymnody of Anne Steele," 158.

[27] "Theodosia," *Poems on Subjects Chiefly Devotional*, new ed. (Bristol: W. Pine, 1780), I:159–60. Lines three and four of stanza one are reminiscent of two lines from Watts, "I bid farewell to every fear" from "When I Can Read My Title Clear" and "Now shall my wants be well supplied" from his long meter version of Psalm 23, "My Shepherd Is the Living Lord." Steele also provided a paraphrase of the Twenty-Third Psalm in the second volume of her *Poems* (147–48).

Along the lovely scene,
Cool waters gently roll,
And kind refreshment smiles serene,
To cheer my fainting soul.

Here let my spirit rest;
How sweet a lot is mine!
With pleasure, food, and safety blest;
Beneficence divine!

Dear shepherd, if I stray,
My wandering feet restore,
To thy fair pastures guide my way,
And let me rove no more.

Unworthy as I am
Of thy protecting care,
Jesus, I plead thy gracious name,
For all my hopes are there.

Suggested Reading

Cynthia Aalders, *To Express the Ineffable: The Hymns and Spirituality of Anne Steele* (Milton Keynes, UK; Colorado Springs, CO: Paternoster, 2008).

J. R. Broome, *A Bruised Reed: Anne Steele, Her Life and Times* (Harpenden: Gospel Standard Trust Publications, 2007).

Michael A. G. Haykin, "Anne Steele and Her Hymns," in *Eight Women of Faith* (Wheaton, IL: Crossway, 2016), 81–92.

Sharon James, "Anne Steele (1717–1778)," in *In Trouble and In Joy: Four Women Who Lived for God* (Faverdale North, Darlington, Eng.: Evangelical Press, 2003), 115–46.

Priscilla Wong, *Anne Steele and Her Spiritual Vision: Seeing God in the Peaks, Valleys, and Plateaus of Life* (Grand Rapids, MI: Reformation Heritage Books, 2012).

Ann Hasseltine Judson (1789–1826), American Missionary Innovator and Theologian

Missions

Laura Rodgers Levens

Ann Hasseltine Judson has shaped over two centuries of history and theology of mission with only fourteen years of mission work. Along with her husband, Adoniram Judson, Ann was one of the earliest modern American overseas missionaries, and they were the first missionary pair supported by a national American Baptist organization. During her time in Burma, Ann oversaw the stability and sustainability of the mission as a matter of community relationships. She created methods of welcoming religious inquirers, taught habits of reading, worship, and prayer as a means to conversion, and published religious tracts in both Burmese and Thai. Ann also published a theological history of her and Adoniram's first decade of work. Ann is remembered in many Baptist quarters for being the first American Baptist female missionary and dying too soon, but it is her exceptional blend of religious imagination and pragmatic wisdom in her work and writings that provides substance and guidance for the next century of Christian mission.

Ann was born on December 22, 1789, in the provincial New England town of Bradford, Massachusetts, a river town located forty miles north of Boston on the Merrimack River. Her father, John Hasseltine, descended from several generations of Bradford Hasseltines. He and his wife, Rebecca, raised three daughters in a rising middle-class merchant family. The Hasseltines were also prominent attendees at the First Congregational Church and on good terms with Pastor Jonathan Allen.

In 1802, Ann enrolled in the recently founded Bradford Academy. Bradford Academy was coeducational, though boys and girls were in separate classes. Ann obtained a more standard, classical education as a new opportunity for American girls, who in prior generations had been trained privately at home. In 1806, a Great Awakening revival swept through Bradford Academy and the First Congregational Church. The whole town was caught up in nightly services, and small groups were devoted to pursuing personal salvation by grace through a recognizable, evidence-based, and often emotional experience of conversion. Ann experienced bouts of anxiety over her salvation, which culminated months later in religious awakening and assurance of regenerate grace. After a time of self-examination to discern that her conversion was real, Ann Hasseltine became a full member of First Congregational Church and began assisting and imploring her family and friends to continue their interest in conversion and full membership. Her father, her sisters, and several close school friends attributed their perseverance in conversion to Ann's encouragement and guidance.

Ann and the Bradford community also increased their commitment to acts of benevolence and world mission support during the revival period. Ann was very involved in prayer meetings, benevolent works, and the female mission society as a teenager and young adult. During Ann's involvement, the female mission society focused on providing rural education and supporting missionaries among Native Americans and across the globe. After her graduation from Bradford Academy in 1807, Ann voluntarily taught school in rural villages near Bradford as a part of mission society and church work. No colleges would allow middle-class women to study among the men, but Ann convinced her pastor to tutor her in college level self-study of religious works like Jonathan Edwards as if she were in seminary.[1]

In 1810, at the age of twenty-one, Ann and the congregation of First Church welcomed the Massachusetts Congregational Assembly to Bradford. Because of the community's reputation for revival and mission interest, Bradford was an opportune place for the Assembly that year for Ann, Pastor Jonathan Allen, and others who favored the creation of an American-supported international missions enterprise. During the event, a

---

[1] Concerning Ann Judson's theological studies, see James D. Knowles, *Memoir of Mrs. Ann H. Judson* (Boston: Lincoln & Edmands, 1831), 23. According to Dana Robert, Ann Hasseltine's religious self-study rivaled the characteristic "male student enrolled in Andover Seminary" (*American Women in Mission* [Macon, GA: Mercer University Press, 1997], 7). J. D. Kingsbury describes the revivalist and mission impulse among the First Church of Bradford that provided a special energy for the General Assembly and preparation for Ann Judson's future in *Memorial History of Bradford, Massachusetts* (Haverhill, MA: C. C. Morse and Son, 1883), 106–12, 171–75.

group of seminary students from Andover Theological Seminary presented a letter expressing their commitment to foreign missions. They further petitioned Congregationalist clergy to form an American Mission Board. One of the seminary students presenting the petition was named Adoniram Judson, whom Ann met during the Assembly. Adoniram was born on August 9, 1788, in Malden, Massachusetts, and educated at Brown College and Andover. Shortly after the Assembly concluded, Adoniram asked Ann to marry him and join him overseas in foreign mission.

Ann received Adoniram's proposal as two questions in one. Would she commit to missionary work for life, even if she never saw her family and beloved Bradford again? Would she commit to being his partner as a wife and colleague? Ann meditated upon these questions in much the same way that she sought awakening faith and conversion. In her letters and journals, Ann penned her decision as a means of pursing a calling, or a vocation as a missionary. Detaching herself from "earthly objects," Ann sought to "go where God, in his providence, sees fit to place me" while investigating her own intentions and wondering "whether my love to Jesus was sufficiently strong to induce me to forsake all for his cause." In the end, Ann agreed to the proposal as a matter of trust in God and in Adoniram's shared sense that embarking on this new venture would be their way to "grow in grace," "live near to God," and attempt to be useful.[2]

Ann married Adoniram on February 5, 1812, in Bradford. Adoniram and his male missionary colleagues were ordained the next day in Salem, Massachusetts, and Rev. Jonathan Allen, Ann's pastor, addressed both the men and women in his sermon during the service.[3] Thirteen days later the Judsons sailed to India on the ship *Caravan* with two mission colleagues, Samuel and Harriet Atwood Newell. During their trip, Ann continued her

---

[2] Ann Judson, letter to Ms. Lydia K., Beverly, MA, September 8, 1810, in Knowles, *Memoir of Mrs. Ann H. Judson*, 50–51; Ann Judson to her parents, Madras, 1813, in Ann Hasseltine Judson, *An Account of the American Baptist Mission to the Burman Empire* (London: J. Butterworth & Son, 1823), 16.

[3] Ann Judson attended the ordination service and her missionary role was addressed by her pastor in the sermon, but there is no nineteenth century evidence that Ann left her pew to kneel at the altar during the ordination. This myth about Ann "slipping from her pew" to commit to mission arose in the early twentieth century. See Laura Rodgers Levens, "Reading the Judsons: Recovering the Literary Works of Ann, Sarah, Emily, and Adoniram Judson for a New Baptist Mission History," *American Baptist Quarterly* 32, no. 1 (2013): 43–44.

religious studies with Adoniram. They both desired a missionary post where they could live among native peoples and avoid employment with European colonial militias or tradesmen. When the Judsons and Newells arrived in British Bengal, an eastern region of the Indian peninsula, in July 1812, Ann discovered that the British colonial powers did not want American missionaries among them either. William Carey and the British Baptist missionaries in Serampore welcomed them, but the British government ordered the Americans' immediate deportation.

While the Judsons looked for a new place to go, Ann and Adoniram studied a contentious issue between American Congregationalists and Baptists over the administration of baptism. Concluding that believer's baptism was the correct manner, Ann and Adoniram petitioned for baptism from the British Baptist missionaries and became Baptists on September 6, 1812. From Ann's perspective, her baptism was a "change of sentiment" due to her growing understanding of the Bible and Christian faith resulting from study, prayer, and meditation. Her change was not a conversion or a denunciation of her Bradford church, though she feared they would interpret her action that way and cease their support. Her fears came true when the American mission cohort decided that the Judsons could not continue as their mission colleagues.[4]

As a result, Ann and Adoniram began writing letters explaining the situation to old supporters and introducing themselves to possible new supporters among Massachusetts Baptists. Their colleague Luther Rice had also changed sentiment about baptism, and he agreed to return to America to raise support while the Judsons searched for a new mission situation. After a short stay in the British-controlled Isle of France (Mauritania) and another thwarted attempt to reenter Bengal, Ann and Adoniram Judson eventually landed in Rangoon, Burma (Yangon, Myanmar), in July 1813. They immediately moved into the British Baptist mission house with William Carey's son Felix and his wife. Ann and Adoniram began learning the Burmese language from a tutor, who first objected to teaching women. After Adoniram reasserted Ann's status as a colleague, they began learning Burmese together by pointing at objects and writing down what they heard.

---

[4] Ann Judson's journal, Calcutta, September 1, 1812, in Knowles, *Memoir of Mrs. Ann H. Judson*, 77; Ann Judson to Nancy Gage, September 7, 1812, in the *Massachusetts Missionary Baptist Magazine*, May 1813, 294.

By 1815, the Judsons were on their own and the mission in Rangoon, Burma, became an endeavor supported by the American Baptist Triennial Convention. At the age of twenty-six, Ann was principally responsible for running the mission household and representing the mission at Burmese court. Acting as the mission's diplomat, Ann visited government grounds, petitioned for favors, and explained their peaceful intentions. The Rangoon government accepted her presence as a symbol of trust between the mission and the Burmese. Ann visited the vicereine so many times to ensure the mission's stability and welfare that the two women developed a friendship and continued over the years to look after one another.

Ann also gave birth to a son, Roger Williams Judson, in 1815. She was later devastated when her son died of fever at eight months old. Shortly after little Roger's death, Adoniram Judson's health broke down and the Judsons almost left Rangoon because of his inability to work. News of missionary reinforcements, the vicereine's care, and time for recovery kept Ann and Adoniram in Rangoon. George and Mrs. Hough joined them in 1816, along with a very large printing press. Encouraged by Adoniram, Ann wrote a theological catechism in Burmese and translated some of Adoniram's Burmese work into Thai.[5] Using the *Catechism*, Ann Judson gathered her first society of Burmese women for literacy education, religious instruction, and conversation while Adoniram continued translation work.

---

[5] Ann became one of the earliest composers of theology in the modern mission movement and was a model second-hand translator from Burmese to Siamese. Based on Ann Judson's letters, Ann composed a *Catechism* in Burmese in 1816 (published in 1817 and reprinted by the Baptist mission for almost a century). She records in a letter that she wrote "a translation of the book of Jonah, and part of Daniel, not because I consider these books of any more importance than other parts of the scripture, but because they were easier to translate" (Ann Judson to Mrs. Carleton, Rangoon, February 10, 1818, in *The American Baptist Magazine and Missionary Intelligencer* [Jan 1819]:14–15). Her translations were from English into Burmese because Ann never mentions learning biblical languages. Ann's personal translation work probably did not become a part of Adoniram's "first-hand" biblical language to Burmese translation of the Bible. Adoniram records translating the Old Testament in the early 1830s, well after the disruptive events of the Anglo-Burmese War and Ann's death. Ann translated a large collection of Thai sacred stories into English, and she "second-hand" translated her Burmese catechism, Adoniram's Burmese translation of the Gospel of Matthew, and Adoniram's *A View of the Christian Religion* tract into Thai (Ann Judson to her sister, Rangoon, April 29, 1819, in Knowles, *Memoir of Mrs. Ann H. Judson*, 181–82).

Throughout her missionary career, Ann never experienced long periods of safety and stability. Maintaining her place in Rangoon required a high degree of responsiveness to whatever new destabilizing event occurred next. This pattern is already apparent above in Ann's reaction and response to deportation from Bengal, language learning, diplomacy activity, multiple illnesses, and the death of her son. In 1818, Adoniram departed for Bengal to rest and look for a native assistant, but his ship failed to arrive and was feared lost at sea. With no way to find Adoniram or learn of his fate, Ann Judson handled everything at the mission for eight months while the Burmese and British governments traded escalating war threats. When the Burmese government started interrogating foreigners, including Mr. Hough, the Hough family retreated to India. Ann decided to stay in Rangoon. She rode the waves of fear with her strong commitment to guard the mission house community and provided hope with her talents for securing relationships among the local Rangoon people. Adoniram Judson's ship finally reached port after months of delay, and he returned safely to Rangoon.

Ann Judson also made the most out of short periods of stability by sifting the practices she knew from Bradford and adapting them to provide for the context of Burmese religious inquirers. By 1819, the Judsons were confident speakers of Burmese and welcomed the Colmans and Wheelocks as American Baptist missionaries to assist them. Ann and Adoniram together designed a religious structure for worship and daily conversation that mirrored the local *zayats*. The Burmese used *zayats*, spaces decorated with shrines, for communal religious instruction, recitation of sacred texts, and meditation for the Buddhist faith. For the Baptist mission *zayat*, Ann developed a method of religious catechesis that combined literacy training (if necessary), Christian theology instruction, and practices of prayer and self-examination. By choosing a *zayat* structure, Ann and Adoniram signaled to the Burmese their commitment to religious dialogue, sacred texts, and esteem for personal religious commitment. By refusing any images in the *zayat*, the Judsons also indicated their rejection of Burmese Buddhist material culture and reinforced Great Awakening emphases on awareness of sin and conversion experiences.

With its open doors on the side of the road, the *zayat* encouraged multiple people to stop by, hear for themselves, and pick up a printed tract to read at home. In practice, Ann and Adoniram encouraged visitors to return with questions and their family members. Along with mission house administration, Ann oversaw the gathering and growing of the new religious community that would become the Rangoon church. Ann instructed Moung Nau, the first Burmese convert, as he prepared for baptism in June 1819, and continued dialoguing with her women's group. She and Adoniram adapted their worship routines to incorporate Burmese inquirers and include Moung Nau. Ann sought wisdom in understanding the Burmese religious inquirers' connections to their neighbors and family, and she empathized with them over the severe consequences of leaving Burmese Buddhism.

Ann persevered through another low period in 1820, as the Baptist mission in Rangoon almost collapsed again. A new emperor had claimed the throne and was using religion to project his power upon his Burmese subjects. The Burmese government began actively enforcing required religious attendance and adherence to officially sanctioned Buddhist temples. All Burmese religious dissenters—whether anti-temple, nonreligious, or Christian—would be tortured and executed for treason. Faced with these political developments, the American Baptist missionaries decided to leave for a border region. Adoniram and Mr. Colman had traveled to the capitol to petition for religious tolerance, but the emperor had rejected their gifts and they now feared for the lives of the three new Burmese Christians. Ann Judson felt like she was abandoning all for which she had followed God, but she dutifully packed and prayed that the Burmese converts and inquirers would be safe.

At this critical moment, Ann credited the Burmese converts with keeping the American Baptist mission in Rangoon. Moung Nau, Moung Byaay, and Moung Thalah had received instruction from Ann before their baptisms that included a vow not to recant in the face of torture and death. Disagreeing with the missionaries who had decided to leave, these converts used the vow to pressure the missionaries to disregard threats of torture and to stay for the sake of the congregation. Ann wrote to her American supporters that these converts revealed God's mission and changed the missionaries' plans. Ann described them as "a vine planted, small indeed but green and flourishing…and the same invisible hand which planted it, will water and protect it, cause it to shoot out on every side, till the whole country is filled with its branches."[6] Despite the dangers, Ann and Adoniram remained in Rangoon with the Burmese mission community. Ann

[6] Ann Judson to "a friend in Waterville" [Mrs. Chaplin], March 7, 1820, in *American Baptist Magazine and Missionary Intelligencer* (March 1821): 63–68.

and Adoniram closed the roadside *zayat* and transformed the mission house into a semi-private *zayat* until government oppression subsided.

During this time, Ann began experiencing chronic and debilitating abdominal pain that eventually required her to sail back to England and America for medical treatment. She returned to the United States in 1822 and secluded herself in Baltimore under the medical care of her brother-in-law, Dr. Elnathan Judson. Her celebrity status in America alarmed Ann even as she observed general disinterest for mission support and service. As she rested, Ann composed *An Account of the American Baptist Mission to the Burman Empire* (published in 1823) as a support-building history and a theological redirection toward God's redemptive activity. In composing her book, Ann downplayed aspects of her work due to her discomfort with fame and restrictive cultural assumptions about female respectability. In contrast, she composed a vibrant portrayal of God's presence in Burma and mission support as participation and spiritual communion with God. After her health improved, Ann advised the Triennial Convention and spoke at small gatherings on mission practice and missionary character. She inspired both George and Sarah Boardman, among others, to join the Baptist mission to Burma.

Many medical professionals and family members advised Ann Judson to stay in the United States, but Ann remained determined to go back to Burma. In early 1823, at the age of thirty-four, Ann felt well enough to sail across the world again and rejoin Adoniram in Rangoon. While Ann was on medical furlough, Adoniram had continued translation work and care of the Rangoon church community. He had also traveled to Ava, the Burmese capitol, with a new medical missionary colleague, Dr. Jonathan Price. The emperor failed to grant Adoniram's petition for religious tolerance but demonstrated great interest in having Dr. Price at his court. When Ann returned to Rangoon, a small group from the mission house moved to Ava: the Judsons, Dr. Price, Burmese convert Moung Ing, and two Burmese girls Ann had adopted as students and family members. Ann left the Rangoon mission house in the hands of the Burmese Christians and other American Baptist missionaries. She planned to start a school for girls in Ava and use her diplomatic skills to help protect the Rangoon congregation.

Ann shifted her plans upon her arrival in Ava because political relations between the Burmese and British empires had deteriorated once again. None of the American missionaries were welcome in the emperor's court or in his wife's quarters due to suspicions of Western espionage.

Undeterred and hopeful that the political tumult would subside, Ann worked to establish community relationships between the mission house community and the rest of Ava. Ann reconnected with her old friend the vicereine, who now resided in Ava as a widow, and made other Burmese connections to provide the mission house with the necessary goods and goodwill to bring stability.

In May 1824, the British navy invaded Rangoon and started the first Anglo-Burmese War. The American Baptist missionaries in Rangoon were able to evacuate to Bengal, but Ann and her community in Ava were stuck inside Burmese territory. A few days after the attack, Burmese officials burst into the mission house, arrested Adoniram and Dr. Price as British spies, and dragged them away to the prison. Ann, who was pregnant at the time, was left in charge of her adopted girls and the remaining mission house members. She was terrified her husband would be executed or contract a fatal disease in jail. She also feared more searches of the mission home and seizures of its people and resources.

Bribing and petitioning her way through Ava government officials and their female relatives, Ann Judson sought the release of Adoniram and Dr. Price. The government repeatedly delayed or denied her requests, and as a result she began appearing at the Ava governor's house daily to petition for livable conditions and medical care for the prisoners. Ann's friend, the widowed vicereine, gave her Burmese clothing to wear so she could walk the streets and visit Adoniram in prison without interference.[7] Ann depended on the Burmese convert Moung Ing and on her Burmese neighbors for their help with resources for the mission house community.

Ann spent the next two years contending with chaotic and harmful developments for herself and her mission community brought on by the Anglo-Burmese War. For example, a few months after the birth of Ann's daughter, Maria Eliza Butterworth Judson, Ann moved from the mission house into a small lean-to on the governor's grounds to care for a feverish Adoniram. Weeks later, Ann frantically gathered her children and Moung Ing to follow after Adoniram and his fellow prisoners who had been force-marched to a prison in the jungle of Oung-Pen-La.

Between Ava and the jungle prison of Oung-Pen-La, Ann Judson kept the imprisoned Adoniram and Dr. Price alive for eighteen months. While caring for the prisoners in the jungle, Ann and her children endured

[7] Francis Wayland (and Emily Chubbuck Judson), *A Memoir of the Life and Labors of the Rev. Adoniram Judson, D.D.* (Boston: Philips, Samson, 1853), 1:380.

small pox, financial extortion, and food shortage. When the prisoners were returned to Ava, the Burmese government conscripted Adoniram to be their translator for peace negotiations with the British. The return to Ava offered no relief for Ann. She contracted spotted fever (typhus) and would have died without Dr. Price being freed to care for her. During the final months of the war, Ann recuperated in the Ava governor's house and used her status in the governor's household to prevent Adoniram's return to prison.[8]

After the Anglo-Burmese War ended in early 1826, Ann and Adoniram briefly reunited with the Burmese Rangoon church and the Baptist missionaries. Rangoon remained Burmese territory, so the Judsons moved east to British-controlled Burmese territory, and many of the Burmese converts joined them there in search of safety and stability. Ann oversaw the growing Baptist mission community in the British-founded town of Amherst, and Adoniram returned to Ava to seek religious tolerance for Christians remaining in Rangoon. Ann ran day schools and organized regular worship in Amherst until she died of complications from spotted fever at the age of thirty-six on October 24, 1826. With Moung Ing, her girls, and other members of the Rangoon congregation by her side, Ann spoke her last words in Burmese.

It would be an understatement to call Ann Judson well known at her death. She was *world famous* across England and America because of her actions during the Anglo-Burmese War, and her death shortly thereafter cemented her importance to the American and British publics. A posthumous memoir published in 1831 included Ann's journals and letters from her early years in Bradford and offered Ann's vocational journey of abandoning self for God as the general path for Western missionaries. As public interest in her calling and her death grew, later biographers described her as an inspirational "missionary martyr" who sacrificed her desires and died for the cause. Yet through her innovative mission work, Ann Judson also expanded opportunities for women in religious life, developed catechesis methods, cultivated religious communities, and penned her theology of mission as participation in God's ongoing redemptive action. Ann's life work provides more guidance, theological reflection, and future possibilities for mission than any story of her sufferings could ever offer.

---

[8] Ann wrote an extensive account of her activities during the Anglo-Burmese War in a letter to Dr. Elnathan Judson, Amherst, Burma, February 26, 1826, in Knowles, *Memoir of Mrs. Ann H. Judson*, 282–317.

Suggested Reading

Joan Jacobs Brumberg, *Mission for Life: The Story of the Family of Adoniram Judson, the Dramatic Events of the First American Foreign Mission, and the Course of Evangelical Religion in the Nineteenth Century* (New York: Free Press, 1980).

Ann Hasseltine Judson, *An Account of the American Baptist Mission to the Burman Empire: In a Series of Letters Addressed to a Gentleman in London* (London: J. Butterworth & Son, 1823).

James D. Knowles, *Memoir of Mrs. Ann H. Judson, Late Missionary to Burmah: Including a History of the American Baptist Mission in the Burman Empire* (Boston: Lincoln & Edmands, 1831).

Laura Rodgers Levens, "Leaving Home and Finding Home: Theology and Practice of Ann Hasseltine Judson and the American Baptist Mission to Burma, 1812–1826," ThD dissertation, Duke University, 2015.

Laura Rodgers Levens, "Reading the Judsons: Recovering the Literary Works of Ann, Sarah, Emily, and Adoniram Judson for a New Baptist Mission History," *American Baptist Quarterly* 32, no. 1 (2013): 37–73.

Barbara Reeves-Ellington, Kathryn Kish Sklar, and Connie A. Shemo, eds., *Competing Kingdoms: Women, Mission, Nation, and the American Protestant Empire, 1812–1960* (Durham, NC: Duke University Press, 2010).

William Knibb (1803–1845)
Missionary Abolitionist

Social Justice

Kelly Pigott

In August 1845, forty-two-year-old William Knibb landed in Falmouth, Jamaica, to find a large crowd that had gathered to welcome him home. The celebration included a grand parade, with a mile-long procession and over a thousand horses. His wife, Mary, recorded in a letter that "we could see nothing but a forest of heads."[1] Most of the participants were former slaves who wanted to express their gratitude to a man who had helped them not only in their journey to find freedom in Christ but also in their struggle to find freedom from the plantation owners.

One wonders if any of them knew that just a few months prior to this celebration, many Baptists in the United States had formed the Southern Baptist Convention, in part to provide a place in the church for slave owners to continue to hold in bondage their fellow brothers and sisters in Christ. Certainly, none of the revelers knew that a few months later their celebration would turn to mourning as William Knibb passed away after contracting a fever.

The startling contrast of these back-to-back moments in Baptist history reveal the deep divide that has long existed among Baptists concerning race relations. The more well-known story of this particular era is how Baptist pastors in the United States, like Richard Furman, defended slavery by declaring that "…the right of holding slaves is clearly established in the Holy Scriptures, both by precept and example."[2] The lesser-known story is how other Baptists fought to end slavery. Enter William Knibb, born to Thomas and Mary Knibb of Kettering, England, in 1803.

---

[1] Quoted in Peter Masters, *Missionary Triumph Over Slavery: William Knibb and Jamaican Emancipation* (London: The Wakeman Trust, 2006), 49.

[2] Richard Furman, *Exposition of The Views of the Baptists, Relative to the Coloured Population In the United States in a Communication to the Governor of South Carolina* (Charleston, SC: A. E. Miller, 1838), 6.

Unlike in America, Baptists in England were largely unified behind abolitionism. However, this was not always the case. In the early days, organizations like the Baptist Missionary Society (BMS) chose a more neutral stance to prevent jeopardizing evangelistic efforts overseas. But the passionate vision of William Knibb on the issue eventually awakened their conscience, leading to large gatherings of English Baptists who loaned money and support for the antislavery movement. Knibb's success in this, however, was hard won.

As Knibb expressed interest in the ministry as a young adult, it was not at all clear that he would be good at it. He started his career as a printer, working for J. G. Fuller, the son of pastor and theologian Andrew Fuller. He attended a Particular Baptist congregation, Broadmead Church. There Pastor John Ryland baptized him in 1822 and mentored him in the years that followed. On one of his first preaching tours, missionary William Carey accompanied Knibb and remarked, "His manner was not graceful…nor were his words tastefully selected, or always ever accurately combined."[3] Obviously, he improved over time.

Knibb's older brother managed to get an appointment through the BMS to work as a missionary in Jamaica. Unfortunately, the harsh conditions took their toll and Thomas passed away in 1823 at the age of twenty-four. His brother's death devastated William, but the experience compelled him to finish what his brother had started. He pleaded with the BMS to allow him to take his brother's place. It took some persuading, but eventually the Society approved and sent Knibb to Borough Road School in London to receive some training, as Knibb never attended college. During this time he met and fell in love with Mary Watkins. On October 5, 1824, they were married, and one month later the young newlyweds sailed to Jamaica as missionaries.

Knibb and his brother were by no means the first Baptist missionaries in Jamaica. Decades before, George Leile, a freed slave turned founding pastor of the First African Baptist Church in Savannah, Georgia, had started a vibrant mission in Jamaica as the first American Baptist missionary.

Thus, upon landing in Jamaica, Knibb became a part of a long-established Baptist work. With no formal ministerial training, his first duties were to teach. As he immersed himself in the world of his students, it

---

[3] G. A. Catherall, *William Knibb: Freedom Fighter* (United Kingdom: Joney Publishing Company, 1972), 9.

didn't take long for Knibb to notice the exploitation and cruel treatment of the slaves by many of the estate owners. He wrote to his mother, "The cursed blast of slavery has, like a pestilence, withered almost every moral bloom. I know not how any person can feel a union with such a monster, such a child of hell. For myself I feel a burning hatred against it, and look upon it as one of the most odious monsters that ever disgraced the earth."[4]

He had to be careful, however, because powerful institutions defended slavery and viewed it as a vital part of Britain's success mainly due to great wealth brought to the empire through sugar production. Aware of this predicament, the BMS cautioned the young Knibb in a letter: "We are anxious to offer you a few words of advice in relation to your new engagement, as a token of our affectionate goodwill towards you. You are aware that the state of society in Jamaica is very different from that under which it is our privilege to live in this country, and that the great majority of its inhabitants are dependent upon their superiors...." The letter acknowledged that though conditions were painful to watch, "as a resident in Jamaica, you have nothing whatever to do with its civil or political affairs; with these you must never interfere."[5] Whether or not Knibb submitted to this ultimatum is a matter of contention among sources. Evidence suggests he at least felt at liberty to confront slave owners when they interfered with the spiritual formation of the slaves. If his efforts happened to highlight the mistreatment of slaves, so be it.

For example, colonial authorities imprisoned one of Knibb's deacons, Sam Swiney, for attending a "dissenting" church, the label given to non-Anglican groups like Methodists, Presbyterians, and, of course, Baptists. He was lashed twenty times and forced to do hard labor in chains. Knibb wrote a story about it in the local newspaper, which eventually led to the dismissal of two magistrates. Though the law sided with Knibb on this issue, the affair contributed to a growing perception among many that the young missionary had an agenda as an "agitator." Even leaders in the BMS were a little troubled by Knibb's activism, calling him an "officious meddler." Knibb wrote back, "...thankful that I am one of the 'officious meddlers' and not one of the honoured and applauded traffickers in human blood."[6]

---

[4] Ibid., 16.

[5] Quoted in Philip Wright, *"Knibb: the Notorious": Slaves' Missionary 1803–1845* (London: Sidgwick and Jackson, 1973), 31.

[6] Catherall, *William Knibb*, 32.

Making the situation worse for Knibb was the conflict between the established Anglican church and Dissenters. There was already a natural animosity between the two groups stemming from prior events in the English Reformation, but this was magnified as the Anglicans fully supported the slave owners and the dissenting pastors tended to side with the slaves. In addition, a rumor gathered strength that some Dissenters were actually spies working for the Anti-Slavery Society that had recently formed in England.

Tension escalated in Jamaica as the antislavery movement in England began to enjoy some successes. In 1831 the British House of Commons began to seriously consider passing laws to gradually eradicate slavery. The slave owners in Jamaica felt the pressure, creating an atmosphere of fear and paranoia. Increasingly, slave owners viewed Knibb as a ringleader for an abolitionist conspiracy, and many of them were not beyond fighting dirty, spreading rumors in an attempt to discredit Knibb. Powerful people looked for any opportunity to silence and even eradicate the Baptist missionary. They got their opportunity in December 1831 in what became known by many names, including the "Great Jamaican Slave Revolt" and the "Baptist Wars."

Events of the revolt are difficult to determine. It lasted for around eleven days, with skirmishes and property damage and deaths and a lot of confusion. The rebellion started with Samuel Sharpe, a slave and a Baptist deacon from Montego Bay. As one can imagine, there were many versions of what was ultimately behind Sharpe's efforts. The plantocracy was convinced that the Baptist ministers, specifically Knibb, incited the slaves to revolt. On the other side, abolitionists argued that the slave owners feared the momentum of the antislavery movement in England and intentionally agitated the slaves in the hopes of garnering sympathy and an exemption from any laws passed.

The groundwork for the revolt appears to have been a growing hope among the slaves that the king of Great Britain was about to free them. Along with this, however, was a fear that the slave owners would not comply. Knibb was recorded as stating that he explicitly attempted to dispel the rumor and encouraged his church members to obey their masters. Nonetheless, many slaves felt like they needed to take matters into their own hands.

According to one account, Sharpe found discarded newspapers highlighting the antislavery discussions in the United Kingdom. He became convinced that the British Empire planned to set the slaves free and require estate owners to pay for the labor. Sharpe confronted Knibb, stating, "We have worked enough already and will work no more; the life we live is too bad, it is the life of a dog, we won't be slaves no more, we won't lift hoe no more, we won't take flogging anymore."[7] He then gathered other like-minded slaves, and they devised a plan whereby during the Christmas break they would stop working and demand to be paid. Sharpe originally intended to use a nonviolent approach. However, as word spread about the plan, other slaves did not share this vision. Soon, others planned an open revolt.

On December 27, an enslaved woman was beaten for some minor infraction. Her husband intervened and beat the assailant. No one intervened to defend the white man who had beaten her, and this sparked the rebellion. Word spread that the time had come, and that night, enslaved people lit fires and destroyed plantation property. Over the next couple of days, additional skirmishes broke out and more buildings were burned. The colonial government declared martial law on December 31 and called out the militia. Greatly outgunned, slave owners and militia defeated the uprising and forced the rebellious slaves to surrender. By the end of the rebellion, the death toll included 207 slaves and 14 whites, though many felt that this official number was too low. The aftermath was even worse, with over 600 slaves imprisoned and charged. Approximately half the rulings resulted in execution, totaling 312.[8] Many people accused the courts of bad management and bias.

Among those arrested and imprisoned was William Knibb. Almost immediately the plantocracy accused Knibb and fellow Baptist ministers of instigating the rebellion. White mobs rioted and harassed the slaves and the BMS leaders, eventually destroying chapels (including the one Knibb preached in) and threatening lives. Knibb himself received several death threats. The plantocracy singled out Baptist slaves in particular for beatings, ushering in what became known as the "reign of terror."[9]

Eventually, Knibb and the Baptist leaders decided it was best that he leave and go back to England, which was exactly what the slave owners had hoped. So in 1832 he returned home. But the plantocracy strategy

---

[7] Doreen Morrison, *Slavery's Heroes: George Liele and the Ethiopian Baptists of Jamaica 1783 –1865* (Liele Books, 2015), 134.

[8] Mary Reckord, "The Jamaica Slave Rebellion of 1831," *Past and Present* 40 (July 1968): 121–22.

[9] Masters, *Missionary Triumph Over Slavery*, 27.

backfired, for, once in England, Knibb no longer felt constrained by the fragile politics of Jamaica, and he spoke freely of what he had witnessed. One of his first public addresses was to the BMS: "I appear as the feeble and unworthy advocate of 20,000 Baptists in Jamaica who have today no places of worship in which to meet, their chapels have been destroyed and no Sabbaths, and I believe and solemnly avow my belief, that by far the greater part of that twenty thousand will be flogged every time they are found praying." Knibb's oratorical skills had come a long way since he was last in England, and he held the audience spellbound. When he finished and sat down, he did so to "repeated rounds of deafening applause." Immediately a resolution was passed to support abolition.[10]

However, Knibb was just getting started. Reportedly he said, "Now I'll have slavery down. I will never rest, day or night, till I see it destroyed root and branch."[11] To this end he travelled the countryside, speaking to any group who would listen, which helped contribute to a groundswell of antislavery sentiment. Eventually, committees of both the House of Commons and the House of Lords invited him to speak. When asked pointed questions about the treatment of the slaves, Knibb gave blunt answers.

Finally, in December 1833, Parliament passed the Abolition Act, declaring that on August 1, 1834, slavery would be abolished. Unfortunately, the act also described a long and complicated process whereby the slaves would have to complete apprenticeships. During this time, they would only be partially free. In this, the slave owners found a way of continuing to exploit the slaves and to keep them working on the estates for little or no pay.

Knibb returned to Jamaica in 1834 and played a key role in holding the plantocracy accountable to the law. For this, he faced persecution, threats, and further attacks on his character. Once again, the slave owners underestimated Knibb's abilities. He, along with other colleagues, managed to get the attention of the British government. When Parliament formed committees to investigate the success of the apprenticeship program, Knibb's testimony again proved influential. As a result, the government ended the program early, declaring that on August 1, 1838, the slaves would be set completely free.

In the final decade of Knibb's life, he continued his efforts as a missionary and abolitionist. He spent some of his time in England, speaking

---

[10] Wright, *"Knibb: the Notorious,"* 116.

[11] Ibid., 112.

on social justice issues pertaining to the newly freed slaves. He spent some of his time in Jamaica, where he continued to preach and baptize. His church in Falmouth grew to around 2,500 and planted six churches in the region.[12]

After Knibb died at the young age of forty-two, Mary lived for another twenty years, devoting her time to teaching young girls in Kettering. Many of their children and grandchildren served as missionaries. Knibb was not without his critics. Some charged him with being too complacent prior to the rebellion. Others viewed him as too much of a provocateur. Nonetheless, his legacy both as a missionary and as an abolitionist continues to inspire. On the 150th anniversary of the abolition of slavery in Britain, Knibb received the Jamaican Order of Merit, the first white man to be so awarded.

Though for good reasons Baptists have a reputation among many for being on the wrong side of history when it comes to slavery, the lives of William and Mary Knibb serve as a reminder that contrarian stories exist. Many Baptists fought not only the establishment but also sometimes their own community of faith because of the dictates of their conscience. If there is a lesson to be learned, it is that when Baptists listen to their contrarian voices, they tend to be at their best.

Suggested Reading

Pete Masters, *Missionary Triumph over Slavery: William Knibb and Jamaican Emancipation* (London: The Wakeman Trust, 2006).

Philip Wright, *Knibb "the Notorious": Slaves' Missionary, 1803–1845* (London: Sidgwick and Jackson, 1973).

---

[12] Masters, *Missionary Triumph Over Slavery*, 48.

John Mason Peck (1789–1858), Missionary Educator in the Early American West

Missions

Brian Franklin

For almost his entire adult life, John Mason Peck traveled throughout the United States as a Baptist missionary, educator, writer, pastor, and fund-raiser. Over those four decades, from 1817 to 1858, he always returned to his adopted home near St. Louis in what was then known as the West—the states and territories of the Mississippi Valley. His story serves well as a window into American Baptist thought and practice during the first half of the nineteenth century: what they cared about, the visions they dreamed for their nation and denomination, and the ways in which their principles led to paradoxes and cautionary tales for today.

John Mason Peck was born in Litchfield, Connecticut, on October 31, 1789. Since he was the only son of Asa and Hannah (Farnum) Peck, John's birth assured the continuation of an American Peck family line that stretched back to their ancestors' arrival in Connecticut in 1634. John grew up in a Congregationalist family, with parents who maintained a farm and a stable home yet remained in relative poverty. Later in life, John described his childhood as a combination of schooling and farming, and his spiritual life as "spent like the generality of youth in willful opposition against God."[1]

In December 1807, Peck faced two life-changing forces that ended his boyhood wanderings. First, at a local revival, he encountered God in what he later described as a conversion experience. This weeks-long experience paralleled Peck's second life-altering encounter: meeting Sally Paine. Sally (who assumed the name Sarah in adulthood) attended the same revivals, also professed conversion, and joined the local Congre-

[1] Rufus Babcock, ed., *Forty Years of Pioneer Life: Memoir of John Mason Peck* (Carbondale: Southern Illinois University Press, 1965), 16.

gational church. The two met, grew in "esteem for each other," and were married eighteen months later in May 1809.[2]

In 1811, after the birth of their son Eli (their first of ten children), the Pecks moved to upstate New York, near Sally's family. Having grown up in Congregationalist families, both John and Sally would have been baptized as infants and would have planned to baptize their children as well. However, during this period of family growth, the Pecks began to reconsider their theological beliefs. Soon thereafter, they rejected the doctrine of covenant baptism and were baptized into the Baptist church at New Durham, New York, in October 1811. When John told his congregation of his desire to preach, they promptly called and licensed him. Over the next five years, Peck served as pastor of two nearby churches.[3]

While he preached in New York during the War of 1812, Peck found his heart drawn toward missions. He read about the first American foreign missionaries, including Adoniram and Ann Judson, who sailed for India in 1812 as representatives of the American Board of Commissioners for Foreign Missions (ABCFM). But rather than look abroad, Peck turned his eyes closer to home, toward the American territories of the Mississippi Valley. He identified the Valley as a land ripe for missionary labor, whose people were "not more than one third…supplyed [*sic*] with preachers."[4]

Peck's missionary aspirations began to come to fruition when he met Luther Rice in June 1815. Rice had sailed to India with the ABCFM missionaries in 1812. Like the Judsons, he had converted from Congregationalist to Baptist principles after leaving on that mission. While the ABCFM team stayed in south Asia, Rice sailed home to raise funds and promote a more centralized Baptist missionary organization. He succeeded at both in 1814 with the establishment of the General Convention of the Baptist Denomination in the United States of America for Foreign Missions (commonly referred to as the "Triennial Convention" because it would meet every three years). It was on a fundraising tour for this organization in June 1815 that Rice found himself in upstate New York at John Mason Peck's home. In early 1816, the Pecks offered themselves to the Triennial Convention as missionaries to the West.

---

[2] Babcock, *Forty Years*, 19–20.

[3] Ibid., 26–27.

[4] Ibid., 37–38, 51; John Mason Peck to Luther Rice, April 6, 1817, letter written on *Minutes of the Mississippi Baptist Association* (Natchez: Andrew Marschalk, 19 October 1816), St. Louis Mercantile Library, John Mason Peck Collection, Appendix 1, Item 106.

After one year of theological study in Philadelphia, Peck and his colleague James Welch received a call from the Triennial Convention board to undertake an experimental domestic mission to St. Louis and the Missouri Territory. The Pecks—now a family of five—set out on a four-month journey to St. Louis. After arriving, John spent the next three years traveling throughout the Missouri and Illinois regions and organizing some of the earliest churches, schools, female mite societies, and mission societies in the West.

After these three years of excitement and success, the following two years brought trouble, tragedy, and change for the Peck family. In mid-1820, the Triennial Convention announced that it would withdraw financial and organizational support from Peck's mission. Over the next sixteen months, two of their children died, their firstborn Eli (age 10), and their fourth born, William Carey (age 3). After two years without any outside support, Peck secured a partnership with the Massachusetts Baptist Missionary Society in early 1822. With the periodic $5/week from this new appointment, and a renewed sense of mission going forward, the Peck family moved in April to the place that would become their permanent home: Rock Spring, Illinois, just eighteen miles outside of St. Louis.

After the move to Rock Spring, John Mason Peck began to settle into the life for which he has come to be known. "Mr. Peck was a *Western Man*...the embodiment of Western character," recalled Jeremiah Jeter, pastor of the Second Baptist Church in St. Louis and future president of the Foreign Mission Board of the Southern Baptist Convention. Jeter's audience of the 1820s would have known what the word "Western" meant: the states and territories of the Mississippi Valley.[5]

Peck wrote incessantly about the West and the Valley during his early years of ministry. He edited and wrote for *The Pioneer* (1829), the first Baptist periodical in the West. His *A New Guide for Emigrants to the West* went through three editions in the 1830s as Americans devoured his descriptions of western people, places, and customs. He annotated maps and compiled a *Gazetteer of Illinois*. Peck even set his pen toward infrastructure improvement. After experiencing a disastrous shipwreck aboard the passenger riverboat *Shepherdess* in January 1844, Peck wrote to the U.S. Congress and successfully lobbied for an appropriation of funds to clear obstructions in western rivers.[6]

[5] Babcock, *Forty Years*, 346–47.

[6] Ibid., 328–30.

Peck's voluminous writing points also to his passion for education. Upon arrival in the West in 1817, Peck immediately began establishing Sunday schools and common schools for children in the St. Louis area. He raised money for libraries. Above all, he longed to educate pastors in the West, for the West. Before he even left New York in 1816, Peck had already opened correspondence with Luther Rice about his vision for a "great, central, mammoth, Baptist Metropolitan College and Theological Seminary." That vision experienced its first life in 1827 with the founding of Rock Spring Seminary, among the first institutions of higher learning anywhere between the Alleghenies and the Mississippi River.[7]

Peck's tireless work for widespread access to education endeared him to many, but it also made him many enemies. His most persistent opponents allied themselves with a loosely organized group called (derisively) the Anti-Mission Movement. During the first half of the nineteenth century, tens of thousands of citizens mostly in the Mississippi and Ohio River valleys spoke against the growing system of religious societies. They viewed these as unscriptural and intrusive organizations. Antimissionists published scathing editorials, burned pledge notes, interrupted meetings, and organized their churches against these societies. John Taylor of Kentucky, Alexander Campbell of Virginia, and Daniel Parker of Illinois proved some of Peck's fiercest opponents.

These leading Antimissionists remained diverse, but they all agreed on at least one thing: John Mason Peck represented all that was wrong among American Baptists (and Protestantism generally). Their ongoing dispute revealed a cluster of paradoxes at the heart of Baptist theology, ecclesiology, and practice. Baptists tended to value the local in early America, yet they found themselves spreading nationally during the antebellum era. Baptists supported cooperative organizations aimed at benefiting society, but they also believed that the highest religious authority rested in the local church. Baptists championed the separation of church and state, but if the state offered to support religious endeavors, Baptists splintered on how to move forward.

For Peck, this entire dispute was much simpler. The "*radical* evil, which lies at the bottom of all other evils amongst western Baptists," Peck complained to his friends, "is the *deplorable ignorance of the ministry*. This

---

[7] Rufus Babcock, "Personal Recollections of John Mason Peck, D.D.," in *Christian Watchman and Reflector* 39, no. 20 (May 1858): 1.

is the Hydra monster that has produced almost every other evil."[8] In his diagnosis, Peck was on the right track. Plain folk of the West *did* foster suspicion of organized education, especially when it came from the East and when it called into question their views about biblical qualifications for pastors. But in his delivery, Peck was often very wrong. He dismissed his opponents as acting out of "sheer selfishness" or out of pure jealousy, like little trees overshadowed by "big trees in the woods."[9] He tended toward patterns of classifying groups of people, a potentially helpful tool for a writer but a poor practice when wielded by a preacher in prejudicial ways.

During the 1830s and 1840s, Peck solidified his reputation as one of the most prominent Baptists in the United States through his wide-ranging promotion of religious societies. This was the golden age of what historians have called the Protestant Benevolent Empire, an extensive network of groups dedicated to spreading the gospel and improving the daily lives of people. By the 1830s, the nation's disparate collection of local benevolent societies had centralized their efforts into organizations with national visions and scale.

Peck joined forces with many of these national organizations, including the American Bible Society, the American Sunday School Union, and the American Baptist Publication Society, to name a few. He believed their organizational power was essential to success in the Mississippi Valley and that this region would prove crucial to the nation's future. For these causes, he embarked on regular fundraising tours across the nation. He met with all sorts of people along the way, from small-town Baptist pastors to world-renowned figures, including President John Quincy Adams in Washington, DC, and Charles Dickens in St. Louis during Dickens's 1842 American tour. In 1835, Peck began a tour to raise money for the seminary. He returned with $20,000, including a $10,000 gift from Boston doctor Benjamin Shurtleff, after whom the trustees would rename the seminary Shurtleff College.

In 1831, Peck struck up a friendship with Jonathan Going that proved pivotal for American Baptist missions. Going, also a Baptist pastor, undertook his own tour of the West in mid-1831. He arrived at Peck's home on June 20, and the two of them set out on a three-month tour of Illinois, Missouri, Indiana, and Kentucky. On their last night together, in

---

[8] John Mason Peck to Lynd, Stevens, and Johnson, July 25, 1833, American Baptist Historical Society, John Mason Peck Papers.

[9] Babcock, *Forty Years*, 110–11.

Shelbyville, Kentucky, Peck recorded in his journal, "Here we agreed on the plan of the American Baptist Home Mission Society." Only months later, in April 1832, the ABHMS held its first annual meeting in New York. This society grew rapidly and sent missionaries throughout the United States, picking up where the Triennial Convention had left off a decade before.[10]

Peck's nationalistic vision, and his commitment to national unity above all civic virtues, required that he be a political man. For the most part, Peck navigated these waters well, attempting to steer away from partisanship. But the combination of his Baptist convictions and his nationalism—both rock-solid—led him toward two political stands in the 1840s and 1850s that, although common then, prove more troublesome now.

The first episode revolved around Peck's support for the Mexican-American War of 1846–1848. In early 1848, near the end of the war, Peck published an editorial in the local *Bellville Advocate*, based on his recent public speech that celebrated the American military victory at the Battle of Buena Vista. His editorial defended the Polk Administration's original justification for war: that Mexico shot first. "The conviction in my mind is irresistible," Peck argued. "The government of the United States committed no aggression on Mexico."[11]

Peck's publication drew the sharp critique of a freshman U.S. congressman from a few miles away in Illinois: Abraham Lincoln. It "disappoints me," Lincoln confessed in a letter to Peck. Lincoln thought of Peck as "intelligent, right-minded, and *impartial*," but the editorial suggested to him otherwise. Five months after challenging Polk and the U.S. Congress with the bold Spot Resolutions, Lincoln went on to similarly eviscerate Peck's defense of the war. He closed prophetically with a question based on Jesus' words: "Then I ask, is the precept 'Whatsoever ye would that men should do to you, do ye even so to them' obsolete?—of no force?—of no application?"[12]

Lincoln's critique signaled a deeper and more existential irony in Peck's life: his middle-road position on slavery and equality. Peck was a man divided by his commitment to maintaining moral, denominational,

---

[10] Babcock, *Forty Years*, 244, 265–66.

[11] Abraham Lincoln to John Mason Peck, 21 May 1848, in *Abraham Lincoln Papers: Series 1, General Correspondence, 1833 to 1916*, available at https://www.loc.gov/item/mal0011100

[12] Ibid.

and civic loyalties that warred with one another on the battlefield of American slavery. No doubt, Peck lamented slavery and its devastating consequences. He called it a "bitter draught" for both slave and enslaver, and "a violation of man's nature and of the Christian law of love." Yet slavery remained an abstract evil for most of Peck's life. It wasn't until New Year's Day 1842, on a trip through Nashville, that he witnessed his first slave auction:

> To-day I attended for a few moments a sale in the marketplace. A negro boy was sold, who appeared about twelve years old. He stood by the auctioneer on the market-bench with his hat off, crying and sobbing, his countenance a picture of woe. I know not the circumstances...and it filled me with indescribable emotions.[13]

Unfortunately, Peck's disapproval of slavery generally stopped with his expressed sorrow. He opposed the expansion of slavery but rejected abolition. He lamented the poor condition of slaves but also claimed it was "certainly not as oppressive" as the condition of the poor in "England, Ireland, and many parts of Continental Europe." He wished for the freedom of enslaved African Americans but only if they remained separate, ideally via colonization in Africa. Equality was out of the question, Peck assured his readers in 1853. He never had, and never would, give African Americans "the least expectation" that they would ever possess "social and political equality whilst they live amongst us."[14]

Peck developed his theology and ideology of slavery with careful attention to classic Baptist ideas regarding the scope of governmental power, the separation of church and state, and the role of individual conscience. Regarding slavery, he expressed the interplay between these ideas perhaps most clearly in a January 1851 address he delivered at the state house in Springfield, "The Duties of American Citizens." The Illinois House of Representatives invited Peck to exhort Illinoisans to comply with a new and controversial national law: the Fugitive Slave Act. Passed by the U.S. Congress in September 1850, this federal law threatened penalty to American citizens who aided escaped slaves or failed to cooperate in their lawful recapture.

---

[13] John Mason Peck, *A New Guide for Emigrants to the West*, 2nd ed. (Boston: Gould, Kendall & Lincoln, 1837), 113; Badcock, *Forty Years*, 300.

[14] John Mason Peck, *Christian Times*, October 20, 1853, in Roger D. Bridges, "John Mason Peck on Illinois Slavery," *Journal of the Illinois State Historical Society* 75, no. 3 (Autumn 1982): 214.

Peck devoted his entire address to defending obedience to this law. Christians, Peck argued, owed particular duties to God and other duties to "the powers that be." This idea, he emphasized, functioned in "entire accordance with a fundamental principle of the [Baptist] denomination," the separation of church and state, and citizens' duties to these separate spheres.[15]

With these ideals in mind, Peck argued that it remained the duty of all American citizens, especially Baptist Christians, to obey the Fugitive Slave Act. He labeled supposed moral opposition to the law as "religious fanaticism" characterized by "wild, anarchical, licentious doctrines," akin to the "phrenzy" of nullification and secession in the South. Peck closed with a warning to those who opposed this law. "Cease your agitation," he warned. No number of "lectures and protests, and denunciations, and resolutions" had ever pricked a slaveholder's conscience. He advocated that Baptists cease preaching against something they believed immoral—a strange and disappointing note for a Baptist preacher to end on.[16]

When Rufus Babcock visited Peck in summer 1850, cholera was ravaging St. Louis. And yet Babcock found Peck supplying pulpits, supporting the seminary, editing newspapers, preparing a discourse upon the death of President Zachary Taylor, and doing the work "of one or two men besides."[17] This whirlwind of work could describe any day in Peck's latter years. In his final decade, he wrote or edited several books, including a biography, *The Life of Daniel Boone*. He pastored multiple churches in the St. Louis area (including both a German and African American church) and briefly one in Kentucky. In July 1852, Peck experienced a capstone of his career when Harvard bestowed upon him an honorary Doctor of Divinity. His peer recipients of honorary degrees were Horace Bushnell, Francis Wayland, and Alexis de Tocqueville.

Peck's final years were marked by tragedy. In November 1852, the seminary, including almost the entirety of Peck's library, burned to the ground. Peck had collected materials for four decades with an eye toward writing a magnum opus history of the Mississippi Valley. After the fire, all that remained were the materials he kept at home: his journals, personal

---

[15] John Mason Peck, "The Duties of American Citizens" (St. Louis: T.W. Ustick, 1851), 5, at St. Louis Mercantile Library, John Mason Peck Collection, Appendix 2 (Other Pamphlets), item 343.

[16] Ibid., 5, 10, 21–22.

[17] Babcock, "Personal Recollections," 1.

book manuscripts, and letters. Peck mourned, and then he redoubled his collection efforts.

Peck's deepest tragedy visited almost exactly four years later. On October 24, 1856, his wife Sally died. Peck was crushed. He floundered for words to describe "to *what extent* she was the *help-mate*, pre-eminently, in every department of labor" he ever undertook. As he was literally "worn out" both physically and emotionally, Peck's work pace slowed. On March 14, 1858, surrounded by family and friends at home, John Mason Peck died.[18]

John Mason Peck left many legacies, but two in particular stand out. Peck spent his entire life writing and collecting materials about the Mississippi Valley. By early 1858, when he knew the end was near, Peck resolved to preserve his life's work. In his will, he gifted all of his materials to the St. Louis Mercantile Library for preservation, with the single condition that all of it be made "accessible to all persons engaged in historical researches."[19] He named Rufus Babcock his literary executor and charged him with compiling a memoir from his remaining journals and letters. Babcock published that memoir in 1864, and providentially so because soon after he returned Peck's journals to the Mercantile, the library moved locations. During the move, they mistakenly sent all of Peck's materials to a paper mill, which turned them into wrapping paper.

Peck left a second striking legacy in his influence on the Baptist denomination, especially in the United States. When Peck's memoir first hit the market for sale in May 1864—during the Civil War—advertisers were effusive. "There is not an intelligent Baptist in this country who has not heard of the life and labors of John M. Peck," wrote the editors of the *Christian Watchman and Reflector*. "Dr. Peck was no ordinary man," they assured their readers. In his death, "the Baptist cause and the Christian church had lost a faithful, brave, and earnest standard-bearer."[20] These editors were correct indeed. When he died in 1858, Americans (especially Baptists) knew exactly who John Mason Peck was and what he had contributed to American religion, education, and society. Baptists and Americans today should know the same.

---

[18] Babcock, *Forty Years*, 356–58.

[19] "A Guide to the John Mason Peck Collection of the St. Louis Mercantile Library Association" (St. Louis: St. Louis Mercantile Library Association, 1989), 9.

[20] *Christian Watchmen and Reflector* (Boston, MA), 26 May 1864, p. 2; June 30, 1864, p. 3.

Suggested Reading

Rufus Babcock, ed., *Forty Years of Pioneer Life: Memoir of John Mason Peck* (Carbondale: Southern Illinois University Press, 1965).

Roger D. Bridges, "John Mason Peck on Illinois Slavery," *Journal of the Illinois State Historical Society* 75, no. 3 (Autumn 1982): 179–217.

John Mason Peck, *A New Guide for Emigrants to the West*, 2nd ed. (Boston: Gould, Kendall & Lincoln, 1837).

Emily Chubbuck Judson (1817–1854), *The Scribe of Missions*

Missions

C. Delane Tew

Emily Chubbuck Judson made her mark on the Baptist mission effort through her pen as a highly acclaimed author and chronicler of mission work in Burma. She was the third wife of the legendary missionary to Burma, Adoniram Judson. Emily wrote the story of her husband's second wife, Sarah, and after his death she worked diligently alongside Frances Wayland to research, write, and edit Adoniram's official biography, which spread the story of Baptist mission efforts in Burma throughout America. She passionately recorded the actions of Adoniram to reach the people of Burma with the gospel message, the hardships he endured, and his desire to encourage American Baptists to support the mission effort. As Adoniram's wife, Emily was able to participate in mission work herself as well as care for her stepchildren and the daughter she and Adoniram had together.

Life was not easy for young Emily Chubbuck. Born in 1817, Emily grew up in poverty, with her father moving from job to job and unable to support the family adequately. When she was eleven, Emily went to work in a mill to bring money to the family. Emily's education was a patchwork of short stents in small village schools and self-education. Illness often hindered her efforts, a condition that would plague her periodically throughout her life. Even with the bleakness of life, or perhaps because of it, Emily began writing by the age of nine, regardless of the fact that she lacked a formal education. At the age of fifteen, she started teaching while enjoying publication of her work in local papers. Her first poem, written in a notebook, was a self-portrait written for a cousin: "...Her hair is dark, a glossy brown, / Sometimes bound up but oftener, / In wild confusion o'er her face, / And destitute of every graies [sic]...."[1]

---

[1] In George H. Tooze, ed., *The Life and Letters of Emily Chubbuck Judson*, vol. 7 (Macon, GA: Mercer University Press, 2013), 3.

In 1838, the *Hamilton Village Paper* published a number of Emily's writings. By age nineteen, with her teaching and her writing she was the sole support for her parents and her older sister, Catherine (Kate). Emily's skill and intelligence opened a door for her when in 1840 she received a scholarship to the Utica Female Academy. Leaders of the school agreed that after her studies she would teach at the school in order to pay off her tuition. In 1841, Emily became assistant instructor of the department of English. That same year, she published her first book, *Charles Linn, or how to observe the Golden Rule.*

Emily also had her writings published in several popular magazines of the day. *Knickerbocker* magazine published her poem, "Where are the Dead?" and other poems were published in *Lady's Book* and *Mother's Journal.* Over the next four years, Emily wrote and published four collections of moral short stories for children as well as children's religious books for the American Baptist Publication Society. Emily's works were published under both her own name and under the penname Fanny Forester. Because she wrote both religious and literary stories, she reached a wide audience. The growth of her popularity took a significant step in 1844, when N. P. Willis, editor of *Evening Mirror*, began to publish her writing in his magazine. This was the era of writers such as Ralph Waldo Emerson, Henry David Thoreau, and other transcendentalists. A friend of Emily's commented that she was being categorized with the group. Fanny Forester's popularity grew, enabling Emily to receive an unprecedented $5.00 per page from magazines that wished to publish her writings.

Emily's publication of a collection of her magazine stories in a book titled *Trippings in Authorland* in 1845 changed her life course. In the same year, missionary Adoniram Judson sailed back to the United States with his wife Sarah, their three oldest children, and Sarah's son from a previous marriage. Their two youngest, Henry and Edward, had been left in Burma with another missionary couple. Sarah had been gravely ill, and loved ones hoped that she would convalesce during the furlough while the older four children would settle in America to be educated. Sadly, Sarah died during the voyage and was buried on the island of St. Helena. Back in the United States, Adoniram sought an author to write Sarah's biography. He came across *Trippings* and grew curious about the author Fanny Forester.

Emily and Adoniram met on Christmas Day 1845. Because of her health, her doctors had encouraged Emily to spend the cold winter months in Philadelphia, Pennsylvania. Adoniram was in the same city encouraging Baptists to continue supporting the efforts of the American Baptist

Missionary Union. On Christmas morning a mutual friend, Arthur D. Gillette, brought the fifty-seven-year-old Adoniram to meet Emily, twenty-nine years old. By January 2, 1846, Emily acknowledged her love for this stately missionary. During their brief courtship, many of their meetings focused on details of Sarah's life for the memoir. Letters from Adoniram soon came to demonstrate his love for Emily; the gift of a watch that had belonged to Ann Hasseltine Judson, his first wife, emphasized his growing dedication to Emily.

Adoniram said goodbye to Philadelphia and Emily by the end of January, leaving for a speaking tour, but not before he and Emily were engaged. Emily returned to her home in Utica, New York, to prepare for her wedding and travel to Burma. During this time, Emily researched and dealt with copyists on publication of a collection of her writings, *Alderbrook*. Adoniram stepped in to aid in its publication. He also paid in full all debt owed by Emily's parents. Emily continued to publish writings under the name Forester through 1847. She feared the public would criticize Adoniram for marrying an author of such frivolous fiction and poetry. Unfortunately, this fear came true. She received criticism not only from the religious world but also from fans of Fanny Forester, who lamented that such a gifted woman would waste her life away in a distant, dangerous country. But Adoniram never faltered in his love for her. In the face of public consternation, Emily and Adoniram married on June 2, 1846, and sailed for Burma the next month. On board the ship the night before their departure, Emily wrote, "Our 'Cradle' rocks upon the tide; / My heart is rocking too; / And warm tears gather blindingly, / And shut the shore from view. / I scarcely know why I should weep; / But 'tis so strange to be / An exile from my native land, / Upon the stormy sea!..."[2]

Emily had a heart open to mission work from a young age. At the age of eleven, she had read of the life and death of Adoniram's first wife, Ann. At the time, she thought of becoming a missionary herself. Emily was baptized at the age of seventeen. While she was teaching, she wrote her pastor about her desire to serve on the mission field. He encouraged her to wait for God to open the door for her. She must have recalled those events as she crossed the oceans in 1846.

The seas on their voyage to Burma were fortunately calm, and the uneventful crossing allowed time for Emily to begin learning Burmese

[2] Ibid., 406.

under the tutelage of her husband. Using time on board and after her arrival in Burma, Emily began working on her *Memoir of Sarah B. Judson, Member of the American Mission to Burmah.* Arriving in Burma, Emily met her two new stepsons, Henry and Edward, with a loving heart. She continued to write poems, and numerous editors wrote to her asking for pieces they could publish. Emily also concentrated on building a new life. Upon her arrival, she immediately took on the task of building a home for Adoniram and his two young sons whom he had left with fellow missionaries while he was away in the United States. Their first home together was in Moulmein, a center of missionary work in the country. However, Adoniram had a passion to work in Rangoon where no missionaries lived, and he moved his family there.

In Rangoon, the Judsons shared their house with bats and a wide variety of insects and vermin, and the interior surfaces of their entire living space were often covered with mold. Emily's letters described her inability to secure even the basics of adequate nutrition for the family, as she rarely found fruits and vegetables in the market. Scarcer still among the vegetarian Buddhists was meat to feed her family. In this atmosphere, all members of the family experienced grave illness. Adoniram suffered repeated bouts of dysentery, Henry had "Rangoon fever," Edward became deathly ill with erysipelas, a violent skin disease, and Emily herself suffered a variety of fevers that left her too weak even to sit up. In her letters, she described crawling to the children's beds to care for them. Still, when her health allowed, she continued studying the language and working on Sarah's memoir, completing it on June 1, 1847. The family remained in Rangoon only seven months. Following their return to Moulmein, Emily gave birth to Emily Frances Judson on Christmas Eve 1847. Early in January, Emily wrote arguably her best-known poem, "My Bird," about her infant daughter. "Ere last year's moon had left the sky, / A birdling sought my Indian nest, / And folded, O so lovingly! / Her tiny wings upon my breast. / From morn till evening's purple tinge / In winsome helplessness she lies; / Two rose leaves, with a silken fringe, / Shut softly on her starry eyes...."[3]

Emily had begun learning Burmese from her husband when they left America. Eventually, she learned it well enough to conduct prayer meetings for the Burmese women. In a letter, she described holding two women's prayer meetings in one day, the first at 6:00 a.m. and another

[3] Ibid., 455.

after breakfast. She also continued the work Sarah Judson had begun on "Scripture Questions," with a volume on the book of Acts. She finalized the manuscript for Sarah's biography while in Rangoon and had it published in 1848. This work, writes Laura Rodgers Levens, contributed "to nineteenth-century American ideologies of womanhood, Christian behavior, and the agency of missionary women. Emily, as Fanny Forester, used the complexities of Sarah's character, as well as her distinctive traits in comparison to Ann Judson, to ponder the 'power' of femininity and Christian humility for her readers."[4] Through this memoir the world learned of Sarah's continued evangelistic efforts among the Karen tribes[5] following the death of her first husband, George Boardman.

In 1848, Emily decided that she could not continue writing for magazines while fulfilling her duties as wife and mother and engaging in mission work with the Burmese. From that point, Emily would only write letters to friends and family. However, she often had requests from her widening circle of acquaintances for a piece of poetry in memorial of family members or times of celebration. In letters home, Emily was at times defensive of her earlier literary career. She explained to friends that she had used her God-given talent to the best of her ability and that now she was dedicated to spreading the gospel. She also learned that the desire for anything from her pen pushed editors to obtain letters she had written to family at home. They often took only the parts of her letters that made it seem like she was unhappy on the mission field. Editors continued to beg Emily for new works, and one even promised her twenty percent of the price of a book, twice the usual royalty. Though Emily no longer wrote for the literary magazines, she did contribute pieces to religious and denominational magazines describing the life and works of missionaries as well as life in a foreign land.

Emily's health, weak since childhood, continued to limit the work she was able to do. Then, in 1849, she realized she was pregnant again. As the new year opened, Adoniram's health faltered. The couple took a trip to the seashore at Amherst, confident that the sea air would help them both. Adoniram did not improve. Doctors counselled that a sea voyage was his

[4] Laura Rodgers Levens, "Reading the Judsons: Recovering the Literary Works of Ann, Sarah, Emily, and Adoniram Judson for a New Baptist Mission History," *American Baptist* Quarterly 32 (Spring 2013): 55.

[5] The best source on the Karen people is Amy Neiman, Eunice Soh, and Parisa Sutan, "Karen," *ethnomed*, https://ethnomed.org/culture/karen.

only hope. As a result of difficulties with her pregnancy, Emily had to watch from the shore as his ship sailed on April 8, 1850. Adoniram died on board just four days later in the Bay of Bengal and was buried at sea. Emily did not learn of his death until August 9. Her baby boy had been stillborn on April 23.

Emily was torn between staying in Burma to continue the mission work begun by Adoniram and caring for her children in the face of continued health issues. Pulled by the desire to have all the Judson children under one roof, Emily, with her two stepsons by Adoniram and her daughter, Emily Frances, sailed for America on January 22, 1851, spending time in Calcutta and London before arriving in America in October. The family first settled in Hamilton, New York. Emily relied on payments from the mission board and from her writing to cover their expenses. For two summers, she successfully gathered all six of the Judson children plus Adoniram's stepson. Emily took great care to guide the children in their education and in their spiritual lives, joyously celebrating the baptisms of the three oldest.

Other than the children, Emily's main concern was the writing of Adoniram's biography. Together with the mission board, Emily decided that Dr. Francis Wayland, president of Brown University, should pen the book. Emily wrote numerous letters to family, friends, and religious leaders asking for any correspondence they might have from Adoniram. Dr. Wayland depended on Emily to help arrange the material, leading her to move to Providence to work more closely with him. Before they could complete the volume, word came that Edward Fletcher was writing an unauthorized biography of Adoniram. Emily greatly feared that his work would negatively impact the legacy of her husband. She also feared that this book would limit the sales of the Wayland book, as she would receive royalties from it but none from the Fletcher work. Despite her efforts, the Fletcher work was published.

Emily also worked on publishing a collection of her poetry, which she titled *Olio of Domestic Verses.* Always concerned with being able to support the Judson children financially, Emily negotiated to keep this book's copyright for herself for seven years before it transitioned to the publisher. Turning to explaining the missionary effort to the public, Emily wrote a collection of essays and other writings, published in 1853 with the title *The Kathayan Slave and Other Papers Connected with Missionary Life.* Levens writes, "Her dramatic stories of Adoniram's experiences in prison and as a humble gospel preacher in *Kathayan Slave* left a lasting imprint of

Adoniram's character and missionary methods upon American Baptist memory…."[6]

Emily did her best to care for the three youngest Judsons and to provide for them with her writing through 1854, welcoming the older Judson offspring as often as they could visit. Unfortunately, her health began to deteriorate drastically. Emily found homes for the children, settling the youngest, Emily Frances, with her longtime friend Ann Maria Anable. Overcome with weakness, Emily relied on her brother, Wallace, to write her correspondence. Emily's sister, Kate, cared for her in her final days. Emily died on June 1, 1854.

Emily left behind an amazing body of literature. As acclaimed author Fanny Forester, she was highly respected for her keen insight into human nature as well as her creative use of words. As a missionary, she was much loved by the Burmese she taught and by Baptist men and women in the United States who admired her courage. As a scribe of missions, she told the story of Sarah Judson and Adoniram Judson in a way that fanned the flames of missionary support in Baptist churches.

Suggested Reading

Rosalie Hall Hunt, *Bless God and Take Courage: The Judson History and Legacy* (Valley Forge: Judson Press, 2005).

Laura Rodgers Levens, "Reading the Judsons: Recovering the Literary Works of Ann, Sarah, Emily, and Adoniram Judson for a New Baptist Mission History," *American Baptist Quarterly* 32 (Spring 2013): 37–73.

George H. Tooze, *The Life and Letters of Emily Chubbuck Judson*, vols. 1–7 (Macon, GA: Mercer University Press, 2013–).

[6] Ibid., 56.

William J. Simmons (1849–1890), African American National Leader, Preacher, Educator, Editor, Organizer

Education

Laura Rodgers Levens

During one of the darkest periods of American history, William James Simmons was a force to be reckoned with. As a minister, school president, journalist, and church statesman, Simmons strove against slavery and segregation, "the sum of human villainies," on behalf of African Americans. He devoted his life to ensure that the rise of Jim Crow would not "crush out the life" of African Americans.[1] He worked to build up Black schools, newspapers, women's organizations, and a religious denomination. Known as a large-hearted man, Dr. Simmons promoted an expansive vision wherein Black women and men could rise to the heights for which they were created.

William was born in Charleston, South Carolina, to two slaves, Edward and Esther Simmons, on June 29, 1849. While William was still very young, his mother escaped from slavery with him and his two sisters, Emeline and Anna. They traveled north through the Underground Railroad to Philadelphia, where they stayed in the home of his uncle, Alexander Tardieu (or Tardiff). Over the next few years, Esther Simmons and her brother Alexander struggled to support the household while avoiding slave traders and others looking to profit from returning fugitive slaves. The family moved across Pennsylvania several times to avoid discovery and capture. They also suffered from smallpox without medical care, and William was educated privately by his uncle due to the looming danger of capture and re-enslavement.

In 1862, at the age of thirteen, William Simmons was apprenticed to Dr. Leo H. DeLange, a White dentist in Bordentown, New Jersey.

---

[1] William J. Simmons, Preface to *Men of Mark: Eminent, Progressive and Rising* (Cleveland: George M. Revell, 1887), 6.

Simmons proved to be an able and competent dental assistant, but he often contended with racism from patients and even Dr. DeLange. He applied to dental college in Philadelphia, but the college rejected him due to racial prejudice. He stayed in dentistry until September 16, 1864, when he ran away from Dr. DeLange and enlisted in the Forty-first United States Colored Troops. Simmons participated in several battles around Virginia as a Union soldier and was present at the surrender of Confederate General Robert E. Lee at Appomattox. After the end of the Civil War, he worked as a dentist in Philadelphia before returning to work for Dr. DeLange in New Jersey.

William Simmons professed conversion and joined the Baptist church in Bordentown in 1867 at the age of eighteen. The Baptist church was White, and here he experienced better treatment and collegiality than in his prior years. Bordentown's pastor, Rev. J. W. Custis, took interest in Simmons and encouraged him to go into ministry. The church supported him financially through three years of education at Madison University (later known as Colgate) and Rochester University. In 1868, Simmons began working at a Baptist church in Rochester as a way to earn more financial aid, and he also began ministering among the Black community there. Unable to complete the degree at Rochester due to eye strain, he moved to Washington, D.C., and enrolled in Howard University in 1871.

Howard University was a dramatic cultural shift for William Simmons. Unlike with Madison and Rochester, donors established Howard University as a historically black college. Missionaries opened Howard as a school of theology for freed slaves in 1866, and in 1867 an act of the United States chartered it as a university. Known in the twentieth century as "the capstone of Negro education," Howard was governed by White men and educated Black men and White women while William Simmons attended from 1871–1873. Simmons connected with the Black community and families in D.C. and showed excellent administrative potential by rebuilding a school and being hired as a principal of Hillsdale Public School. He also established professional connections and support from influential White educators, scientists, newspaper editors, and others during this period.

Simmons married Josephine A. Silence of Washington, D.C., on August 25, 1874. Shortly after, they moved to Florida in pursuit of financial security and to explore Simmons's professional possibilities. He preached in small churches, invested in land and agriculture, worked as an academy principal, and served in political office as a deputy clerk and county commissioner. Committed to political activism and the Republican Party, he campaigned for Rutherford B. Hayes in 1876.

When the Reconstruction era ended in 1877, so did Simmons's political career and professional opportunities. In the decade after the Civil War (1865–1877), African American men had enjoyed integrated employment opportunities, schools, political offices, White philanthropic interest, and voting rights in a concerted effort to revive post-war America as a land of opportunity for both Black and White. After 1877, Whites in both the North and South made a concerted effort to disenfranchise African Americans and instill a White majority in state and federal governments. White politicians, judges, businessmen, and journalists enforced social rules and passed laws to enact segregation through what would become known as Jim Crow laws. The following decades became a time of disillusionment, fear, and struggle for African Americans, as episodes of lynching and vandalism rose in number. For Simmons, it must have seemed like the prowling slave traders had returned to steal his freedom.

At the age of twenty-nine, Simmons had done too much in the world to content himself with hiding. William and Josephine Simmons, now a family with small children, moved back to the community and schools of Washington, D.C. He taught public school and pastored a small church there, only returning to Florida to be ordained as a deacon and licensed to preach in Ocala in 1879. Also in 1879, Simmons moved his family to Kentucky to begin a pastorate at First Baptist Church of Lexington. In 1880, they moved to Louisville, where he assumed the principalship of the Normal and Theological Institution. Small and in debt, the General Association of Colored Baptists of Kentucky (GACB) administered the school, which made it Black *owned* and Black *governed*. Here, Simmons found his place to explore his talents, grow his influence, and build a place of Black education and opportunity.

Black Baptists in Kentucky had been among the earliest to organize themselves after the Civil War. In 1866, they purchased land in Frankfort with plans to open a college for ministers and teachers. Operations stalled due to lack of funds and personnel, but by 1879 the GACB had sold the Frankfort property, bought property in Louisville, and opened Normal and Theological Institute as a small industrial and secondary education school of thirty students. The Board of Trustees had barely any funds for school resources and teacher salaries. After the first year, members of the board, led by William H. Stewart, convinced the First Baptist Church of Lexington to release William J. Simmons from his pastorate so could he return to his prior profession as an educator and school administrator.

Simmons viewed the Normal and Theological Institute as a great experiment on behalf of African Americans and Black Baptists in the South. He worked with great optimism and hope for the future and felt himself at home in a field "of which he was justly proud, and for which he felt himself fully prepared and competent." Simmons envisioned the Kentucky school growing into a "high grade college," and in 1881 he visited the American Baptist Home Mission Board and convinced them to contribute annual funding to the school.[2] Simmons used the momentum to raise more funds across Kentucky. He also preached convincingly about the importance of African American investment in education. Black Baptists responded by raising funds and sending students to Louisville in droves.

As principal, William J. Simmons hired male and female teachers to teach coeducational industrial and liberal arts classes. When the first high school class graduated, he added a college department fashioned after the liberal arts curriculum of Howard University. In 1884, the Normal and Theological Institute was renamed State University, and Simmons became president. In 1885, Wilberforce University honored Simmons with an honorary Doctorate of Divinity, and he presided over three hundred students, faculty, and staff in college, industrial, and preparatory programs. State University offered industrial classes such as sewing, shoe making, chair caning, cooking, photography, and printing much along the same model provided by Booker T. Washington in Tuskegee, Alabama. It also offered professional classes in business, missionary work, music, and law. In 1886, Charles H. Parrish, C. F. Sneed, and Sarah E. Nelson became the first college graduates. The college graduating classes remained small compared to the other programs throughout Simmons's tenure, but Simmons was very proud of the quality of education and character of the college graduates. He employed several of them as teachers in the school.

William J. Simmons's pride in State University and his matter-of-factness about the general state of Black education and social influence attracted supporters among Black and White Baptist crowds. During the

---

[2] R. B. Butler, "Historical Report of Education Work of the Baptists of Kentucky," in *Golden Jubilee of the General Association of Colored Baptists in Kentucky: The Story of Fifty Years' Work from 1865–1915*, ed. Charles Henry Parrish (Louisville: Mayes Printing Co., 1915), 127.

American Baptist Home Mission Society Jubilee in 1882, Simmons captured the audience with playful banter, saying that "no school this side of the eternal world…is better than my own" and giving frank descriptions of the deplorable government support for Black public education in Kentucky. With no dedicated public schools for Black students outside of Louisville and a bare fifty cents per student allotted to cover the three-month "school year," Simmons appealed to the ABHMS to assist the South, "especially the quarter in which I live, …we are starving for the Gospel and starving for books." Throughout his speech, he unabashedly declared African Americans "awake" and "in dead earnest…to elevate themselves"; they were hard workers, paid their preachers, and gave all they could to build their own churches and schoolhouses. Simmons appreciated the support from ABHMS and other White supporters, but he also required their attentive appreciation of the African American "brightest lights" and the injustices they endured.[3]

Among his African American community, Simmons encouraged male and female students to develop all of their talents toward being "useful and great."[4] Under Simmons's leadership, State University offered all levels of education to male and female students, including liberal arts education. Simmons did not confine women to domestic skills, and he spoke of their importance as future teachers and community leaders. He employed female professors in all departments and entrusted them with administrative roles. State University graduates Lucy Wilmot Smith and Mary V. Cook joined the faculty as Latin Professor and Model School Principal, respectively, and also worked alongside Simmons in his organizing endeavors.

Early on in his project to build the Normal and Theological Institute into a prestigious university, Simmons expanded his vision to galvanize African American organizing across the nation. After the end of Reconstruction, Simmons lost faith in political parties to advocate for African Americans. He joined the National Convention of Colored Men in 1883

---

[3] Quotes from William J. Simmons, "What the Colored People Are Doing," *Baptist Home Missions in North America: Including a Full Report of the Proceedings and Addresses of the Jubilee Meeting, and a Historical Sketch of the American Baptist Home Mission Society, historical tables, etc. 1832–1882* (New York: Baptist Home Mission Rooms, 1883), 85–88.

[4] Henry M. Turner, "Introduction: Accompanied by a Sketch of the Life of Rev. W. J. Simmons, A. B., A. M., D. D.," in William J. Simmons, *Men of Mark: Eminent, Progressive, and Rising* (Cleveland: George M. Rewell, 1887), 46.

to stay politically involved, but he never campaigned for the Republican Party again. The way forward, to Simmons, would happen when African Americans built their own institutions. Socially minded churches, newspapers, schools, and civic groups would inform and energize African American people to advocate for themselves against segregation and oppression.[5]

Dr. Simmons considered State University as a beacon of opportunity for Kentucky *and* a platform for influencing African Americans across the nation. When William Stewart bought the *American Baptist* newspaper in 1882, Simmons was elected editor and given free reign. Simmons transformed the local Black newspaper into a national organ by drawing journalists and editorials from across the South to write on the issues and interests of African Americans. He was the first to pay journalist and activist Ida B. Wells-Barnett for her columns. Mary Cook and Lucy Wilmot Smith wrote articles and edited columns devoted to women's issues. In 1886, Simmons expanded the paper's women's department into a monthly periodical called *Our Women and Children*, consisting of "stories, poetry, and articles on marriage, housework, children, women's religious activities, and racial concerns." As a director and editor of *American Baptist* and *Our Women and Children*, Simmons pressed justice issues and wrote editorials with strong calls for African Americans to have loyalty to themselves over any political party.[6] He also took on leadership positions in the National Negro Press Association and was elected president in 1886.

With school and newspapers, William J. Simmons blazed the trail for the Black Social Gospel, which was the theological precursor for Martin Luther King Jr. and the twentieth century Civil Rights Movement. Many of Simmons's contemporaries criticized him for "replacing religion with politics," though Simmons regularly preached on saving grace and State University trained students in Bible and traditional theology. Simmons matched the dignity, redeemed personhood, and Spirit-oriented creativity taught by traditional Black Baptist religion with his awareness of social aspects of humanity and righteous indignation over the hellish oppression condoned by American society. He led the struggle for Black freedom by

[5] William J. Simmons, editorial in *American Baptist*, quoted in Turner, "Introduction," 47.

[6] Turner, "Introduction," 46–47; Evelyn Brooks Higginbotham, *Righteous Discontent: The Women's Movement in the Black Baptist Church, 1880–1920* (Cambridge, MA: Harvard University Press, 1993), 78.

articulating a vision and fostering opportunities for African American Baptists to uphold their God-given humanity and gospel transformation in the here and now.[7]

William J. Simmons's trailblazing work continued with his endeavors to organize African American Baptists to accomplish social change. Simmons convinced Kentucky Black Baptists to care about the school and welcomed women as well as men in the work of religious organization. Through his experience with the ABHMS, Simmons recognized the potential for women's efforts in Black denominational organizations. When the GACB refused to allow women into their membership and meetings, Dr. Simmons agreed to help Kentucky women organize into their own state organization. In 1883, he welcomed Mary Cook, Lucy Wilmot Smith, and other women into his church. Simmons convened the meeting, promptly turned it over to female leadership, and left them to set the agenda. Naming themselves the Baptist Women's Educational Convention of Kentucky, the women supported mission work and raised funds for State University.

In April 1886, William Simmons published an open letter in the *American Baptist* with a call for Black Baptists to organize into a national body. Simmons believed that despite the independent streak in African American Baptist congregations, they could come together to grow in spiritual power and social power. Simmons presided over the first meeting of the American National Baptist Convention (ANBC) in August 1886 in St. Louis. The ANBC elected Simmons president and organized leadership to include Mary Cook, Lucy Wilmot Smith, and other women as well as men. Simmons experienced strong resistance to integrating men and women into the officers' council, but he continued to support and appoint women to leadership roles in the denomination.[8]

William Simmons took on yet another denominational leadership

---

[7] Gary Dorrien, *The New Abolition: W. E. B. Du Bois and the Black Social Gospel* (New Haven, CT: Yale University Press, 2015), 2–12.

[8] Simmons disagreed with the female leadership over their petition to create a separate national women's auxiliary to the ANBC in 1890. Simmons continued to support women's rights for higher education and careers but thought that integrated ANBC leadership committees would suffice. Perhaps he could not see as well as the women how fragile their leadership status in the convention continued to be. Within five years of Simmons's death, there were no female officers in the ANBC or in its successor, the National Baptist Convention (est. 1895) (Higginbotham, *Righteous Discontent*, 153–55).

role in 1887, but this time with the White Northern Baptists. The ABHMS appointed Simmons as District Secretary for the Colored Baptists in the South, in recognition of his leadership among Black Baptists and appreciation for his organizational prowess. As the first African American elected to a position within the ABHMS, Simmons traveled the South and solicited reports about the home mission efforts as well as the continued needed assistance of Black Baptists across the South. Simmons's ANBC and journalist colleagues applauded the ABHMS move, hoping the society would increase their attention to Black Baptists' social concerns.

Due to his multiple leadership positions among White Baptists, Black Baptists, educators, journalists, and political organizers, historians christened William J. Simmons an "ecclesiastical politician" who marshalled a vast benefactor system.[9] His colleague and ANBC successor Dr. E. M. Brawley characterized Simmons as "a good preacher, a splendid organizer and a man of vast executive power" who "could do more work than any two men we know."[10] Positions of authority, however, were only important to Simmons as long as he could deploy his organizational energies to build up the African American people.

Part of Simmons's determination to build and organize was undoubtedly to counter the tide of Jim Crow segregation, lynching, and propaganda against Black humanity. But Simmons worked even harder out of pride in the collective abilities and dignity of his people. He wanted his book, *Men of Mark: Eminent, Progressive, and Rising* (1887), to propel Black youth and the Black community at large to aspire for education and the strength of character that makes a difference in their world. An enormous compilation of 172 biographies, *Men of Mark* pulses with the same optimism for African American talent and achievement that Simmons carried into all of his endeavors. And, ever the educator, Simmons included copious examples of African American speaking and writing as training material for the next generation of influential, progressive leaders.

Until his untimely death, William J. Simmons worked on behalf of African American people through building their institutions. Through it

---

[9] Gary Dorrien, *The New Abolition,* 400–401; and James Melvin Washington, *Frustrated Fellowship: The Black Baptist Quest for Social Power* (Macon, GA: Mercer University Press, 1986), 160.

[10] Dr. E. M. Brawley, *The Baptist Tribune*, 30 June 1887, quoted in *Baptist Home Mission Monthly* 9, no. 8 (August 1887): 207.

all, he preached and urged his colleagues to strive for the "noble soul to be what God intended, despite the laws, customs and prejudices." Tragically, Simmons died of heart failure on October 30, 1890, at the young age of forty-one. He left behind a wife, seven children, many presidencies, and a new agricultural and industrial school development known as the Eckstein-Norton Institute at Cane Spring, Kentucky. At his death, Simmons was lauded as "the prince of educators and preachers," "one of the greatest Negro leaders of the Nineteenth Century," and "one of the foremost Baptists in the world." His institutional legacy lives on in State University, now known as Simmons College of Kentucky, and in the current National Baptist Convention, USA; National Baptist Convention of America, Inc.; and the Progressive National Baptist Convention. Though memory of Simmons faded during the early twentieth century, one can hear echoes of Simmons's theology of the "noble soul" in Martin Luther King Jr.'s calls to be judged not by race but by character.[11]

Suggested Reading

Gary Dorrien, *The New Abolition: W. E. B. Du Bois and the Black Social Gospel* (New Haven, CT: Yale University Press, 2015).

Evelyn Brooks Higginbotham, *Righteous Discontent: The Women's Movement in the Black Baptist Church, 1880–1920* (Cambridge, MA: Harvard University Press, 1993).

Charles Henry Parrish, ed., *Golden Jubilee of the General Association of Colored Baptists in Kentucky: The Story of 50 Years' Work from 1865–1915* (Louisville: Mayes Printing Co., 1915).

William J. Simmons, *Men of Mark: Eminent, Progressive, and Rising* (Cleveland: George M. Rewell, 1887).

James Melvin Washington, *Frustrated Fellowship: The Black Baptist Quest for Social Power* (Macon, GA: Mercer University Press, 1986).

---

[11] William J. Simmons used the phrase about the "noble soul" in his remarks about Frederick Douglass (*Men of Mark*, 65). Charles H. Parrish records August 1890 as the month of Simmons's death, in Charles Henry Parrish, ed., *Golden Jubilee of the General Association of Colored Baptists in Kentucky: The Story of 50 Years' Work from 1865–1915* (Louisville: Mayes Printing Co., 1915), 109. Dr. Charles H. Parrish, newly elected president of State University and husband of Mary V. Cook, led the movement to successfully rename the school "Simmons University" in 1918. For Simmons's eulogies, see "Two New Appointments," *Baptist Home Mission Monthly* 14, no. 2 (February 1892): 72; and Gary Dorrien, *The New Abolition*, 404.

Fannie Exile Scudder Heck (1862–1915), *Baptist Mother of Missions*

Missions

Karen O'Dell Bullock

The tiny newborn child cried her first sounds as the old nurse lifted her and cooed softly, wrapping her in a soft blanket. No doctor attended this birth. No family gathered to support the young mother. Born in a rented cabin while her mother was fleeing the Civil War, this quiet baby would grow to become one of the most influential Baptist women in America. Her life became a marvelous testimony of courage, mission, faithful service, and inspiration.

Earliest Years

Fannie Exile Scudder Heck was born the second of ten children to Jonathan McGee and Mattie Anna Callendine Heck in Buffalo Lithia Springs, Virginia. Her mother, descendant of *Mayflower* settlers, of a signer of the *Declaration of Independence*, and of the Scudder missionary families of New England, was only thirteen when she first met the tall, handsome young lawyer who was a full dozen years her elder.[1] Jonathan was an enterprising and energetic man whose ancestors had fled the Palatinate in Germany to escape religious persecution. A graduate of Rector College who studied

[1] Rosalie Hall Hunt, *Out of Exile: Fannie Heck and the Rest of the Story* (Greenville, SC: Courier Publishing, 2019), 47. Hunt states that Fannie's many-generations grandfather, Richard Clark, had arrived in Plymouth on the *Mayflower* in 1620 and had signed the *Mayflower Compact*. One of his descendants had signed the *Declaration of Independence*, and another, Dr. John Scudder, was America's first missionary doctor to India, serving for more than four decades. Richard Clark sailed for Ceylon, now Sri Lanka, in 1819 with the American Board of Commissioners for Foreign Missions. His heritage included seven missionary sons and two daughters. The great Medical College and Hospital at Vellore, India, was founded by his granddaughter Ida S. Scudder. See David M. Stowe, "Scudder, John," in *Biographical Dictionary of Christian Missions*, ed. Gerald H. Anderson (New York: Macmillan Reference USA, 1998), 610.

law in Morgantown, Virginia, he had already been admitted to the bar, established a large practice, and purchased miles of land along the Monongahela River. He also served as a Justice of the Peace and as a Commonwealth attorney. For two years Jonathan courted the lovely and capable Mattie Callendine and, at the end of this period, had won the approval of both of Mattie's parents to propose marriage. Jonathan and Mattie were reared in devout Christian families and spoke often of centering their married life on Christ. Mattie was converted and joined the Baptist church two weeks before their wedding in Morgantown on March 10, 1859, just as the Civil War was erupting.[2]

Two years later, and already a new father of their firstborn child named Mary Louise, Jonathan was commissioned a Colonel of the Thirty-first Regiment of Virginia Volunteers, which he raised and equipped. The Union Army threatened the territory around Richmond, so Jonathan moved Mattie and baby "Loula" first to Staunton, Virginia, and then to Raleigh in North Carolina. Almost immediately, in July 1861, at the Battle of Rich Mountain against General George B. McClellan, he was captured and paroled with others.[3] It took some time for him to be released, however, and Jonathan was worried about his family. He had heard of a refuge for wives and children of soldiers who were fleeing to safety, and he secured a cabin for Mattie at Buffalo Lithia Springs in Virginia, about nine miles west of Clarksville, in a region that would become West Virginia.[4] Expecting another child, Mattie made her way there with Loula and a devoted family nurse. Soon, surrounded by other families in exile, Fannie was born. Her middle name marked the occasion.[5] She was two months old before her father saw her for the first time.

---

[2] Catherine W. Bisher, "Heck, Jonathan McGee," in *Dictionary of North Carolina Biography*, 6 vols., ed. William S. Powell (Chapel Hill, NC: University of North Carolina Press, 1988), 92.

[3] Bisher, "Heck, Jonathan McGee," 93.

[4] The state of Virginia had been divided for some time. The northwestern counties were far removed from Richmond, the state's capitol, and their economic and political interests, combined with strong support for abolition, had caused a deep divide. By 1861, the western portion of the state split from Virginia and, after three conventions, was admitted to the Union as a new and separate state, called West Virginia, on June 20, 1863, during the war. The capitol was moved from Wheeling to Charleston in 1870.

[5] Years later, Fannie took another name to be her own—that of her great-grandmother, Jane Scudder Chadwick, a devout Baptist woman who had helped to found

In 1863, the Heck family moved yet again, this time to Jones Springs in Warren County, North Carolina, where Fannie's father had purchased a retreat with natural spring water. This time, the Hecks opened up their cabins to families of war refugees, inviting a number of guests to make their temporary homes there. Jonathan worked to supply war provisions. By April 1865, as the fighting decimated their countryside, Jonathan and Mattie learned that Sherman's March was headed their direction and fled with their little ones to escape. Fannie was two years old at the time, and making their situation infinitely more acute, she contracted measles. While they were on the run, hiding in the woods by day and traveling by night, her condition worsened with typhoid pneumonia. Her parents feared for her life. Then they received word that President Lincoln had been assassinated.[6] As the Union Army surrounded the hills and battles raged, the little family took shelter in a cabin, hiding for more than two weeks in safety. Nursing Fannie during those long days and praying through the agony of their circumstances solidified the young parents' dependence on God. At last, Fannie pulled through, and they packed their wagon and returned home.

Following the war, Fannie's family moved to Morgantown again and then, in 1868, to Raleigh, where Jonathan was among several men whose energies and expertise joined to rebuild the southland. In the next few years, he was often gone from home on his many business ventures. He proved to be an astute and successful promoter of southern resources and opportunities for agricultural, manufacturing, commercial, and residential investments, including iron, coal, and copper production. Jonathan built a large Second Empire-style home for his family on Blount Street in downtown Raleigh and helped to establish the Oakwood estates section of the

---

the Baptist Church at Morgantown, Virginia. See Memory F. Mitchell, "Heck, Fannie Exile Scudder," in *Dictionary of North Carolina Biography*, 92.

[6] President Lincoln was shot by actor John Wilkes Booth on the evening of April 14, 1865, while the Lincolns attended *Our American Cousin*, a play at Ford Theater in Washington, D.C. He was taken to the Petersen House across the street, where he died at 7:22 a.m. the following morning. Heck family history tells of the visitors who came to stay at Jones Springs during the final months of the Civil War, including the wife and daughter of Robert E. Lee, whose daughter, Annie Carter, died in 1862 and was buried in the Jones family plot there (see Bisher, "Heck, Jonathan McGee," 93).

growing city.[7] Fannie lived there for the rest of her life.

Formative Influences

Anna Chadwick Callendine, Fannie's maternal grandmother, came to live with the family in 1866. Fannie adored her grandmother, spending many hours in her room each day reading the Bible, talking about family history, and learning about missionaries. Some of Fannie's own Scudder family members were still serving in India at the time, and at Anna's knee, Fannie learned to pray for the gospel of Christ to be shared with all the peoples of the world. She loved to memorize Bible verses too, and Anna would hear her recitations and talk to her about God's promises. One of their favorite books to read together was a leather-bound copy of Ann Judson's biography. In later years, Fannie named this book as one of her most formative influences and said she determined at this age that she would serve God however she could be used.[8]

Fannie was ten years old when she began her formal schooling at Professor Hobgood's seminary, a school for girls that her father and other men of Raleigh had founded in the large seventeen-room Polk mansion, just a block away from her home. Jonathan was a trustee at Wake Forest College and successfully compelled the brilliant Reverend William Royall and his son-in-law, Franklin Hobgood, a recent Wake Forest graduate, to become co-principals of the school. When Reverend Royall stepped away because of ill health, Professor Hobgood became the head of the school, which then took his name. Here Fannie learned French and German from Miss Walthall, a graduate of Vassar, drawing and painting from Mr. Norton, and English, math, moral philosophy, sciences, and Latin. She also took piano with Professor Meyerhoff. Deportment and "social polish" completed her curriculum.[9]

Fannie was a shy girl, yet she determined to overcome her timidity. A natural, kind-hearted leader, Fannie listened well, cared deeply, and proved to be someone the whole family relied on when anyone was ill, for

---

[7] This neighborhood is now called the Blount Street Historic District. The first substantial house built in Raleigh after the Civil War was the impressive Second Empire Heck-Andrews House at 309 North Blount Street, which still stands today. The house, which features a three-story tower and a dramatic mansard roof, set the tone for construction on what quickly became a fashionable street with houses built by industrialists, railroad executives, and planters. This is the home where Fannie grew up.

[8] Hunt, *Out of Exile*, 45.

[9] Hunt, *Out of Exile*, 48.

Fannie presented a calm, comforting, and capable presence. During these years of girlhood, Fannie and her family never missed a Sunday service at any of their homes. If there were no church, Jonathan and Mattie would start a Sunday school and soon have dozens of children and adults learning Bible lessons and worshiping together.[10] After the move to Raleigh, the First Baptist Church became a home to the whole family. Devoted to the church, Fannie's parents taught Sunday school, and her father was a leader in North Carolina's Baptist denominational work, contributing freely with time and wisdom and funds.

The Southern Baptist Convention met in Raleigh in 1872, and Fannie attended with her father, fascinated by what she heard. The Heck home hosted Dr. J. B. Taylor, Secretary of the Foreign Mission Board; Reverend A. D. Phillips, missionary to Africa; and the Drs. John A. Broadus and James Boyce from Southern Seminary. Fannie spoke with Dr. Taylor about his friendship with Adoniram Judson, which again set Fannie's heart afire for missions.

In 1874, the same year that Fannie's father became president of the North Carolina Baptist Convention, a post he held for many years, something happened at First Baptist Church, Raleigh, that also changed Fannie's perspective on the roles of women in denominational life. That year, her home church elected deaconesses to serve the congregation alongside the deacons. A momentous decision, it had resulted from many months of prayer and intensive Bible study. After proceeding thoughtfully under the leadership of Thomas Pritchard, the church voted to elect four women to this role, a decision enthusiastically supported by Fannie's father.[11]

The following year, when Fannie was thirteen years old, she left home to attend Hollins Institute, formerly Valley Union Seminary, in Hollins,

---

[10] Jonathan and Mattie started Sunday schools among the newly freed African Americans as well. Years later, Fannie recalled her first memories of Bible study, where both Black and White Christians worshiped together. The *Emancipation Proclamation* was issued six months after her birth.

[11] These women were Miss Sallie Towles, Mrs. A. M. Lewis, Mrs. W. B. Swepson, and Miss Anna Justice. For many years, the women of FBC Raleigh had cared sacrificially for others, even leaving their homes as Sherman was on the march through their city so that they could care for the wounded soldiers housed in the basement of their church. See Jane Reavis Purser, *In the King's Service: A History of the Woman's Missionary Union, 1886–1986: First Baptist Church, Raleigh, North Carolina* (Raleigh, NC: The Union, 1986), 1.

Virginia, about six miles north of Roanoke. This school had a reputation for rigorous academics and strict discipline. Its principal, Charles Lewis Cocke, had written that "young women require the same thorough and rigid mental training as that afforded to young men," and he took his task seriously. Hollins was the first chartered women's college in Virginia and the first to establish an English department directed by a full professor.[12] At Hollins, Fannie methodically went about her studies, determined to learn well. She loved history best, followed by English and elocution, and spent a great deal of time in the library. She was excited to learn that Lottie Moon, a recent graduate of Hollins, had left for China two years before, and she yearned to share the news with her grandmother and parents.

On Fannie's first summer visit home from Hollins, Dr. Henry Tupper, of the Foreign Mission Board of the Southern Baptist Convention, stopped for a visit at the Heck home. He was representing the mission board when he asked Mattie Heck to consider founding women's societies across North Carolina for mission support, as the women of South Carolina were doing. The mission board had realized the importance of Baptist women in the success of mission engagement, since women did much of this work already as individuals and in small groups. Fannie was seated at the table the afternoon Dr. Tupper proposed the project and Mattie agreed. Her mother, ever attentive and involved in charity and gospel work from their home, had been Fannie's closest role model. To see her mother now take up such a responsibility was life-changing for her daughter.[13] Fannie pledged to help her.

Greatest Joy and Sorrow

Fannie graduated from Hollins just weeks before she turned seventeen and received the grace of Christ for salvation. Her pastor, Reverend Skinner, baptized her a few months later when she turned eighteen, and she joined the First Baptist Church, her home fellowship. Immediately, her church invited her to teach a class of younger boys, whose teacher had been called away on business. She accepted and began to study her Bible even more intensely. The boys' Sunday school class began to grow. Fannie also

[12] Nancy Parrish, *Lee Smith, Annie Dillard, and the Hollins Group: A Genesis of Writers* (Baton Rouge, LA: Louisiana State University Press, 1998), 25–26. Hollins was also the first college in America to name a woman as its president when Matty Cocke was elected in 1901.

[13] Hunt, *Out of Exile*, 54–55.

attended a Wednesday night prayer service and a Thursday evening Women's Missions group, serving wherever she could.

During these years, Fannie began to receive the attention of a young man who had grown, across the months, to be a dear friend. Their interests, both intellectually and spiritually, were well matched, and they grew to love each other. For Fannie, this was her greatest joy. Just as they had come to an understanding about marriage, however, he contracted consumption, or tuberculosis, and died a year later. His illness and death broke Fannie's heart. She remained faithful to his memory, and to the love she held for him, for the rest of her life.[14]

In 1883, concerned for her health and grieving heart, Fannie's parents asked her to join Professor Winston of Richmond College, who had arranged to take a group of young women to Europe on a three-month tour. They would see the sites where the great literature of the world had been written, a subject dear to Fannie. They hoped that the trip would inspire her, stimulate her mind, and also help her heart to heal from her recent sorrows. Twenty-one years old that June, Fannie steamed away to Rome, Florence, Venice, Paris, London, and Ireland. When she returned, she seemed to have regained a measure of peace. She had asked God to make her useful and committed herself to follow his leadership. Fanny unpacked her bags and quietly went to work, convinced that God had given her spiritual gifts and called her to a life of service.

Fannie on Mission

She resumed her Sunday school class, began attending mission and prayer meetings, and a family friend invited her to help with a project in a poorer section of Raleigh. John Pullen was starting a little church in South Fayetteville Street, down by the tracks of the Southern Railway. He asked Fannie to organize a Sunday school for children and to disciple a group of young girls. Without the advantages of education or training, these children needed her help. She enlisted her childhood friend, Sallie Bailey, to work with her. Soon Fannie and Sallie had organized Sunday afternoon sewing classes, where dozens of girls gathered to learn this valuable skill, and wood-carving classes for the boys. While they stitched and whittled, Fannie told fascinating stories, mostly from the New Testament. Within

[14] Hunt, *Out of Exile*, 73–85. This young man, who is never named in Hunt's account, gave to Fannie a beautiful travel writing desk that remained, with her Bible, her most cherished possession.

a year, there was a large Sunday afternoon Sunday school on the site. In addition, John, Fannie, and Sallie visited in the homes, befriended the parents, and invited them to services. Whole families came to Sunday school. Fannie and Sallie gathered outgrown clothing, particularly warm coats, and delivered them to the children, invited them to tea parties, and helped raised funds to build a church. When they decorated the church for Christmas, it was the first time the children had experienced such a celebration.[15]

Fannie had felt a deep concern for the poor, which focused into a passion for social work as she matured. She began to say that missions is not related to geography; in fact, one could be engaged in missions even at home. She then began working with others to found the Associated Charities organization, seeking to organize relief efforts in Raleigh more effectively, and served as its first president. Fannie was not only mindful of the needs within her own community but also aware of the college girls who came to Raleigh to what was then the Baptist University for Women, now Meredith College. She gathered small groups of young women to learn about and pray for missionaries, involving them in service to Christ.

In January 1886, when the State Mission Board formed a Woman's Central Committee of Missions, the board personally invited Fannie Heck to become its first president.[16] For several years the committee functioned as an arm of the Baptist State Convention, and, as one of two voted representatives of this body, Fannie attended the formation of the Woman's Missionary Union (WMU), Auxiliary to the Southern Baptist Convention, which was founded in Richmond on May 11, 1888. This was the first national Baptist organization for women, whose purpose it was to support the denomination's mission causes around the world.

Woman's Missionary Union Leader

In 1890, the Women's Central Committee of Missions of the North Carolina Baptists was authorized to affiliate with the SBC WMU, and in 1891 the committee made its first report to that organization. A year later, WMU president Mattie Macintosh stepped down from her position and the WMU nominated Fannie Heck, the beautiful, elegant speaker, to succeed McIntosh. Though she was only twenty-nine at the time, her deep faith, fine writing ability, and strong leadership skills made her a prime candidate. She was elected to office, and WMU looked with excitement

[15] Hunt, *Out of Exile*, 89–93.

[16] Purser, *In the King's Service*, 7.

toward the work God would do through its new president. The first two years saw vigorous growth.

In 1894, however, Fannie's father passed away, leaving the entire family devastated.[17] Fannie, suffering from a debilitating loss of vision and extreme headaches at the time, became even more ill when a fever ravaged her body. Several weeks passed before she could take up a pen. The combination of grief and sickness put such a strain on her that, for the sake of her health and the WMU, Fannie resigned her post. She sent her annual message to be read in her absence at the meeting in Dallas: "As the Good Shepherd leads some into new green pastures, others He maketh to lie down; ah, sorely against their wills. But not for long should such repining last. We would not, dare not, cross His mighty will with ours and so we rest, sure, safe, and full content that God knows best."[18]

The national WMU was grieved to lose its dynamic leader, but two years later, when Fannie had returned to health, the women welcomed her back to the presidency in 1896. Though glad to return to the ministry and women she loved, Fannie was still recovering from her loss, changed by the pain she had suffered. She trusted that God would provide her with strength for the days ahead. She resigned again in 1899 and devoted herself for the next decade to many other areas of service. When a change of leadership occurred in 1906, Fannie was reelected president again and served until 1914. She was a dynamic, invigorating, and motivating force.

Fannie's writing and speaking schedule was intense. She wrote endless leaflets; a book titled *In Royal Service*, the first twenty-five-year history of the WMU; the words to "The Woman's Hymn" and the compilation of the first WMU hymnal; and a monthly paper called *The Missionary Talk*. She was coeditor of *Our Mission Fields* (now *Royal Service*), a quarterly of the SBC WMU. Also, under her leadership, state WMU offices began to employ staff members.

In 1908, WMU elected Edith Crane as the corresponding secretary, and she came to help Fannie Heck to administer the vast organization. This left Fannie able to concentrate on setting the vision and structure for a future WMU, including missions education programs designed and

[17] Jonathan McGee Heck died in 1894 in Philadelphia, where he had gone for cancer treatments. His body was returned to Raleigh, where he was buried at the Oakwood Cemetery, not far from the family home. Fannie's mother, Mattie, lived until June 29, 1928, outliving her daughter Fannie by thirteen years.

[18] Quoted in Hunt, *Out of Exile*, 179.

implemented for young women and men (Young People's Union); for boys (Royal Ambassadors); for girls (Girls' Auxiliary); and for small children (Sunbeams). Everybody had a place in missions. These programs, adopted and welcomed into Baptist churches, educated generations of laypeople from childhood to maturity in the essential work of reaching the world with the gospel. They helped to unite Baptists at local church, associational, state, and convention levels.

Fannie also continued to serve as president of the North Carolina WMU from the time of its organization in 1886 until her death. During her tenure in North Carolina, the number of societies grew from 14 to 1,200, with the annual contribution to missions increasing from $1,000 in 1886 to nearly $50,000 by 1915. While leading at this level, her deep concern about the lack of educational opportunities for children and adults in the remote western counties of North Carolina never lessened. She journeyed to the area and continually urged Baptists to take up this cause. As a result of her work, the North Carolina Baptist Convention created the Mountain Mission School in 1900, which helped to bring a greater knowledge of Christ to the mountain people. Along the way, she was instrumental in founding a Young Women's Christian Association and a Young Men's Christian Association in Raleigh.

Global Reach

Heck's influence was educational and global as well. In appreciation of her participation in the Student Volunteer and Young People's Missionary Education movements and of her love of Meredith College students, the WMU installed the Heck Memorial Fountain on its campus in Raleigh. Fannie also helped to organize the Woman's Missionary Union Training School (now Carver School of Missions and Social Work) in Louisville, Kentucky, in 1907. The WMU designed a specialized curriculum of mission study courses for women and young people there. The Heck Memorial Chapel at Southern Seminary stands today in honor of her contribution.

In addition, Fannie was a delegate to the first Ecumenical Conference, held in New York in 1900, and she spoke at the Baptist World Alliance in Philadelphia in 1911, a year after it was inaugurated in London. Finally, in 1913, just a few months before she became too ill to travel, she represented North Carolina at the Social Service Conference in Memphis, Tennessee.

Final Days and Legacy

In 1914, Fannie was diagnosed with cancer and spent her last year in the Hygeia Hospital in Richmond. Her room, called "Blue Sky Room," "Sunshine Corner," and "House of Peace," was named by doctors and nurses who attended her. Fannie's cheery presence reflected her hope in Christ. She went to be with the Lord on August 25, 1915, having fulfilled the purpose for which she was born and an "exile" no longer. She was home. Her passion to bring the good news of Jesus Christ to those who had never heard it permeated her life. Fannie Exile Scudder Heck's life and work, through the WMU, engaged thousands of Baptist churches to become missional, both at home and abroad. For this, and so much more, she is remembered as Baptists' beloved "Mother of Missions."

Suggested Reading

Catherine Allen, *Laborers Together with God* (Birmingham, AL: SBC Woman's Missionary Union, 1987).

Rosalie Hall Hunt, *Out of Exile: Fannie Heck and the Rest of the Story* (Greenville, SC: Courier, 2019).

Rosalie Hall Hunt, *We've a Story to Tell: 125 Years of WMU* (Birmingham, AL: SBC Woman's Missionary Union, 2013).

Henry L. Morehouse (1834–1917), Bridge Builder between Missions and Social Justice

Missions

Michael E. (Mike) Williams, Sr.

In the twenty-first century, Americans may consider it routine or normal to experience rapid change. They are used to the frequent upheaval that comes from living in a time when technology may be outdated as soon as it is available on the store shelves and instantaneous communication is the norm rather the exception. Confronted with such instant differences, Americans also face the continuous reality that immediate transmission of information often leaves them overwhelmed and occasionally feeling hopeless. In the last half of the nineteenth century and through the first decades of the twentieth century, Americans also experienced a time of tremendous turmoil, but it was a time that provided visionary hope as well. Beginning with the divisive and explosive issue of slavery and the bloody crucible of civil war, through the agonizing pain and disappointing incompleteness of reconstruction of the South, the new century saw the development of immense riches of the great financial empires. A flood of immigrants poured into the United States during the final decades of the nineteenth century and the first decade of the twentieth century, and American Christians matched these changes with decades of church and denominational growth. Founded on Christian reform organizations created during the Second Great Awakening and spurred by the great pulpit orators whom church historian Sydney Alhstrom calls "the Princes of the Pulpit," as well as great revivalists like Dwight L. Moody and social reformers like Baptist Walter Rauschenbusch, American Christians and Baptists in the United States could approach the beginning of a new century with optimism despite the myriad challenges and strong undercurrent of emerging theological and hermeneutic conflict.[1] Among Christians in the North and South, several denominational giants led the efforts to expand the work of Baptists abroad and in the United States. Henry L. Morehouse of Northern Baptists stood as one of the greatest of those denominational servants.

Born in 1834, Henry Lyman Morehouse grew up on farms in Bangall and East Avon, New York, and attended the Bangall Baptist Church as a child. He attended the Genessee Wesleyan Seminary before he entered the University of Rochester in 1854. He excelled in academics, including election to Phi Beta Kappa, and experienced conversion and baptism. After graduation, he administered the family farm and actively engaged in the presidential election of 1860 as an ardent supporter of the new Republican Party and Abraham Lincoln. Feeling called to vocational ministry, he rejected a political career and enrolled in Rochester Theological Seminary. Upon graduation, he served for a time with the Christian Sanitary Commission, made up of civilians ministering and providing medical aid to the Union Army. After serving amid the horrors of war, Morehouse accepted the pastorate of the tiny Baptist church in East Saginaw, Michigan. He served that congregation for eight years before accepting the pastorate of East Avenue Baptist Church in Rochester, New York, which he served for six and a half years. Throughout both pastorates, each church grew substantially, and Baptists in both Michigan and New York recognized his preaching, pastoral, and administrative skills as well as his deep commitment to the mission activities of Baptists in the North and to the denomination as a whole. After Morehouse's death, a career Baptist foreign missionary wrote of Morehouse's tenure in Rochester, "He brought…a warm heart, a zeal for souls and a capacity for work.…I dare not say that Doctor Morehouse made foreign missionaries of us; but as our pastor he certainly put before us an object-lesson of service as a high ideal in such a way that we could not be satisfied with any lower ideal."[2]

Through his successful work in Michigan, which was considered a pioneer area by many Northern Baptists, and because of his denominational work, Morehouse rose to the attention of his fellow Baptists. In 1879, the American Baptist Home Mission Society summoned him to

---

[1] Sydney Ahlstrom, *A Religious History of the American People* (New Haven: Yale University Press, 1974), 738–40.

[2] Lathan A. Crandall, *Henry Lyman Morehouse: A Biography* (Philadelphia: American Baptist Publication Society, 1919), 3–47.

serve as corresponding secretary, essentially chief executive. Baptists hoped to capitalize on a growing economy with Morehouse's vigorous leadership, and Morehouse did not disappoint them.

Baptists of the Triennial Convention created the American Baptist Home Mission Society (ABHMS) in 1832 "to promote the preaching of the gospel in North America."[3] Strongly influenced by the work of pioneer Baptist missionary John Mason Peck, the society primarily focused on supporting missionaries in the developing West in new or relatively new states like Ohio, Indiana, Kentucky, Illinois, Michigan, and Missouri as well as newly opening territories like Minnesota and Iowa. After 1849, this westward expansion of mission work included California and New Mexico. As European immigrants began to flood into the country in the 1840s and 1850s, more than 2.2 million between 1847 and 1854 alone, the society refocused energies and resources to ministry among immigrants. The division of Baptists and the creation of the Southern Baptist Convention in 1845 interrupted the society's work in the South, but by the time Morehouse came to the helm in 1879 as corresponding secretary, the ABHMS had affiliated in some way with two-thirds of the Baptist state associations and conventions in the South.[4]

Unfortunately, despite the consistent and ambitious work of the ABHMS, a lack of funds severely hampered its work. While the society sponsored 236 missionaries and teachers, operated eight colleges or seminaries that educated more than 1,000 students, and supported construction of ten church buildings in the 1878–1879 budget year, it operated on a budget of a little less than $90,000. Though these were astonishing results on limited resources, the ABHMS's operations exploded once the society unleashed the Morehouse whirlwind upon the home mission enterprise. Capitalizing on an economic boom as the nation recovered from the Panic of 1873, Morehouse initiated an aggressive expansion of the society's work. From his days as a pastor in Michigan, he recognized the importance of aiding young and struggling congregations with the construction of their buildings. In 1881 he created the Church Edifice Gift Fund. By 1885, Northern Baptists had collected more than $100,000 that it

---

[3] Henry L. Morehouse, "American Baptist Home Mission Society," in *A Century of Baptist Achievement*, ed. A. H. Newman (Philadelphia: American Baptist Publication Society, 1901), 204.

[4] Ibid., 205–06, and H. Leon McBeth, *The Baptist Heritage: Four Centuries of Baptist Witness* (Nashville: Broadman Press, 1987), 401.

issued as outright grants to churches. Immediate and outstanding results occurred. From the ten church buildings constructed in 1879, Northern Baptists' projects grew and resulted in the construction of ninety-eight church houses in 1883 from the gift fund. Church construction increased from fewer than 300 in the eight years prior to Morehouse's time as head of the ABHMS to more than 700 in the last eight years before he left the corresponding secretary's office in 1893. Nor did Northern Baptists only progress in raising funds for church construction. Total annual receipts had almost quadrupled in the first ten years of Morehouse's service.[5]

But Henry Morehouse's contributions to Baptist and Christian life in the United States went far beyond raising funds. He worked to unify two separate Women's Home Mission societies. Although unsuccessful at the time, his efforts brought each into closer relationship with the ABHMS. Under his leadership, the ABHMS supported the efforts of Sophia Packard and Harriet Giles to begin a school for African American Baptist women in Atlanta that was named the Atlanta Baptist Female Seminary, close to the institution then known as Atlanta Baptist Seminary and then renamed Atlanta Baptist College in 1897. In 1888, with the support of Baptist philanthropists John D. Rockefeller, Sr., and Laura Spelman Rockefeller, the ABHMS retired the debt on the college and renamed and chartered the school as Spelman Seminary for Women after Laura Rockefeller's parents.[6]

Morehouse also challenged the ABHMS to be more aggressive in its work among Native Americans—initially in Oklahoma but then spreading into the Southwest and onto the Great Plains as the U.S. Army herded the migratory tribes onto reservations and the U.S. government took away many of their ancestral privileges. When Morehouse served as corresponding secretary, the ABHMS started work among many nations such as Choctaw, Seminole, Creek, Sac and Fox, Arapaho, Cheyenne, Comanche, and Caddo but especially among the Delaware and Cherokee. Bacone College, originally founded in Tahlequah, Oklahoma, in 1880 by ABHMS missionary Almone Bacone, relocated to its permanent location in the Creek nation in Muskogee, Oklahoma, in 1885 and became a

[5] H. L. Morehouse, "Report of the Corresponding Secretary," *The Baptist Home Mission Monthly* 14 (July 1892): 234; Crandall, *Henry Lyman Morehouse*, 65.

[6] Crandall, *Henry Lyman Morehouse*, 56–57; David Charles Laubach, *American Baptist Home Mission Board Roots, 1824–2010* (Valley Forge, PA: American Baptist Home Mission Societies, n.d.), 11–12.

leading institution providing education for Native Americans. Like Spelman, Bacone drew much of its early support from the Rockefeller family. At the formal creation of the Northern Baptist Convention in 1908 held in Oklahoma City, Native American leader Lone Wolf addressed the convention with a moving tribute to Morehouse. Lone Wolf stated, "My people were sick and Doctor Morehouse brought the medicine that made them well." By 1900, Morehouse happily reported that Baptists among the Native American nations in Oklahoma numbered approximately 4,300.[7]

Morehouse also actively advocated work among the immigrant masses that flooded United States soil in the last decades of the nineteenth century and first decades of the twentieth century. Despite the fact that labor unions and anti-immigrant forces lobbied hard to limit and even halt immigration, Morehouse strove to aid the immigrants primarily coming from southern and eastern Europe and ministered to and evangelized them once they came to the United States. During his first term as corresponding secretary, the ABHMS continued its aggressive work among German and Scandinavians—primarily Swedish—as well as beginning work among Czech, Polish, Portuguese, Finnish, Jewish, Dutch, and Japanese immigrants. The society also assumed mission work among Chinese in California that had been abandoned by Southern Baptists and began ministry among Chinese in Chicago and New York.[8]

During this same era, the American Baptist Home Mission Society began work in both Canada and Mexico. Morehouse and the society did not view these nations as foreign missions but assumed leadership of the mission work as falling under the umbrella of Home Missions much in the same way as the Southern Baptist Convention has more recently viewed that part of mission activity as North American missions. After 1898, when Cuba and Puerto Rico became, respectively, a protectorate and territory of the United States after the Spanish-American War, the society took the same approach to those islands as with Canada and Mexico.[9]

After critics had attacked Morehouse's administration, he stepped aside in 1893 to fill a newly created position as field secretary. This position liberated Morehouse from the day-to-day administrative operations

---

[7] Morehouse, "American Baptist Home Mission Society," 213; Crandall, *Henry Lyman Morehouse*, 76–79; and "A unique history; a promising future," at the Bacone College website, https://www.bacone.edu/about.

[8] Morehouse, "American Baptist Home Mission Society," 211–12.

[9] Ibid., 210, 211, 214; Crandall, *Henry Lyman Morehouse*, 72–75; *The Baptist Home Mission Monthly* 17 (July 1895): 220–22; "Articles by the Field Secretary," 167.

of the society and allowed him to travel much of the year, visiting various ministries of ABHMS and making recommendations to the home office for additional funding or new areas of activity. By 1900, Morehouse proudly issued a report that tallied the overall progress made by the ABHMS and documented the success. He wrote that the total receipts of the society advanced from over $4.2 million in the eleven years of 1879 to 1890 to more than $4.9 million in the ten years between 1890 and 1900. He added that the total in excess of $9.2 million more than tripled the total from the previous forty-seven years. Even allowing for inflation, this demonstrated outstanding growth. He also reported that the society had increased in several key areas such as "permanent funds for missions and education, from $55,615.28 in 1879 to $519,257.01 in 1900; church edifice permanent funds from $229,633.48 to $320,826.34; annuity funds from $97,258 to $445,053.97; school and mission property in value from $302,879.94 to $995,265." But the growth of the ABHMS was not limited to the development of financial resources and property. Morehouse also reported that the society's work had expanded "from thirty-four States and Territories to fifty-four; the laborers increased from 238 to 1,180; the nationalities represented from seven to twenty; schools for the colored people and Indians from eight to thirty; the enrollment from 1,041 to 4,848; while 1,617 church edifices were built by direct aid." He concluded by summarizing, "The whole number of missionaries appointed was 17,671; of the churches organized 2,749; of baptisms reported, 80,746."[10]

These accomplishments were important, but Morehouse's greatest contribution was helping establish the American Baptist Education Society (ABES) and working in support of higher education for African Americans. John Rockefeller's biographer, Ron Chernow, describes Morehouse as the "driving force behind" the ABES. For years, Rockefeller had looked for an avenue to handle the multitudes of philanthropic requests that he received, and he had written Morehouse for advice five years earlier. Rockefeller and Morehouse formulated a system of matching grants to encourage others to give. Chernow also writes that Morehouse enlisted a former Baptist pastor as the director of the new society. This thirty-five-year-old minister was Frederick Gates. Gates became the primary conduit for the vast sums of money that the richest man in the U.S. and its best-known Baptist continued to channel into Northern Baptists' coffers, especially in funding Baptist higher education and support for African American

[10] Morehouse, "American Baptist Home Mission Society," 215.

higher education. Morehouse and Gates, along with Thomas Goodspeed, advocated the creation of a flagship Baptist institution of higher education that would spearhead efforts to raise Baptist scholarship to the highest levels. As Chernow writes, Gates "portrayed this new Baptist university as the nucleus of a national educational network," writing to Morehouse that it would be "A scheme so vast, so continental, so orderly, so comprehensive, so detailed" that it would "capture a mind so constituted as Mr. Rockefeller's is." Crandall adds that "While Doctor Morehouse had little or no direct part in the campaign to raise $400,000 with which to meet Mr. Rockefeller's conditional offer of $600,000, he was the constant and trusted advisor of the two men [Gates and Goodspeed] who carried this important undertaking to a successful termination."[11]

At virtually the same time, Morehouse began to advocate for greater attention to the needs of African American higher education. In 1895, Booker T. Washington delivered his famous "Atlanta Compromise" speech before the Atlanta Exposition. A few months later and only about a month before the Supreme Court handed down its infamous *Plessy v. Ferguson* decision that Henry Louis Gates, Jr., and many other historians have identified as "cementing 'separate but equal' as law of the land" and the evils of the Jim Crow South, Morehouse responded with a short call of only four paragraphs for the education of the "talented tenth" that black activist W. E. B. Du Bois would less than a decade later advocate as the answer to Booker T. Washington. Washington announced his position for industrial and vocational training such as that offered by his Tuskegee Institute in Alabama. In *The Independent*, Morehouse, while not identifying Washington, spoke directly to Washington's proposal. He wrote, "In the discussion concerning Negro education we should not forget the talented tenth man." He added, "The talented tenth man, with superior natural endowments, symmetrically trained and highly developed, may become a mightier influence, a greater inspiration to others than all the other nine or nine times nine like them." Further, he wrote in defense of other alternatives for education. Morehouse said, "Without disparagement of the faithful men of moderate abilities, it may be said that in all ages the

---

[11] Ron Chernow, *Titan: The Life of John D. Rockefeller, Sr.* (New York: Random House, 1998), 241, 242, 309, 310; letter from Frederick T. Gates to H. L. Morehouse, 9 October 1888, as cited in Chernow, *Titan*, 310; and Crandall, *Henry Lyman Morehouse*, 132. For more on the relationship between Gates and Rockefeller, see Chernow, *Titan*, 309ff.

mighty impulses that have propelled a people onward in their progressive career, have proceeded from a few gifted souls." Morehouse went on to write,

> It is this talented tenth man of our colleges that in after years reflects more honor on his *alma mater* than the other nine; it is this tenth man that is the recognized leader in his profession and the leader of public opinion. To him, rather than to the other nine, the many look for suggestion and advice in important matters....This being true, I repeat that not to make proper provision for the high education of the talented tenth man of the colored people is a prodigious mistake. It is to dwarf the tree that has in it the potency of a grand oak. Industrial education is good for the nine...but that tenth man ought to have the best opportunities for making the most of himself for humanity and God. The powers of this talented tenth man are often latent; unsuspected by others and even by their possessor, and are evoked only under favorable conditions, sometimes comparatively late in the youthful period of life. In a...course of study...the particular aptitude of the pupil may be discovered, the secret springs of power be opened; and the man, having discovered himself, leaps forward to pre-eminence among his fellows. Scores of such men and women are among the students in the schools for the colored people of the South. A mere common education will not disclose their uncommon powers; they need the test of the best....[P]rovision should be made for the higher education of the talented tenth as well as ordinary education for the other nine. The great need of the colored people of the South is wise leadership along all lines of development; men of large and comprehensive views acquired by contact and communion with the world's great thinkers; such men are needed to-day even more than nine times as many with a little more practical knowledge concerning the use of the saw, the jack-plane and the blacksmith's forge. In our educational work for the colored people, therefore, proper provision should be made for the talented tenth.[12]

Subsequently, Du Bois adopted and expanded Morehouse's phrase and ideas, and while Morehouse himself may have been influenced by Abraham Lincoln and a black Republican newspaper, this challenge to Washington certainly indicated where Morehouse's sympathies lay.[13]

---

[12] H. L. Morehouse, "The Talented Tenth," *The Independent* 48 (23 April 1896), 1, at https://babel.hathitrust.org/cgi/pt?id=pst.000020204716;view=1up;seq=557.

[13] Henry Louis Gates, Jr., "Who Really Invented the 'Talented Tenth'?" 18 February 2013, *The Root*, https://www.theroot.com/who-really-invented-the-talented-tenth-1790895289. Morehouse likewise may have been responding to a sermon by AME bishop Henry McNeal Turner given at the first gathering of the National Baptist Convention in

Morehouse resumed his role as the corresponding secretary in 1903 and continued until his death in 1917. In many ways, these years were the most rewarding of his life, despite the fact that they came during his seventh decade. In 1907, as the ABHMS celebrated its seventy-fifth anniversary, the society asked him to give its keynote address during which he gave a review of its ministry. Morehouse endorsed the creation of the Northern Baptist Convention in 1908 with the cooperation of the ABHMS. He originally met with his southern counterpart, I. T. Tichenor, at the volatile Fortress Monroe meetings in 1895 to settle territorial disputes, and subsequently he met with SBC representatives for further comity agreements in Washington, D.C., in 1909 and at Hot Springs, Arkansas, in 1913 that laid the foundation of cooperation between the SBC and NBC for decades into the twentieth century. In 1905 he began work as a pioneering and important member of the Baptist World Alliance and became one of the BWA's key supporters.[14]

Perhaps the greatest tribute to Morehouse's influence came from African American Baptists and their supporters in higher education. A conference held at Spelman Seminary (now Spelman College) published a tribute to Morehouse in 1909 that stated, "The vast influence of your life work...for the welfare of humanity and especially of the Negroes of the South, can never be measured till the revelations of eternity." Appreciation for Morehouse's contribution in this area culminated in 1913, when trustees renamed Atlanta Baptist College in his honor. The history of the college recorded that "his kindly spirit and his great tact have accounted for his unusual success in the education of the Negro." Morehouse College became one of the leading institutions of higher education for Blacks in the nation. Its distinguished alumni include Martin Luther King, Jr., as well as many other significant African American leaders.[15]

October 1895 when he proclaimed, "God is a Negro." See Andre E. Johnson, *Black Theology* 13, no. 1 (April 2015): 29–40, at https://www.academia.edu/24786033/God_is_a_Negro_The_Rhetorical_Black_Theology_of_Bishop_Henry_McNeal_Turner.

[14] Charles White, *A Century of Faith* (Philadelphia: Judson Press, 1932), 278; Crandall, *Henry Lyman Morehouse*, 109–10; F. Townley Lord, *Baptist World Fellowship: A Short History of the Baptist World Alliance* (Nashville: Broadman Press, 1955), 9; Rober Baker, *Relations between Northern and Southern Baptists* (Fort Worth: Evans Press, 1948), 120–22, 132, 141–42, 176–77, 183–86; and *The Baptist Home Mission Monthly* 17 (July 1895): 221.

[15] *The Baptist Home Mission Monthly* 31 (June 1909): 307; Benjamin Brawley, *History of Morehouse College* (Atlanta: Morehouse College, 1917), 103.

Though declining in health, Morehouse stayed at the helm of the American Baptist Home Mission Society and died only a day after returning to his office after a three-month leave for health reasons. Upon his death, the ABHMS published a tribute that stated that missionaries and teachers on the field had multiplied more than six times, expenditures had increased tenfold, and more than seven times the numbers of Black students were being educated in American Baptist-sponsored schools than there had been when he had begun his tenure.[16]

Certainly, some of Morehouse's language and programs held remnants of racial paternalism and elitism consistent with Northern Baptists of his era. However, he should not be separated from his culture and time. Like most of his contemporaries, he was a product of the time in which he lived. Despite this, he must be regarded as a man ahead of his time. Especially considering the challenging times in which he lived, he held progressive ideals while maintaining his cultural and biblical conservatism. His openness to immigrants at a time when many of his contemporaries promoted closing or severely limiting immigration as well as his advocacy for education among Native Americans and especially African Americans displayed his genuine care for other ethnicities. Above all, Henry L. Morehouse demonstrated that missions and evangelism should never be separated from the quests for education and social justice or vice versa. As the ABHMS tribute stated, "He was a rare executive, a statesman of wise and clear vision, a consecrated and tireless worker, a devoted friend, and above all, a Christian gentleman. The world is better because Henry L. Morehouse lived."[17]

Suggested Reading

Lathan A. Crandall, *Henry Lyman Morehouse: A Biography* (Philadelphia: American Baptist Publication Society, 1919).

Bill J. Leonard, *Baptist Ways: A History* (Valley Forge, PA: Judson Press, 2003).

H. Leon McBeth, *The Baptist Heritage: Four Centuries of Baptist Witness* (Nashville: Broadman Press, 1987).

---

[16] "Tribute to Dr. Morehouse," *Missions* 8 (September 1917): 646.

[17] Ibid., 647. See also Adolph H. Grundman, "Northern Baptists and the Founding of Virginia Union University: The Perils of Paternalism," *Journal of Negro History* 63, no. 1 (January 1978): 26–41, at https://www.jstor.org/stable/2717358?seq=1#metadata_info_tab_contents; "Tribute to Dr. Morehouse," *Missions* 8 (September 1917): 646.

Hannah Maria Norris Armstrong (1842–1919), *Canadian Missions Pioneer*

Missions

Melody Maxwell

Hannah Maria Norris boarded the steamship with the determination of a young person fully committed to God. If Nova Scotians would not fund her mission, she believed, God would provide a way. She closed her eyes and steeled herself for the long journey across the sea to Boston. Just as she was settling in, Maria heard voices calling her name. Puzzled, she looked up and saw several prominent Baptist leaders approaching her. "Miss Norris," they urged, "don't do this!" The men asked her to give Baptists of the province another chance in supporting her work. Both her mission and the churches would benefit, they explained, and they were willing to take up her cause. Surprised, Maria pondered this new offer. Could it be of God? With a deep breath, she turned and began slowly walking back down to the harbor with the men. Perhaps she wasn't alone in this endeavor after all.

Hannah Maria Norris, known to her family as Maria (pronounced muh-RYE-uh), was born on November 30, 1842, in the seaside town of Canso, Nova Scotia, Canada. The daughter of a Roman Catholic father and a Congregationalist mother, Maria became a Baptist in 1866. Friends urged her to wait for the harbor ice to thaw before she was baptized, but instead she had a hole cut in the ice in order to act on her conviction.[1]

An excellent student, Maria studied at the Normal School in Truro, Nova Scotia, and returned to her hometown as a teacher. In addition to this role, she taught Sunday school and regularly visited a settlement of indigenous Mi'kmaq people, evangelizing them in their own language—

---

[1] "Mrs. Hannah Maria Norris Armstrong," *The News* 32, no. 10 [Rangoon, Burma] (October 1919): 50, Hannah Maria Norris Armstrong Collection, D1997.004, Box 6, HMNA-0-1 1997 2-831, Esther Clark Wright Archives, Acadia University, Wolfville, Nova Scotia.

foreshadowing her future missionary career. In 1868, Maria began teaching at the Acadia Ladies' Seminary in Wolfville, Nova Scotia. Soon she began to sense a prompting from a "still small voice"[2] that encouraged her to consider missions work in Burma, the land in which the first Canadian Baptist missionaries had served. She inquired about this possibility with the Foreign Mission Board of Maritime Baptists, whose leader responded that no funding was available. He also likely hesitated to send a single woman as a missionary, an unusual action at this time.

Determined to follow God's call, Maria sought other means of funding for her missionary endeavor. She requested support from a wealthy relative, who promised the money but later changed his mind. It was then that Maria planned to sail quietly to Boston to inquire with the American Baptist Missionary Union, and from there to sail to Burma. However, Baptists in Halifax learned of her plan and persuaded her to disembark the boat and seek support from local Baptists. Convinced of this idea, Maria soon leaped into action.

First Maria contacted the Foreign Mission Board again, urging them to accept her request for service. This time they responded favorably: "We will send her out as our Missionary subject to the concurrence of the Convention, so soon as the Board shall be furnished with the funds necessary."[3] The board recommended that Maria seek support from women in Baptist churches in the Maritimes. In addition, the following year the Baptist Convention of the Maritime Provinces voted to undertake its own missions efforts, apart from those of American Baptists. The initiative of Maria and her supporters resulted in new missions endeavors for Maritime Baptists.

Maria set about raising support with her characteristic vigor. Aware that women in New York had recently formed the Woman's Union Missionary Society, Maria enlisted a mentor to help her write a constitution for similar societies in Nova Scotia. She then began visiting women in churches across the Maritimes. She first visited her hometown of Canso, Nova Scotia. On June 18, 1870, women in the Baptist church in that town organized the first women's missionary society in Canada. Other towns followed in rapid succession: Amherst, Nova Scotia, on July 5; Windsor, Nova Scotia, on July 11; Falmouth, Nova Scotia, on July 12; and so forth,

---

[2] Mary Cramp, *Retrospects: A History of the Formation and Progress of the Women's Missionary Aid Societies of the Maritime Provinces* (Halifax: Holloway Bros., 1892), 5.

[3] Ibid., 9.

until by the end of August, thirty-two women's missions groups had been formed. Maria's tireless work had mobilized women across Nova Scotia and New Brunswick for direct missions efforts. This work provided them with experience in leadership, business, and ministry, among other areas. It also gave single women the opportunity to serve in new roles overseas. These efforts were part of the broader transatlantic woman's missionary movement of the late nineteenth century, in which Protestant women of many denominations were engaged in sending and supporting thousands of single women missionaries. Within Canada, Baptists in the Maritimes, prompted by Maria Norris, led the way in this work. Women's societies from across the region joined in 1884 to form the Woman's Baptist Missionary Union, later United Baptist Woman's Missionary Union, and known today as Atlantic Baptist Women. This organization has played a significant role in Atlantic Baptist life, providing women with a vision, voice, and financial power within a male-dominated convention.

Thus successful in her efforts to recruit women's support, Maria Norris wasted no time in preparing to go to Burma using the $1300 raised from the women's missionary societies. On September 21, 1870, she left home, with a tearful goodbye to "the dear Mother I was not to see again outside of heaven."[4] Soon she was at sea, arriving in Rangoon, Burma (present-day Yangon, Myanmar), the following January. She claimed the promise of Isaiah 41:13 upon her arrival: "I [God] will help thee."[5] Quickly acquiring language skills, Maria taught school while sharing the message of salvation with the Karen people. During one trip she made to Thailand, a band of armed robbers intended to kill her but changed their minds at the last minute. Maria felt that God's hand was upon her and her ministry.

As news of her missions work spread, other Baptists from the Maritimes felt called to similar endeavors. The "Serving Seven" were sent out together in 1873. Among this group was William Armstrong, whom one biographer asserts had agreed before Maria left for Burma to marry her.[6]

---

[4] Untitled list of dates, Hannah Maria Norris Armstrong Collection, D1997.004, Box 5, G-17 1997 2-563, 1, Esther Clark Wright Archives, Acadia University, Wolfville, Nova Scotia.

[5] "Dates from Mother's Daily Light," Hannah Maria Norris Armstrong Collection, D1997.004, Box 4, D8, Esther Clark Wright Archives, Acadia University, Wolfville, Nova Scotia.

[6] Darcy Elliot, "Motherly Mission: Ideal Motherhood, the Women's Missionary Movement and the Experience of Hannah Maria Norris Armstrong (1842–1919)," bachelor's thesis, Mount Saint Vincent University, 2008, p. 88.

The two were wed on January 31, 1874. The following year the couple moved to India to work with the Telugu people, whom Maritime Baptists had chosen as the recipients of their new mission (and among whom Baptists from Ontario were already working). During this time the Armstrongs had two children: Katherine (Katie) and Ernest. A third child, Frederick (Fred), was born later.

In 1880, poor health forced the family to return to Canada for a time of rest. The women's missionary groups formed to support Maria were doubtless grateful for the opportunity to talk with her about her missions efforts. However, the Armstrongs decided to return to the mission field under the auspices of the American Baptist Missionary Union rather than the Maritime board. They apparently preferred to return to Burma instead of India. Maritime Baptist leaders reported hosting an "all-night session" with William Armstrong, but the sun rose with issues unresolved.[7] The Armstrong family, while still considered by many Maritime Baptists as their own, spent their remaining years of service with the American board, both in Burma and India.

Maria reportedly became fluent in Karen, Tamil, Burmese, and Telugu, and she worked together with William in evangelism, schools, and orphanages among peoples who spoke these languages. In a letter home, she wrote, "Throughout Burma there are inquirers after truth waiting for help....Is not this an open door!"[8] Her missionary zeal enabled her to persevere through years of hardship in foreign contexts in order to share the gospel with those who had not heard it.

In 1887, ill health again forced Maria to leave the mission field. She remained with her children in Canada for five years while her husband returned to Asia—surely a difficult situation for the entire family. During this time, Maria was the only woman to speak before the 1888 Centenary Conference on Protestant Missions in London.[9] This honor demonstrated her global reputation as a pioneering missionary woman. Through her

---

[7] D. A. Steele, *Our Pioneer: Impressions Regarding Mrs. H. M. N. Armstrong* (Amherst, NS: 1920), 30.

[8] Hannah Maria Norris Armstrong, "A Plan for Our Mission Work and Its Needs," Hannah Maria Norris Armstrong Collection, D1997.004, Box 6, HMNA S7, 3, Esther Clark Wright Archives, Acadia University, Wolfville, Nova Scotia.

[9] H. Miriam Ross, "Armstrong, Hannah Maria (Norris)," in *Biographical Dictionary of Christian Missions*, ed. Gerald H. Anderson (Grand Rapids, MI: Eerdmans, 1998), 27.

efforts, not only Maritimers but also leaders from across the Protestant world were encouraged in their missions work.

Upon her return to the mission field, Maria along with William continued their untiring efforts among unreached peoples. They set up a Bible school in Rangoon where educated non-Christians could study in English. This effort consumed much of Maria's attention in the later years of her ministry, although it was not supported by the couple's Baptist colleagues. Undaunted, Maria and William appealed for support from those of other denominations. Maria traveled widely to fundraise for this new project. However, the Armstrongs were unable to see their vision for the school fully realized.[10] Eventually, William became blind and his health failed. He passed away in Burma in 1918. After this, Maria reluctantly returned to Canada to live with her daughter. She had served as a missionary in Asia for more than forty years. A short time after her return to North America, her own health grew poor. Hannah Maria Norris Armstrong passed away on September 4, 1919, at the age of seventy-six, in Toronto.

In death as in life, Maria continued to inspire others to support missions. She had previously written articles about her ministry in multiple missions publications; these same publications published posthumous tributes to the missions pioneer. In the decades that followed, women's missionary groups across Atlantic Canada looked to Maria as their founding mother, finding inspiration from her determined ministry. They retold her story to new generations of women, urging them to greater missions commitment. In 1985, the United Baptist Woman's Missionary Union established the Hannah Maria Norris Chair of Christian Missions and Social Issues at Acadia Divinity College, demonstrating the significance that Maria's legacy carried for them more than a century after her formation of the first Baptist women's societies. In the twenty-first century, Baptist women and men throughout Atlantic Canada and beyond continue to tell the story of Hannah Maria Norris Armstrong to inspire others to greater missions leadership and support.

Suggested Reading

Allen B. Robertson, "Norris, Hannah Maria (Armstrong)," *Dictionary of Canadian Biography*, volume XIV (1911–1920). http://www.biographi.ca/en/bio/norris_hannah_maria_14E.html.

H. Miriam Ross, "Armstrong, Hannah Maria (Norris)," in *Biographical*

[10] Ibid.

Dictionary of Christian Missions, edited by Gerald H. Anderson (Grand Rapids, MI: Eerdmans, 1998), 27.

H. Miriam Ross, "Women's Strategies for Mission: Hannah Maria Norris Blazes the Trail in 1870," in *Canadian Society of Church History Historical Papers* (Canadian Society of Church History, 1992).

D. A. Steele, *Our Pioneer: Impressions Regarding Mrs. H. M. N. Armstrong* (Amherst, NS: 1920).

Augustus H. Strong (1836–1921), Honest Seeker of Moderate Theological Compromise

Theology

Michael E. (Mike) Williams, Sr.

In the years following the American Civil War, a "new intellectual climate" emerged on the American scene that introduced four significant new ideas into academic and theological life in the United States. The introduction of Charles Darwin's evolutionary biology and Herbert Spencer's "social Darwinism" radically revolutionized the U.S. scientific community. The new European biblical studies of higher criticism and textual criticism applied the techniques of modern science to the canon of Scripture. A new academic discipline of comparative religion emerged and found popular public reception. Finally, the new social sciences of psychology and sociology entered American intellectual and academic life. These challenges to traditional education and Christian doctrine smashed into American society during the time of immense sociological change resulting from the upheaval of the Reconstruction Era and the Industrial Revolution. At the exact same time, the young nation grappled with the trials of unprecedented urbanization and explosive immigration.[1]

In the center of an accelerating society transforming from a primarily rural, Anglo-Saxon, and Protestant-dominated culture to a far more theologically, ethnically, and culturally diverse society, many Christians viewed these new ideas as a threat to traditional Christian beliefs. Historian Winthrop Hudson observes that "the psychological and sociological

[1] Winthrop S. Hudson and John Corrigan, *Religion in America: An Historical Account of the Development of American Religious Life* (5th ed.; New York and Toronto: Macmillan Publishing Company, 1992), 233–77; Edwin S. Gaustad, ed., *A Documentary History of Religion in America since 1865* (Grand Rapids, MI: William B. Eerdmans, 1983), 85–91; Sydney E. Ahlstrom, *A Religious History of the American People* (New Haven, CT: Yale University Press, 1972), 763–84.

studies tended to reduce religion to a social phenomenon," while introduction to other faiths caused some to question "the uniqueness of Christian faith" and "both Darwinian biology and the new biblical studies seemed," at least to some Christians, "to undermine the authority of the Bible."[2]

In response to these new ideas, American Christians tended toward one of three responses. Some rejected outright any strain of thought that questioned the traditional expressions of faith. Usually these Christians retreated into some form of narrow sectarianism. Others rejected the conventional designs of orthodoxy as irrelevant and wholeheartedly embraced the new scientific methodologies. A third group sought to provide a mediating position between the more extreme positions and, as Hudson writes, sought "to effect adjustments that would do justice both to the essential elements of the inherited faith and to the newer scientific patterns of thought." Augustus Hopkins Strong fell into this latter group. During what historian William Brackney classifies as "the golden age of Baptist theologies," Strong served as one of the major spokesmen who "attempted to relate doctrinal understanding to the contemporary milieu."[3]

Born in Rochester, New York, in 1835, Augustus Hopkins Strong, except for the few years he spent at Yale and as pastor of a small Baptist church in Massachusetts and of the First Baptist Church of Cleveland, Ohio, spent all of his adult life and ministry in Rochester. When his systematic theology professor from his seminary days at Rochester Theological Seminary, noted Baptist theologian Ezekiel G. Robinson, left Rochester to assume the presidency of Brown University, Strong accepted the professor of theology and president of the seminary position and remained at his alma mater for the next forty years. From this position he became probably the foremost Baptist theologian in the United States, developed what one biographer calls "one of the most respected and theologically diverse seminaries in America," and became "a pastor to pastors."[4]

---

[2] Hudson and Corrigan, *Religion in America*, 257.

[3] Ibid., 258, and William H. Brackney, *Baptist Life and Thought: 1600–1980, A Sourcebook* (Valley Forge, PA: Judson Press, 1983), 263.

[4] Gregory Alan Thornbury, "Augustus Hopkins Strong," in Timothy George and David S. Dockery, eds., *Theologians of the Baptist Tradition* (Nashville: Broadman & Holman, 2001), 140–45; Augustus Hopkins Strong, *Autobiography of Augustus Hopkins Strong*, ed. Crerar Douglas (Valley Forge, PA: Judson Press, 1981), 203; and Kurt A. Richardson, "Augustus Hopkins Strong," in Timothy George and David S. Dockery, eds., *Baptist Theologians* (Nashville: Broadman Press, 1990), 290.

Strong's leadership with the Baptist denomination stretched far beyond Rochester and the seminary. He served as president of the American Baptist Foreign Mission Society as well as the Northern Baptist Convention. His *Systematic Theology* went through eight editions between 1886 and 1907 and served as the most important systematic theology text of that era. His other writings such as *Christ in Creation and Ethical Monism*, *Philosophy and Religion*, and *A Tour of Missions* contributed some of the most significant "theological pieces of the era," as biographer Kurt Richardson suggests. He also forged a significant friendship and eventually family ties with the industrial giant and Baptists' most significant philanthropist of the nineteenth and early twentieth centuries, John D. Rockefeller, Sr. Strong's older son Charles married Rockefeller's daughter Bessie, and even prior to the marriage, Strong frequently accompanied Rockefeller on his travels. Somewhat paradoxically, while he did not agree with every aspect of Walter Rauschenbusch's theology and Social Gospel and, for a time, had a break with him, Strong respected the church historian's scholarship, protected Rauschenbusch from his critics inside and outside Rochester, and ultimately reconciled with Rauschenbusch prior to Rauschenbusch's untimely death from cancer. As Strong's best biographer, Grant Wacker, writes, "He vigorously defended Rauschenbusch's right to assail the capitalist system yet just as vigorously solicited endowments from John D. Rockefeller and other robber barons."[5]

Strong developed his theological foundation under the influence of traditional reformed theology, the Scottish common sense realism of Thomas Reid and other philosophers, and orthodox Baptist thought. As Kurt Richardson writes, "Strong's approach to Scripture was reverent and thoughtful," and his theology professor at Rochester, Ezekiel Robinson, whom Strong identified in his *Autobiography* as "a radical," influenced him "concerning the positive use of historical criticism in biblical study." As his studies continued, Richardson argues that the Rochester theologian "preferred orthodox Lutheran European theologians." William Brackney writes that Lutheran Isaac Dorner, especially, influenced Strong as a "mediating theologian"; in a sense, Dorner represented the very type of theologian that Strong sought to become. However, as Richardson, Carl F. H.

[5] Richardson, "Augustus Hopkins Strong," 290; Ron Chernow, *Titan: The Life of John D. Rockefeller, Sr.* (New York: Random House, 1998), 234, 303–306; and Grant Wacker, *Augustus H. Strong and the Dilemma of Historical Consciousness* (Macon, GA: Mercer University Press, 2005), 4–5, 46, 104–105.

Henry, and Brackney have all demonstrated, Strong's theology evolved considerably over the course of the publication of the various eight editions of his *Systematic Theology* between 1886 and 1907.[6]

In the course of Strong's theological development as a mature theologian, he sought a middle way through which to navigate Baptists and, indeed, all Christians during times of scientific, philosophical, and theological change and stress. He hoped to provide what Brackney describes as "a fresh look at Christology." Ultimately, he became convinced that he held the way forward through adoption of what he called "ethical monism." Strong came to believe that all truth emanated from the person and work of Jesus Christ. His *Christ in Creation and Ethical Monism* sets forth an entirely Trinitarian theology but one that focuses on Christ as the channel for God's ongoing creative work. He hoped that ethical monism might provide the solution to "the problems of existence" presented by "dualistic theory." While conservatives criticized what they regarded as Strong's soft position on Scripture, his adoption of theistic evolution, and their belief that he advocated pantheism, liberals chastised him for a de-emphasis on God's immanence. As Gregory Thornbury concludes, "Strong's dream of the sweeping tide of monism never materialized."[7]

In his study and critique of Strong, Henry records that Strong moved through three periods of his developing theology—"as uncompromisingly fundamentalist," as a theistic evolutionist, and as someone with a view of "intensified divine immanence," represented by "his ethical monism." Henry disregards Strong's last years, especially his *A Tour of the Missions: Observations and Conclusions* published in 1918 and his *What Shall I Believe?: A Primer of Christian Theology* published a year after his death in 1921. James Leo Garrett observes that these two publications "reflect his more conservative period," which this writer believes indicates that he returned to thoughts somewhere between first and second/third periods. Wacker writes of four different ways that Strong has been labelled but concludes "that he is best understood as a mediator between liberalism and

[6] Richardson, "Augustus Hopkins Strong," 292–94; Strong, *Autobiography*, 121; William H. Brackney, *A Genetic History of Baptist Thought* (Macon, GA: Mercer University Press, 2003), 328–29; and Carl F. H. Henry, *Personal Idealism and Strong's Theology* (Wheaton, IL: Von Kampen Press, 1951), 55.

[7] Brackney, *Genetic History*, 330; Augustus Hopkins Strong, *Christ in Creation and Ethical Monism* (Philadelphia: The Griffith and Rowland Press, 1899), 47; Wacker, *Dilemma of Historical Consciousness*, 62–71; and Thornbury, "Augustus Hopkins Strong," 152–53.

orthodoxy." He adds that this viewpoint is the most popular and the one held by other notable historians such as Winthrop Hudson, George Marsden, and Mark Noll. Wacker summarizes that this position argues that Strong "tried to reconcile modernists and fundamentalists by urging a judicious accommodation with modern science. ...by insisting on the authority but not necessarily the inerrancy of Scripture."[8] Certainly, his reluctance to fully embrace inerrancy would be the cause of his rejection by fundamentalists and some conservatives.

Strong's comments included in his *A Tour of the Missions* identify where he ended up after his retirement from Rochester. After recording events on his tour, Strong reflected on his experiences. He titled the first three chapters of his observations and conclusions "Missions and Scripture," "Scripture and Missions," and "Theology and Missions." As Wacker summarizes, while Strong's concerns about the excesses of modernism had been "simmering" for more than ten years, his tour "left him deeply alarmed." He believed that the exclusive use of biblical and historical criticism in hermeneutics led to what Wacker calls "naturalistic assumptions." According to Strong, modernists treated "the Bible as a man-made book, or rather, as a series of books" that ignored a "pre-existent Christ" and disregarded "the influence of the divine Spirit." He warned that such an approach endangered Baptist higher education, Baptist churches, and Baptist missions. In the final chapter, "Missions and Missionaries," Strong largely indicated positive observations on missionaries, stating that he found them well trained and deeply committed. In this chapter, his primary concern related to American Baptist missions support, which he regarded as inadequate compared with that of other denominations. Some of his comments, however, also reflected observations from the previous three chapters. While he insisted that the experiences on the mission field typically "render[ed] the missionary doctrinally sound" and that "Evangelization makes men evangelical," he agreed that rare occasions existed in which other religious ideas misled missionaries into universalism. He argued that part of the problem came from the fact that "They had gotten their preparation for evangelistic work from...teachers of comparative religion, who put [other religions] on the same plane as [Christianity]." He called those who attempted to do so "opposers of the faith" and "destroyers

---

[8] Henry, *Personal Idealism*, 15; James Leo Garrett, *Baptist Theology: A Four Century Study* (Macon, GA: Mercer University Press, 2009), 295; and Wacker, *Dilemma of Historical Consciousness*, 7–8.

instead of builders of Christian civilization" who have "shown the impotence of man-made gospel." Calling "missions...the testing places of Christian doctrine," he further warned that "the school or church that ceases to be evangelical will soon cease to be evangelistic, and when it ceases to be evangelistic will soon cease to exist."[9] This quotation captures the heart of Strong's thinking at the end of his life. It also perhaps reflects his frustration due to the turn of events that will be described below.

Immediate history validated at least some of Strong's concerns. The division he feared was coming between fundamentalists, moderates, and modernists ultimately ruptured the Northern Baptist Convention during the 1920s. Involved on all sides of the conflict, former students of Strong's played significant roles in the controversy. Like Rebekah's womb in Genesis 25, Strong's theological legacy gave birth to two divided peoples. Both sides tried to claim him and at the same time reject him. Eventually, probably the best representatives of Strong's ideas were Curtis Lee Laws, editor of the *Watchman-Examiner* and leader of the Baptist Fundamentalist Fellowship, and Helen Barrett Montgomery, the moderate president of the Northern Baptist Convention. But even Laws and Montgomery lost power to fundamentalists and liberals in their respective organizations. Perhaps the mantle of Strong's theological legacy passed most directly to his friend, Southern Baptist Theological Seminary president E.Y. Mullins, and through Mullins into Southern Baptist life.[10]

Ultimately, as Wacker suggests, Strong emerges as a tragic figure: tragic because of his failure to steer his beloved school and denomination on a middle course that would prevent division, tragic because of his unanswered concerns about a theological drift to which some have believed he contributed and later regretted, and tragic because of his personal life and theological legacy. Primarily because of his own aggressive ambition, he failed to get John Rockefeller to fund his pet project for a Baptist theological flagship institution in New York, and Rockefeller turned the bulk of his philanthropic educational dollars to establishing the University of Chicago. The new university became a school that Strong correctly feared would become a theologically liberal Protestant institution. He failed to keep Rochester Theological Seminary on the theological course he sought for it after his retirement in his futile attempt to get his son John, or even

[9] Augustus Hopkins Strong, *A Tour of the Missions: Observations and Conclusions* (Philadelphia: The Griffith and Rowland Press, 1918), 165–218.

[10] Wacker, *Dilemma of Historical Consciousness*, 110–68.

a moderate like E. Y. Mullins, installed as his successor as president. His older son, Charles, whom he hoped would become a world-renowned evangelical Baptist theologian and philosopher, eventually rejected his faith completely and, by doing so, broke his father's heart. Finally, as discussed above, Strong failed in his attempt to develop a mediating and moderating theology built around his theological innovations, particularly ethical monism, that would be widely accepted as a Protestant evangelical norm at the beginning of the twentieth century.[11]

Despite these disappointments, Augustus H. Strong should not be considered a failure. Strong grappled with truth. Many people step into the harsh trap of unquestioning liberalism or fall into the dark pit of rigid and blind fundamentalism. It takes a special kind of theological curiosity and moral courage to try to bridge the gap between extremes. Strong gave his life to seeking to balance the tension between orthodoxy and modernism. Grant Wacker summarizes Strong well. He writes that "he was a touchingly human figure: too conservative to discard the nurture of his youth, too honest to discount his own religious experiences, yet too intelligent and well-read to ignore the verdict that the modern understanding of history had rendered on the case of orthodoxy." Wacker adds that while he presents "that the key to the riddle of Augustus Strong is that he set out to collaborate with God, but found out that he first he had to reckon with history," he concludes that "Strong himself would have said that it was the other way around" adding, "'When you come to the end of your life,' he wrote the morning before he died, 'will you say that you have never seen God? The answer [must] be that you have never seen anything else.'"[12] Though Strong ultimately failed to provide the *via media* that he sought, his willingness to struggle with the difficult ideas of his age and his curiosity, honesty, and courage serve as an example of the kind of witness to the Baptist and Christian heritage that an increasingly polarized world needs in the twenty-first century.

---

[11] Wacker, *Dilemma of Historical Consciousness*, 12, 172–73; Chernow, *Titan*, 302-307, 309; Strong, *Autobiography*, 356–57; Richardson, "Augustus Hopkins Strong," 301; and Jeff Straub, "'Dear Charles': Entreaties of a Concerned Father to a Wayward Son," 1–22, at https://www.academia.edu/4095842/_Dear_Charles_Entreaties_of_a_Concerned_Father_to_a_Wayward_Son.

[12] Wacker, *Dilemma of Historical Consciousness*, 172, 173.

Suggested Reading

William H. Brackney, *A Genetic History of Baptist Thought* (Macon, GA: Mercer University Press, 2003).

Ron Chernow, *Titan: The Biography of John D. Rockefeller, Sr.* (New York, Random House, 1998).

Kurt A. Richardson, "Augustus Hopkins Strong," in *Baptist Theologians*, edited by Timothy George and David S. Dockery (Nashville: Broadman Press, 1990).

Grant Wacker, *Augustus H. Strong and the Dilemma of Historical Consciousness* (Macon, GA: Mercer University Press, 2005).

John Clifford (1836–1923),
British Baptist Leader and Social Justice Activist

Social Justice

J. David Holcomb

Described by historian David Bebbington as the "most distinguished Baptist minister of his generation in England," John Clifford had a remarkable career that included not only pastoral and denominational leadership but also social and political activism.[1] From his longtime London pastorate at Praed Street Baptist Church in Paddington, Clifford became an influential denominational leader. He served prominent roles in Baptist life including editor of the *General Baptist Magazine*, president of the Baptist Union of Great Britain and Ireland, and the first president of the Baptist World Alliance. Theologically, Clifford embraced modern biblical criticism and sought to reconcile Darwinian evolution with Christian faith. A contemporary of Walter Rauschenbusch, Clifford advocated his own version of the Social Gospel to call on Christians to address the economic, political, and social challenges of their day. His progressive Christian social activism led him to oppose the Boer War as well as challenge the Education Act of 1902 due to its state funding of Anglican and Roman Catholic schools. As an instrumental leader in Baptist life during a tumultuous period of social, political, and theological change, Clifford helped British Baptists understand the public relevancy of their evangelical faith.

Early Life and Influences

John Clifford's affinity for Christian political activism was influenced by his family's experience as industrial laborers in nineteenth century England. Inadequate wages, poor working conditions, child labor, social unrest, and restrictions on civil and religious liberties (especially for nonconformists like Baptists) were commonplace. Clifford's father, Samuel,

[1] David W. Bebbington, *Baptists through the Centuries: A History of a Global People* (Waco, TX: Baylor University Press, 2010), 133.

experienced the vagaries of factory life in the Midlands and found in the local Chartist organization a place to advocate for the expansion of political rights. Clifford's mother, May, supplemented the meager family income by working at home as a lace runner. Born on October 16, 1836, in the village of Sawley, Clifford was the oldest of seven children. He attended school as a child, but by age eleven he found himself working fourteen-hour days as a threader in a lace factory. Of this experience, Clifford wrote, "I began life in a factory and I have never forgotten the cruel impression I received there of men and work."[2]

Despite his father's Calvinism, the Clifford family attended General Baptist churches while living in Sawley and later in Beeston.[3] There his faith was fostered and his eventual call to ministry was encouraged by the pastor, Richard Pike. At age nineteen, Clifford left home and factory work to enroll at the Midland Baptist College. The Baptist institution taught him not to fear the critical study of the Bible and also helped him begin to cultivate a theological rationale for the commensurability of evangelical faith and the Social Gospel.[4]

Pastor and Denominational Leader

In 1858, Clifford became pastor of Praed Street Baptist Chapel in the Paddington area of London. The small congregation enjoyed significant growth during his pastorate, necessitating the move to a larger facility at Westbourne Park in 1877. While pastoring, Clifford continued his academic pursuits and earned degrees in arts, sciences, and law at the University of London. Clifford matched his compelling oratory with his extensive publication record of dozens of books, pamphlets, sermons, and articles as well as serving as editor of the *General Baptist Magazine.* In 1879, the Geological Society named Clifford a fellow, and in 1883, the Freewill Baptist Bates College in the United States granted him an honorary doctorate.

Clifford's rapid ascendancy as a leader of British Baptists is illustrated by the numerous prominent denominational leadership positions he held.

---

[2] James Marchant, *Dr. John Clifford, C.H., Life, Letters, and Reminiscences* (London: Cassell and Company, 1924), 1.

[3] Philip R. Hart, "John Clifford: An English Social Reformer in the Pastorate," *Perspectives in Religious Studies* 16 (Fall 1989): 226.

[4] E. Glenn Hinson, "Baptists and the Social Gospel and the Turn toward Social Justice: 1898-1917," in *Turning Points in Baptist History: A Festschrift in Honor of Harry Leon McBeth*, ed. Michael E. Williams, Sr., and Walter B. Shurden (Macon, GA: Mercer University Press, 2008), 238.

These included president of the London Baptist Association (two terms), president of the Baptist Union of Great Britain and Ireland (two terms), first president of the Baptist World Alliance, and president of the National Free Church Council. In these roles, he championed denominational unity, helping forge, for example, the joining of General and Particular Baptists together in the Baptist Union in 1891. As a leader of Nonconformists in England, Clifford championed Baptist principles of soul liberty, local church autonomy, and separation of church and state.

Theology and Social Activism

Clifford's writings, sermons, and other addresses often sought to reconcile the intellectual antagonisms of his day, including biblical authority and historical criticism, Christian faith and evolution, and evangelical theology and social activism. While Clifford's approach garnered suspicion, if not opposition, from more conservative Baptists, Clifford remained undeterred from marrying his Christological and evangelical faith with modern intellectual currents. Roger Hayden succinctly summarized Clifford's theology as follows: "His interpretation of evangelicalism was Arminian, his appreciation of the new Biblical scholarship acute, and his adherence to the New Testament and its idea of the church unshakable."[5] His embrace of critical methods of biblical study as well as his critiques of biblical inerrancy in his 1892 publication, *The Inspiration and Authority of the Bible*, brought opposition from some Baptists. In fact, Clifford's publication motivated some conservatives to form an organization called the Bible League whose purpose was to defend the Scriptures from modernist impulses. Others saw theological drift in Clifford's deep opposition to creeds. For Clifford, creeds violated freedom of conscience and had been utilized as "weapons of clerical absolutism, tools of theological tyranny, and padlocks of the Bible, and foes of Christian brotherhood."[6]

Divisions in Baptist life came to a head in 1887 when a series of articles were published in Charles Haddon Spurgeon's publication, *The Sword and the Trowel*, warning of the "Downgrade" of doctrine and practice among Baptists. Spurgeon, pastor of the Metropolitan Chapel and one of the most famous preachers in England, published subsequent articles

[5] Roger Hayden, *English Baptist History and Heritage*, 2nd ed. (Oxford: The Baptist Union of Great Britain, 2005), 60.

[6] Quoted in G. W. Byrt, *John Clifford: A Fighting Free Churchman* (London: The Kingsgate Press, 1947), 106.

bemoaning the "New Theology" that was undermining orthodox beliefs on the atonement, the resurrection, and scriptural authority. It was left to Clifford, president of the Baptist Union, to navigate the growing divide between Spurgeon, along with his Calvinist allies who wanted the denomination to adopt a stronger statement of faith, and those who resisted anything that resembled a creed. In hopes of maintaining unity, Clifford orchestrated the adoption of a "Declaratory Statement of Faith." The statement's affirmation of broad theological principles proved unsatisfactory to Spurgeon, who, along with a relatively small number of pastors, withdrew from the Baptist Union. While the "Downgrade Controversy" emerged as one of the most significant conflicts in the history of the Baptist Union, Clifford continued to be called upon for denominational leadership. He must have felt genuine satisfaction three years later when he helped facilitate the uniting of General and Particular Baptists in the Baptist Union.[7]

Influenced by his family's experiences as well as his ministry among the working class in Paddington, Clifford advocated for the Social Gospel earlier than his progressive counterparts in the United States. And, as David Bebbington has claimed, his advocacy "went much further than Rauschenbusch and sought more radical changes to the social and economic order."[8] As early as 1859, Clifford, in his first church report as pastor of Praed Street Chapel, declared that "we exist as a church and congregation not only for our spiritual improvement, but also and especially for saving souls and bodies of the people in the neighborhood." He once described the church as a "social settlement" whose role was to go beyond saving souls to "to the vocation of applying the social teachings of Jesus to the social and economic affairs of life." Praed Street subsequently initiated a number of ministries to fulfill this vocational directive. Among the first was the Mutual Economic Benefit Society where members paid weekly dues and would receive financial and medical aid when ill. Another ministry, The Westbourne Park Institute, offered more than seventy classes and other events each week. These included lectures and instruction in literature, science, and languages as well as building construction and dress making.[9] The need for adequate and affordable housing was another area of concern for Clifford that led his church to create Westbourne Park

---

[7] Bebbington, *Baptists through the Centuries*, 109–10.

[8] Ibid., 133.

[9] Hinson, "Baptists and the Social Gospel," 238–39.

Home. For nineteen years the Westbourne Park Home served as a temporary residence for those who were homeless.

Beyond his church's ministries, Clifford advocated for a number of social reforms, including temperance in alcohol use, increasing the minimum wage, and advocating for women's rights. He most consistently advocated for the Temperance Movement. He frequently bemoaned the evils of the "liquor trade," arguing that it destroyed families and had other deleterious effects on society, including business. Clifford lobbied for a guaranteed minimum wage as well. He believed that pure laissez-faire capitalism treated workers as a means to an end, led to the idolatry of property, and fostered a spirit of competition. In contrast, Clifford contended that a living wage, along with other economic reforms, would diminish exploitation, counter materialism, and foster brotherhood. Women's equality concerned Clifford as well. He advocated women's suffrage and supported the Sex Disqualification Act that passed Parliament in 1919. Women were no longer blocked from law and politics, and Clifford observed that "before long the barrier of sex will be entirely abolished."[10]

Clifford's deep commitment to religious liberty motivated his opposition to the 1902 Education Act. The proposed law would have provided tax support for Anglican and Roman Catholic schools. Clifford vigorously opposed the law as the violation of the consciences of Baptists and other nonconformists. In opposition to the bill, Clifford helped organize the Passive Resistance Movement. Its call for opponents to refuse to pay the religious tax led to the jailing of 170 men. Clifford would find himself in court more than forty times for his refusal to pay the rate as well. The Liberal Party seized on the attention brought by Clifford's noteworthy opposition as well as the attention brought by the Passive Resistance Movement and used them to rally support for their victory in the 1906 Parliamentary elections.[11]

Clifford's advocacy also extended to foreign policy. He criticized the Boer War as imperialistic and rooted in greed and racist motivations. He was particularly opposed to the destruction of Boer farms and the placement of women and children in concentration camps. Formally, Clifford served as president of the organization Stop-the-War and was a member

[10] Quoted in Tom Nettles, *The Modern Era*, vol. 3 of The Baptists: Key People Involved in Forming a Baptist Identity (Fearn, Scotland: Mentor, 2007), 70.

[11] See Dwight A. Honeycutt, "Motivations of a Political Activist: John Clifford and the Education Bill of 1902," *Journal of Church and State* 32 (Winter 1990): 81–96.

of the South African Conciliation Committee. Eventually, he opposed the creation of the Union of South Africa in 1910 due to its discrimination against the Black population.[12]

The Social Gospel that Clifford advocated was reflected as well in his political affiliations. He joined the Fabian Society and held leadership positions in the Christian Socialist League and the National Brotherhood Council. For most of his career he served as an active member of the Liberal Party. By 1890, Clifford had embraced Socialism as an attractive alternative to Communism on the one hand and individualism on the other. Communism, he believed, "exaggerated the social interest at the expense of the individual," while individualism could be "hollow, unreal, and disastrous." Clifford frequently commended Socialism for its harmony with the gospel of Christ. He believed it mitigated against the evils of society brought about by unchecked industrial capitalism while also being "congenial to the Christian understanding of wealth."[13] At times, Clifford went further, declaring that "Socialism in the soul of it is divine." As a result, he believed churches should take "full share in the reformation and rebuilding of society, to welcome every extreme of the Socialist principle."[14]

While Clifford had retired from the Westbourne Park pastorate in 1915, his religious, social, and political activism continued. In 1918, Clifford made waves when he decided to abandon the Liberal Party and join the Labour Party. Despite the fact that he had opposed the Boer War, Clifford eventually supported Britain's involvement in World War I, expressing Wilsonian-like idealism that it might bring about an end to all wars. Nonetheless, Clifford used his prominent voice to oppose conscription and support the rights of conscientious objectors.

Despite his extensive involvement in the public arena, Clifford remained devoted to Baptist causes and the Baptist Union. Perhaps fittingly, he died while participating in a Baptist Union Council meeting on November 20, 1923.

---

[12] Byrt, *John Clifford*, 140–42.

[13] Quoted in Hart, "John Clifford," 240.

[14] Quoted in Michael Walker, "Charles Haddon Spurgeon (1834–1892) and John Clifford (1836–1923) on the Lord's Supper," *American Baptist Quarterly* 7 (June 1988): 139.

Conclusion

Few Baptists rival John Clifford's record of denominational leadership and influence. Even fewer have gained his level of prominence in public life. Clifford's social and political activism, motivated by his commitment to the Social Gospel, exemplified for Baptists the importance of applying the ethical mandates of Scripture to the economic, social, and political problems of the day. Clifford's legacy is, thus, remarkably enduring because the issues that dominated his thought—biblical criticism, the relationship of science and religion, and the application of the Social Gospel—remain central concerns for many Baptists in the twenty-first century.

Suggested Reading

G. W. Byrt, *John Clifford: A Fighting Free Churchman* (London: The Kingsgate Press, 1947).

Philip R. Hart, "John Clifford: An English Social Reformer in the Pastorate," *Perspectives in Religious Studies* 16 (Fall 1989): 225–44.

E. Glenn Hinson, "Baptists and the Social Gospel and the Turn Toward Social Justice: 1898–1917," in *Turning Points in Baptist History: A Festschrift in Honor of Harry Leon McBeth*, ed. Michael E. Williams, Sr., and Walter B. Shurden (Macon GA: Mercer University Press, 2008), 235–48.

Dwight A. Honeycutt, "Motivations of a Political Activist: John Clifford and the Education Bill of 1902," *Journal of Church and State* 32 (Winter 1990): 81–96.

James Marchant, *Dr. John Clifford, C.H., Life, Letters, and Reminiscences* (London: Cassell and Company, 1924).

Virginia Broughton (1856–1934), *National Baptist Educator and Missionary*

Education

Pamela R. Durso

In the late nineteenth century, after devoting twelve years of her life to public education, Virginia Walker Broughton was commissioned as a missionary. She spent the remainder of her life traveling throughout Tennessee and other nearby states, encouraging Black Baptist women to form Bible Bands,[1] raising money for educational and religious causes, and advocating for the formation of women's organizations. She was an effective speaker and writer, an accomplished Bible teacher, and a successful crusader, working in the same circles as Nannie Helen Burroughs and Joanna P. Moore. Her missionary journey is well documented in two autobiographical writings: one published in 1895 and the other in 1907.

Broughton was born March 1, 1856, in Nashville, Tennessee. Her father, Nelson Walker, was born in Virginia and most likely was fathered by his mother's slave owner. According to Walker family lore, Nelson's white half-brother helped him study for and pass the Virginia state bar examination. Nelson's wife, Eliza, was an educated mulatto house slave who worked in the Walker household as a seamstress.[2] When their owners relocated with their slaves to Maury County, Tennessee, Nelson saved money and purchased his and his wife's freedom. He eventually became a

[1] Bible Bands were reading and study groups in which women were encouraged to memorize and interpret Scripture and then instruct other women in the faith. These bands also offered participants training in organizational leadership and domestic skills, and some participants sold Bibles and raised funds for missions. Networking among Bible Band participants resulted in the development of a movement that spanned across states and regions and spread into multiple denominations.

[2] Tomeiko Ashford Carter, ed., *Virginia Broughton: The Life and Writings of a National Baptist Missionary* (Knoxville: University of Tennessee Press, 2010), xxii.

prominent barber, businessman, and lawyer in Nashville. In her 1895 autobiography, Broughton stated that her father was "the first colored lawyer admitted to the bar in Davidson County, Tennessee."[3]

The Walkers had eight children: four girls and four boys. Their daughter Selena was the first Black teacher in Tennessee's Davidson County, and their son John attended Meharry Medical School in Nashville. Founded in 1876, Meharry was the first medical school for Blacks in the South.[4] The couple's daughter Virginia enrolled in 1866 at the newly formed Fisk College and Normal Institute and began the fourth grade that spring. Founded by the American Missionary Association just six months following the end of the Civil War and two years after the Emancipation Proclamation, Fisk was named in honor of General Clinton B. Fisk of the Tennessee Freedmen's Bureau. The general provided the school with facilities in former Union Army barracks near the present site of Nashville's Union Station, and the first classes at Fisk were held on January 9, 1866. Many of the students were former slaves or children of former slaves and ranged in age from seven to seventy.[5]

The same year Virginia Broughton began studying at Fisk, she had a conversion experience. In her autobiography, she wrote, "From a child, she had known the scriptures, and had accepted Jesus as a personal Savior when only ten years old."[6] During her years at Fisk, Broughton excelled academically and graduated with honors in 1875.[7] Later that year, she began teaching public school in Memphis. In the 1870s, few teaching positions were available to Black educators, but Broughton successfully passed a teacher's exam in July 1875, two months after graduation. School officials in Memphis, who did not have enough White applicants to fill all the teacher openings, hired her as a grade school teacher. As a result of her

[3] Virginia Broughton, "A Brief Sketch of the Life and Labors of Mrs. V. W. Broughton: Bible Band Missionary for Middle and West Tennessee" (Memphis, TN: M. L. Jones Publisher, 1895), in Carter, *Virginia Broughton*, 1. Jessie Carney Smith could not verify that Nelson Walker was the first. See Jessie Carney Smith, "Virginia E. Broughton (c. 1856–1934): Feminist, Missionary, Educator, Lecturer, Writer," in *Notable Black American Women: Book II,* ed. Jessie Carney Smith (Detroit, MI: Gale Research, 1996), 57–60.

[4] "Black History Month," Meharry Medical College, https://home.mmc.edu/event/black-history-month-2019/.

[5] "Fisk University History: The End of the Civil War," Fisk University, https://www.fisk.edu/about/history.

[6] Broughton, "A Brief Sketch," 2.

[7] Ibid.

early accomplishments in the field, friends encouraged her to take the principal's exam. She chose not to because one of her Fisk male classmates was taking the exam, and she did not want to compete against him.

In the years following her graduation from Fisk, Broughton sang with the world-famous Fisk Jubilee Singers. The singing group originated in 1871 with students and alumni traveling throughout the country and then throughout Europe, seeking to raise money to keep the debt-ridden school open. The singers struggled at first, but their electrifying performances moved audiences to tears and supplied income for their beloved school. In 1878, while Broughton was in Europe with the singing group, Fisk awarded her a Master of Arts degree.

For twelve years, Broughton was an educator in Memphis, first as a teacher and then principal at North Memphis School and later as a teacher at Kortrecht School, which was founded in 1873 as the city's most advanced public educational institution for Black students and was the first all-brick school building for those students in Memphis. Sometime during her years as an educator, she married John Broughton, a Republican lawyer who served in the County Register's office in Memphis and later in the state legislature. The couple had five children: Emma, Elizabeth, Selena, Virginia, and Julius, Jr.[8]

In 1885, Broughton once again bumped against male competition for a position for which she was qualified. This time she was ready to advocate for herself and to challenge a male colleague's promotion. When Green Hamilton, a younger male teacher, was promoted to head teacher at Kortrecht by Benjamin Sampson, the principal of all the area's Black schools, Broughton challenged the decision. She then garnered support from her fellow teachers and from Fred Savage, a member of the school board. Savage argued Broughton's case before the school board, suggesting that she replace Hamilton. The school board, over the objections of school superintendent Charles Collier, agreed to promote Broughton and demote Hamilton. The board's decision resulted in ongoing conflict, much of which can be attributed to racial tension between Collier, who was White, and Savage, who was Black and brought to light the question of who would control Memphis's Black schools. Broughton publicly spoke out against Sampson and Collier in an article published in a local black newspaper, *The Living Way*. Tomeiko Ashford Carter contends that Broughton even-

[8] Smith, "Virginia E. Broughton," 57.

tually asserted her own parity but of course had to do that within the confines of the patriarchal systems of her time. Carter writes, "Thus, despite her initial reservations about competing for the position not traditionally held by women, it was precisely because she excelled at her job that Broughton was promoted to that very position and later won a similar position at the city's premier school for African Americans."[9]

During Broughton's time at Kortrecth, she was invited by Joanna P. Moore, a popular and influential Baptist leader, to attend a missionary meeting. That 1882 meeting would change the course of Broughton's life. Moore in 1863 became the first White woman appointed by the American Baptist Home Mission Society. She was assigned to work on Island 10 in the Mississippi River, which was near Memphis. There she ministered to 1,000 Black women and children who had relocated to the island so that they could be under the protection of the Union army. After her time on the island, Moore devoted herself to working in Black communities in the South, providing childcare guidance for mothers, offering literacy instruction and domestic skills training, and helping develop the leadership skills of Black women.[10] In 1877, the Woman's American Baptist Home Mission Society gave Moore its first commission;[11] in 1884, she founded the Fireside Schools system, which was not a formal institution but was the organization of study groups for children to encourage Bible study and improve home life;[12] and in 1885, she founded a monthly magazine, *Hope*, which contained Sunday school lessons, Bible Band guides, and letters written by Black women and ministers.[13]

After their initial meeting in 1882, Moore quickly engaged Broughton in missionary work, inviting her to join a Bible study and then training her to form Bible Bands for Black women in Memphis. In her later autobiographical writing, *Twenty Years' Experience of a Missionary*, Broughton

[9] Carter, *Virginia Broughton*, xxvii.

[10] Susan Hill Lindley and Eleanor J. Stebner, eds., *The Westminster Handbook to Women in American Religious History* (Louisville, KY: Westminster John Knox Press, 2008), 153.

[11] Benjamin Brawley, *Women of Achievement* (Boston, MA:Woman's American Baptist Home Mission Society, 1919), 5, https://archive.org/details/womenofachieveme00brawrich/page/n11.

[12] Johnny E. Williams, *African American Religion and the Civil Rights Movement in Arkansas* (Jackson: University of Mississippi Press, 2003), 45.

[13] Lindley and Stebner, *Westminster Handbook to Women in American Religious History*, 153.

noted that the "organization grew and increased in numbers, influence, and spiritual strength.... Soon Bible Bands were organized throughout the city of Memphis and the women of our churches took on new life. Every Monday afternoon women could be seen in all sections of the city with Bibles in their hands, going to their Bible Band meetings."[14] Broughton spent the next few years teaching during the school week and traveling on weekends to rural areas up to fifty miles away, gathering women who would commit to daily study of the Bible. She also organized Bible Bands. Some weeks Broughton returned to Memphis on Monday mornings and went directly from the railroad station to her classroom, often without having slept or eaten breakfast.[15] Although the Bible Band work interested Broughton greatly, she had no plan to leave her lucrative salary as a teacher or undertake full-time missionary work. However, following her mother's death, her own serious illness in 1887, another round of conflict with the school superintendent, and affirmation from women missionaries, Broughton had a change of heart. She resigned her position at Kortrecht and gave herself fully to missionary work.[16]

In 1888, the board of directors of the Bible and Normal Institute (later renamed the Howe Bible and Normal Institute), a school that provided preparation for preachers, teachers, missionaries, and mechanics, commissioned Broughton as a missionary. Her responsibilities included canvassing the Memphis area, organizing women and children locally, arranging for a general district organization, and founding Bible Bands.[17] She also spent time raising money for the school, focusing attention on the girls' dormitory at the institute. Broughton encouraged women in her circles of influence to provide the dormitory with bedding and furnishings. She also urged male pastors to get involved and provide resources and assistance for the school.[18] The school's principal noted, "We make bold to say that there is no more inspiring or important work in the South than that which the women have been doing...in connection with the Bible and

---

[14] Virginia Broughton, *Twenty Years' Experience as a Missionary* (Chicago: Pony Press Publishers, 1907), 9.

[15] Ibid., 18.

[16] Ibid., 14.

[17] Ibid., 21.

[18] Ibid., 25–26.

Normal Institute."[19] By 1908, the institute had enrolled 216 women students in its training classes.[20]

In 1892, Broughton's work expanded as the Women's Baptist Home Mission Society also appointed her as a missionary. She continued her work in founding Bible Bands, traveling throughout Tennessee but also spending time in Arkansas and Missouri. Within two years, she had organized bands in fifty-seven locations in Tennessee alone.[21]

While Broughton was fully committed to the work of missions, her husband was not initially supportive. In *Twenty Years' Experience of a Missionary*, Broughton, writing in third person, recorded a conversation between the two of them. "One day he asked her, 'When is this business going to stop?' She replied, 'I don't know; but I belong to God first, and you next; so you two must settle it.'"[22] Later she noted that "God verily did settle the question" and convinced her husband that his wife had been called to a special ministry and "to hinder her would mean death to him."[23] Two of their daughters, Emma and Elizabeth, were quicker than their father in supporting Broughton's missionary work. As a child, Elizabeth often brought tea to her exhausted mother following one of her missionary trips. Both daughters were converted before their father, and following his profession of faith all three were baptized on the same day by Rev. H. Smith.[24]

For ten years, Broughton spent time planning and leading ten women's district association meetings held in West Tennessee. Hundreds of women participated in the meetings, during which Broughton and other women leaders spoke. In *Twenty Years' Experience as a Missionary*, Brought

[19] H. R. Traver, "The Bible and Normal Institute," *The Baptist Home Mission Monthly* 15, no. 8 (August 1893): 272.

[20] Smith, "Virginia E. Broughton," 58.

[21] Ibid.

[22] Broughton, *Twenty Years' Experience as a Missionary*, 46.

[23] Ibid., 46–47.

[24] Ibid., 50–51. The Broughtons had five children: Emma, Elizabeth, Selena, Virginia, and Julius Jr. Emma exhibited great musical abilities as a child and graduated from the Howe Institute and the Musical Conservatory of Chicago. She later became a music teacher, married, and had three children. Elizabeth also studied at Howe Institute and Moody School for Girls in Northfield, Massachusetts. She later graduated from Roger Williams University and taught school. Later she became a medical doctor and served as a missionary in Africa. Selena died in childhood. Virginia graduated with honors from Fisk University in 1907. Broughton's only son, Julius, Jr., became an accomplished shoemaker.

described the Durhamville meeting as having the most "powerful spiritual manifestations" and the women speakers as being used "mightily of God to encourage women to live pure, virtuous lives and train up a consecrated, intelligent ministry from the youth of the race to lead the race forward as God directed in His Word."[25] As a result of the meetings, a general awakening took place, and reform was evident as improvements were made in the home and in the church life of participants. Women gave up "the vile habits of beer drinking and snuff-dipping" and used their "little mites" in buying Christian literature and contributing to missionary and educational work.[26]

In addition to organizing meetings, Broughton participated in revivals. In a revival in Woodlawn, she "labored earnestly and persuaded many to accept Jesus through her clear and simple presentation of God's plan of salvation and through her fervent prayers." At another meeting in Woodlawn for children, Broughton had "the privilege of leading a number of children to the Savior's loving arms."[27] Not only were women and children converted; men too had life-changing experiences during these revivals. During one service, Brother Summer became deeply convicted of sin. Broughton and the other women missionaries prayed earnestly for him, and "God was present and the burdened soul was relieved and his sorrow changed to joy in his acknowledging Jesus as his personal Savior."[28] At another service held at First Baptist Church of Nashville, Broughton was moved by the Spirit to kneel beside a man and pray for his conversion. She later wrote, "The power of the Holy Spirit was manifestly present and the man's heart was so melted under this glowing fire of the Holy Spirit that he soon made a bright profession of religion. In telling his experience of conversion he said: 'I felt if I went to hell after such a prayer was made for my escape it would be warm, indeed, for me.'"[29] In her autobiography, Broughton described these revival seasons as "time of special refreshing and spiritual edification" and gave thanks to God "for any part the dear Lord permitted our missionary to share in them.... we praise God and give him all the glory for the dear ones...being saved in these revival meetings."[30]

---

[25] Ibid., 31.
[26] Ibid., 32.
[27] Ibid., 74.
[28] Ibid., 77.
[29] Ibid., 75–76.
[30] Ibid., 77–78.

In 1899, Broughton moved her family to her hometown of Nashville, where she served as one of Joanna Moore's secretaries at the headquarters of the Fireside School and as assistant editor of the monthly magazine, *Hope*. In 1902, Moore, who was in failing health, devised a plan by which to transfer the supervision of the Fireside School to a Black missionary. She recommended that Broughton be named as the school's supervisor. Broughton's work was exemplary during these months, which she attributed to the wise counsel and encouragement she received. Yet Moore struggled to let go of control of her beloved school. After six months, she negotiated a return to her position and soon once again took over solo management of Fireside.[31] Broughton then returned to Memphis in order to continue her missionary leadership.

In addition to her missionary work, Broughton served as an advocate for the formation of women's conventions at both the state (Tennessee) and national levels. She was vocal in defending the organization of a state convention for Black Baptist women, and, with other women, she declared that such a convention would promote middle-class values among Black families, bring in financial support for churches, and found and support social service programs that would benefit communities. Meanwhile, she also worked on a national level, calling the National Baptist Convention, USA (NBC), to approve the formation of a women's convention.

In 1890, Broughton traveled to St. Louis to attend an NBC gathering and served as a speaker at the convention. In her presentation, "The Ideal Woman," she called for a separate and distinct organization within the NBC. Broughton, Nannie Helen Burroughs, and other women continued to agitate for this organization until they succeeded. In 1895, the NBC created a Woman's Auxiliary with Broughton serving as its recording secretary. The next year, the NBC closed the auxiliary down, the male leaders choosing instead to appoint women to various convention boards. Yet the women refused to abandon their dream, and in 1900, the national Women's Convention was formally established.[32] From June 14, 1902, until the end of 1903, Broughton wrote a monthly "Women's Department" column for the NBC's official newspaper, the *National Baptist Union*, addressing such topics as childrearing, tithing, and obedience to God. She would later serve as the editor for this column and as an editor for *Missionary Herald*. In addition to columns and articles, Broughton also wrote

[31] Ibid., 83–85.

[32] Smith, "Virginia E. Broughton," 59.

Woman's Work: As Gleaned from the Women of the Bible and the Bible Women of Modern Times and *Systematic Bible Study by Periods: Twelve Bible Lessons.*

Virginia Broughton died on September 21, 1934, of complications from diabetes.[33] A woman of great giftedness and dedication, she had given her entire adult life to the service of others, first as a teacher and principal and then as a missionary, speaker, writer, revival leader, and women's rights advocate. In her 1895 autobiography, she named her missionary efforts "the crowning work of her life," concluding that "there can be no longer doubt as to woman's divine appointment to assist in the great work of evangelizing the world, for the women's organizations throughout this country have demonstrated the fitness of women to work for Jesus, and manage their business so discretely that the wisest men are now bidding them welcome as co-workers in all the great evangelical movement of the age."[34] Broughton's missionary work was certainly influential among Black women and Black churches in Tennessee and surrounding states, but over the course of her life, her circle of influence grew well beyond her region. Her Bible teaching, practical writing, and inspiriting speaking brought change to the lives of thousands of women, men, and children, while her leadership and fundraising skills made her one of the most prominent women in the early years of the National Baptist Convention, USA.

Suggested Reading

Virginia Broughton, "A Brief Sketch of the Life and Labors of Mrs. V. W. Broughton: Bible Band Missionary for Middle and West Tennessee" (Memphis, TN: M. L. Jones Publisher, 1895), in Carter, ed., *Virginia Broughton*.

Virginia Broughton, *Twenty Years' Experience as a Missionary* (Chicago: Pony Press Publishers, 1907), 9, onlinebooks.library.upenn.edu/webbin/book/lookupname?key=Broughton%2C%20Virginia%20W%2E.

Tomeiko Ashford Carter, ed., *Virginia Broughton: The Life and Writings of a National Baptist Missionary* (Knoxville: University of Tennessee Press, 2010).

Jessie Carney Smith, "Virginia E. Broughton (c. 1856–1934): Feminist, Missionary, Educator, Lecturer, Writer," in *Notable Black American Women: Book II,* ed. Jessie Carney Smith (Detroit, MI: Gale Research, 1996), 57–60.

[33] Carter, *Virginia Broughton*, xxvii.

[34] Broughton, "A Brief Sketch," 2.

Leslie Lee Gwaltney (1876–1955), Prophet of the Press, Peacemaker, and Imperfect Voice for Social Justice

Social Justice

Michael E. (Mike) Williams, Sr.

The First Amendment to the U.S. Constitution includes the most cherished rights in American history, especially the first liberty, freedom of religion, and continuing with freedom of speech and freedom of the press. Baptists in the United States have certainly benefitted from the first freedom as well as being advocates for it, but the next two freedoms protected in the First Amendment have also influenced Baptist life significantly. Weekly religious newspapers in the United States began in the early nineteenth century with the Presbyterian publication, *The Christian Secretary*. The first weekly Baptist newspaper, *The Christian Watchman*, began publication in 1819, followed by *The Columbian Star* in 1822 by Baptist leader Luther Rice and others. *The Columbian Star* eventually moved south to Georgia and became *The Christian Index*, and it remains the oldest continually published religious newspaper in the country. As Baptist churches and institutions expanded across the country in the nineteenth century, a plethora of state Baptist newspapers emerged. Baptist pastors and laymen originally owned and operated many of these newspapers, but gradually private owners either transferred or sold these publications to state Baptist conventions. Often these private owners and editors used the newspapers to promote primarily but not exclusively Baptist institutions, ministries, and programs while selling advertising to private businesses and reporting general, national, and sometimes even international news. In some situations on the frontier, religious newspapers, like Baptist newspapers, frequently provided the primary or even the only news source for isolated communities or individuals. They also met a need for reading materials where bookstores, libraries, and even mail routes were in limited supply.[1]

---

[1] "About *Christian Secretary* (Hartford [Conn.]), 1822–1896," Chronicling Historic American Newspapers, National Endowment for the Humanities, at

Editors of these religious newspapers projected a loud voice in denominational matters as well as political realms.

Born at the end of the Reconstruction Era in rural tidewater Elberon, Virginia, about halfway between Petersburg and Norfolk, Leslie Lee Gwaltney promised to be an outstanding student due to his studies in the local school and his avid love of reading. Though he felt called to ministry, his father hoped that he would become a physician. After the two compromised on a business career, for a brief time Gwaltney studied business and worked in a Richmond department store. The young man eventually enrolled at the local Baptist college, Richmond College, and then moved to Union Theological Seminary, where he studied Greek and Hebrew. After marrying, beginning his family, and serving small, rural Baptist churches, he moved to the Southern Baptist Theological Seminary in Louisville, Kentucky, where he completed a Master of Theology degree. That same year, 1908, First Baptist Church of Prattville, Alabama, called him as their pastor.[2]

Gwaltney's move to Prattville exposed him to conditions he had never experienced while attending school in Richmond and Louisville and serving country churches. As Wayne Flynt writes in his monumental *Alabama Baptists: Southern Baptists in the Heart of Dixie*, the membership of Prattville Baptist Church "consist[ed] of businessmen, farmers, and workingmen" from the local cotton gin company and from local textile mills as well as "many indigent widows." Gwaltney recorded that normally such a mix of "these classes work together harmoniously in a church," but at least while he served in Prattville they did. Samford University professor and contemporary of Gwaltney, James H. Chapman, recorded in a short biography of Gwaltney that this introduction to pastoral ministry in the mill town, "crystalized...a Christian social service philosophy" and called it "his testing laberatory [*sic*]."[3]

---

https://chroniclingamerica.loc.gov/lccn/sn92051442/; "Our History," *The Christian Index*, at https://christianindex.org/our-history/; and *Encyclopedia of Southern Baptists*, s.v. "CHRISTIAN INDEX, THE."

[2] L. L. Gwaltney, "Birth and Rearing" and "Education and Training," typed autobiographical manuscript, 3–10, James H. Chapman papers, Leslie Gwaltney, AR 639, Box 2, Folder 8, Southern Baptist Historical Library and Archives, Nashville, Tennessee.

[3] Wayne Flynt, *Alabama Baptists: Southern Baptists in the Heart of Dixie* (Tuscaloosa and London: University of Alabama Press, 1998); Gwaltney, "Ministerial

After twenty-two months in Prattville, Gwaltney accepted a call to the pastorate of Greenville, Alabama's First Baptist Church. Greenville, the county seat of Butler County, provided the perfect pastorate for the young, growing pastor. The largest church not only in the Butler County Association but also within a large surrounding area, J. H. Chapman of Howard College (Samford University) recorded later that Greenville was composed of the "cultured, wealthy, respected and influential," and historian B. F. Riley recognized that the congregation as the most important congregation between Mobile and Montgomery. Gwaltney himself wrote, "it was at Greenville that I learned nearly everything I know."[4]

While serving the church in Greenville, Gwaltney experimented in his preaching. He delivered sermons and wrote articles for *The Alabama Baptist*—at the time an independently owned state Baptist newspaper—on controversial subjects such as his opposition to capital punishment and lynching, as well as his support for "theistic evolution," the rights of the working class (including promotion of labor unions), Social Christianity or the Social Gospel as Northerners such as Washington Gladden and Walter Rauschenbusch and their disciples typically referred to it, women's suffrage, child labor laws, and graduated income tax. He managed to challenge his listeners and readers with these ideas outside of conservative Baptist norms because he also stressed orthodox Baptist beliefs on evangelism, atonement, believer's baptism, religious freedom, separation of church and state, and opposition to "sins" like drunkenness, gambling, prostitution, dancing, and pornography while also not promoting controversial views on race. As Wayne Flynt writes, Gwaltney reflected Alabama Baptist culture on race, prohibition, Catholics, the Ku Klux Klan, and separation of church and state.[5]

The Alabama Baptist editor Frank Barnett spent several months on sick leave recovering from a serious illness, and Gwaltney served as interim editor while he also continued in his pastorate at Greenville. Throughout that interim period, Gwaltney filled in capably and addressed many of the

---

Experiences and Churches," 22, AR 639, Box 2, Folder 8, SBHLA, Nashville, Tennessee; James H. Chapman, "Leslie Lee Gwaltney," typed manuscript, 6–7, Chapman papers, AR 639, Box 2, Folder 8, SBHLA, Nashville, Tennessee.

[4] Chapman, "Gwaltney," 5; B. F. Riley, *A Memorial History of the Baptists of Alabama; being an account of the struggles and achievements of the denomination from 1808 to 1923* (Philadelphia and Boston: Judson Press for the Alabama Baptist State Convention, 1923), 332; Gwaltney, "Ministerial Experiences and Churches," 25.

[5] Flynt, *Alabama Baptists*, 320.

same concerns he had preached and written about in preceding years. His ability to do so probably influenced leaders in Alabama Baptist life a few years later. After eight years as pastor in Greenville, the First Baptist Church of Florence, Alabama, called him as pastor. After he served there only slightly more than a year, the Alabama Baptist State Convention purchased *The Alabama Baptist* from Barnett and a short time later recalled Gwaltney's service as temporary editor and invited him to become its editor. He would serve in that position for more than thirty years through times of tremendous cultural change, especially among Southern Baptists, and through the Great Depression and World War II. As historian Wayne Flynt states in his monumental study of Alabama Baptists, in those decades, Gwaltney became "the best known and most highly regarded Baptist in the state."[6]

From this position, Gwaltney sought to implement many of the ideas he had addressed as a pastor and in previous writing for *The Alabama Baptist*. For example, while he devoted much space in *The Alabama Baptist* to promoting state and denomination-wide causes, he delved into many of the hot cultural topics of the day. Having long advocated for voting rights for women, Gwaltney continued to prove to be "the most outspoken Baptist male of women's rights." As the November election loomed in 1920, Gwaltney lauded the approach of the first presidential election in which women would vote. In September he wrote, "Their new privilege will create a new interest in politics and government." He believed that "They will begin to think for themselves on these things, since they can at last put their thoughts in action." Engaging in hyperbole, the editor compared the passage of the eighteenth amendment to the emergence of "our Anglo-Saxon forefathers…in the wilds of Germania" had such reform occurred. Like some others in the Progressive Movement, Gwaltney argued that women of the world, as mothers and wives in particular, could prevent war from occurring once they had political influence. Likewise, he and other Baptist leaders believed that women would support prohibition of alcohol and support reform in issues of public health. Along the same line, a few weeks later Gwaltney printed a plea from Alabama Baptist stalwart W. B. Crumpton. The aged denominational statesman urged women voters to cast votes for candidates who would support the League of Nations.[7]

---

[6] Gwaltney, "Ministerial Experiences," 32–33; Flynt, *Alabama Baptists*, 258.

[7] Flynt, *Alabama Baptists*, 331; *The Alabama Baptist*, September 2, 1920: 3, and October 28, 1920: 5.

The editor's support for women went beyond their voting rights. As the Roaring Twenties unfolded, some Baptists developed a deep concern about the changes among women's hairstyles and apparel as well as a perceived newly found assertiveness. In a May 1923 column titled "Concerning the Feminist Movement," Gwaltney responded to critics of these changes. He began by arguing that he had never sought "to regulate women." Indeed, he argued that men needed more regulation than women. He considered it "folly" to even attempt such management. Furthermore, he argued that he "believe[d] in women," including even "the bob-haired flappers" and wrote "that passing fads and fashion of a half-decade" could not destroy morals "when every decade has had and will have a peculiarity in modes of dress." While elsewhere, Gwaltney expressed concerns about dancing and jazz music, the current fads seemed not to disturb him in the least. He also argued that attempting to keep women in their place harmed men as well as women. As he said, one "cannot put a chain around a slave's neck without becoming a slave"—a remarkable admission in a state weighted down by Jim Crow laws and only a half-century removed from defending slavery with secession and war—and "no man can hold another down in the mud without getting muddy." To those who wanted to silence women in conventions and churches, Gwaltney reminded the readers that if they took the admonition for women to be silent literally, women would not be able even to sing or teach Sunday school. To those who literally interpreted that women should be silent and ask their husbands when they got home, he boldly declared, "the apparent difficulty about that is, the women probably know more about the work of the kingdom than their husbands." Such men would therefore be "horrible instructors." Later in the decade, he lauded the advances made by women in the professions and in state politics and reported that Montana Baptists had ordained a woman preacher. He reminded his readers that in earlier decades, women could not speak to church groups that included men or sing solos or attend Baptist meetings as messengers. Likewise, he proclaimed that women supported the bulk of mission work. In other settings, he stated that some biblical admonitions regarding women undoubtedly came from culture rather than divine proclamation because at other places in the Bible, women clearly played active roles. He even declared that clearly "there were deaconesses in the early church."[8]

[8] *The Alabama Baptist*, May 3, 1923: 3; Flynt, *Alabama Baptists*, 332.

Another controversial area that Gwaltney waded fearlessly into concerned the rights of labor. Taking the side of labor unions brought a negative response from some readers, but Gwaltney held his ground. Indeed, as Wayne Flynt observes, he believed the struggle for labor unions was simply another "aspect of the struggle for religious freedom transferred to the economic arena" and was the next step in the war against child labor that both he and his predecessor at *The Alabama Baptist*, Frank Barnett, had waged in the first decades of the twentieth century, allying with Governor Thomas Kilby and Dr. Hastings Hart of the Child Welfare League of Alabama. Gwaltney supported collective bargaining but criticized the actions of strikers in 1921 as representative of a "Bolshevik spirit." He praised Governor Kilby for calling out the state militia only as a last resort and congratulated him for his prompt and decisive action when it became necessary. A hundred years later, the reader might determine that Gwaltney straddled the fence, but as he explained in observations made in 1926, taking sides or not taking sides in the struggle led to criticisms from both. That year after attending a session of the Northern Baptist Convention, he asked why only a representative of labor addressed the session and no corresponding representative of capital spoke. Gwaltney questioned why no "captain of finance" spoke to the session "on the glories of capitalism." Sarcastically—and parenthetically—he added, "if there are any glories in it." While Gwaltney did attempt to steer a middle course in the conflict between capital and labor, more often he tended to slide to the side of labor, perhaps a reflection of those early pastoral years in Prattville.[9]

On the issue of convict labor, Gwaltney held no middle ground. Quoting a column in the *Birmingham News* that criticized Alabama's newly inaugurated governor, W. W. Brandon, and his plan to defer action on the state's notorious convict leasing system, Gwaltney wrote, "How gratifying it is to see the South's greatest daily challenging the iniquitous convict lease system." He challenged the new governor "to see that which is morally wrong can legitimately neither play for time nor be justified on the ground of mere expediency." When Brandon failed to end the system, Gwaltney lauded candidate Bibb Graves in the campaign for governor in

[9] *The Alabama Baptist* with Elizabeth Wells and Grace Thornton, in *The Alabama Baptist: Celebrating 175 Years of Informing, Inspiring and Connecting Baptists* (Birmingham: *The Alabama Baptist*, 2017), 51; Wayne Flynt, *Alabama in the Twentieth Century* (Tuscaloosa: University of Alabama Press, 2004), 195; *The Alabama Baptist*, 23 September 1920, p. 4; October 7, 1920, p. 4; October 28, 1926, p. 4; Flynt, *Alabama Baptists*, 342.

1926, focusing attention on the evils of convict leasing in the mines of Alabama, declaring that "sin likes to go undercover." He trumpeted, "The whole convict lease system was eternally wrong...in the sight of God and man." Unfortunately, it took the death of a White convict to finally force the issue, and in 1928, Alabama finally ended the dreadful system.[10]

On another major Baptist issue of the 1920s, Gwaltney found himself again in what historian Flynt calls "the eye of the storm" of another Baptist hurricane. In this case, theological conflict formed the basis of the storm, typically labeled by historians as the fundamentalist-modernist controversy. For decades, conservative Christians feared that new scientific discoveries and theories, different systems for interpreting the Bible, and changes in the traditional structure of higher education and religious order threatened the fabric of faith, Christianity, and even the political structure. Far more complex than a confrontation between fundamentalists and liberals or fundamentalism and modernism, or a battle between evolutionary theory and the Bible, the struggle reached an apex in the 1920s with the Scopes trial in Tennessee, but it continued to transpire throughout the remainder of the 1920s. Many fundamentalists split from mainstream denominations and formed new denominations or independent bodies to continue their agenda. Some denominations adopted essentially scientific modernism and/or theological liberalism as these fundamentalist factions withdrew. However, as Flynt states in *Alabama Baptists*, "most American evangelicals" found themselves "suspended between fundamentalism and modernism, dissatisfied with some elements of both."[11]

---

[10] *The Alabama Baptist,* March 25, 1926, p. 4; August 26, 1925, p. 4. See also Douglas A. Blackmon, *Slavery by Another Name: The Re-Enslavement of Black Americans from the Civil War to World War II* (New York: Anchor Books, 2008). Blackmon's Pulitzer Prize-winning account focuses on the convict leasing system in Alabama as representative of the South. It is an excellent work; unfortunately, it fails to present much information about Christian reformers like Gwaltney and others who, while they certainly remained prejudiced and paternalistic toward African Americans, exhibited many of the characteristics of the Social Christianity referred to above and had genuinely progressive attitudes and actions as demonstrated by this brief account.

[11] Flynt, *Alabama Baptists*, 344–45. The literature on this topic is exhaustive, especially as these battles occurred again in the 1980s and 1990s and continue even today. Probably the best single study of both the background to this period and the period itself is George Marsden, *Fundamentalism and American Culture: The Shaping of Twentieth Century Evangelicalism, 1870–1925* (New York: Oxford University Press, 1980). On the years of the struggle after 1925, Marsden's *Reforming Fundamentalism:*

A complete discussion of this topic falls outside the scope of this chapter, but suffice it to say that while Gwaltney found himself "tranquilly confident of his own scientific and biblical understanding," he tried to steer Alabama and Southern Baptists in a middle way between the fundamentalist and modernist extremes. While several leading pastors and Alabama and Southern Baptists supported Gwaltney in his progressive-conservative middle way, other Baptist press editors, pastors, and laypeople blasted Gwaltney at every turn. Despite the attacks, Gwaltney played a leading role in the election of a conservative-moderate, E. Y. Mullins, as president of the SBC in 1921 and in two subsequent reelections, and he supported Mullins as he steered the SBC to a "compromise" confession of faith in 1925. How Gwaltney managed to do so would demand a much longer explanation than is possible in this study. Suffice it to say that Gwaltney agreed with conservatives and fundamentalists on enough critical issues that it helped him maintain his position, and Gwaltney had proven himself as a journalist who allowed both sides to present their arguments in a fair forum, *The Alabama Baptist*. Alabama Baptists also knew Gwaltney. The weeks he spent traveling around the state, appearing in their churches, supporting the denomination's causes, preaching revivals, and serving as a pastor had solidified a trust that enabled him to weather this particular hurricane.[12]

Unfortunately, Gwaltney, like all human beings, remained a deeply flawed person still captive to certain aspects of his culture, especially those of racial and religious prejudice that were unfortunately so common even among Southern Baptist liberals and moderates of this era. While his racism typically found milder expressions, and he frequently denounced lynching as barbaric, he also defended segregation and exhibited a prejudiced racial paternalism offensive to later Baptist eyes and ears. He even wrote mild defenses of the Ku Klux Klan and issued anti-Semitic statements and bitter anti-Catholic diatribes indicative of Klan opinions.[13] While a lengthier study might attempt to explain his actions, there may no excuse for them, even in light of the context of Deep South culture in the first half of the twentieth century. They demonstrate that all people,

---

Fuller Seminary and the New Evangelicalism (Grand Rapids: Wm. B. Eerdmans, 1995 ed.) is helpful though not as comprehensive, clear, or thorough as his 1980 classic.

[12] Flynt, *Alabama Baptists*, 344–53.

[13] Ibid., 353–59.

even those who are open-minded and progressive, may have their blind spots.

As mentioned above, these issues are representative of the kinds of issues that Gwaltney dealt with as a pastor and as a newspaper editor and denominational leader for over thirty years. Like many Southern Baptists of his era, he remained conservative in many social issues, like alcohol consumption, and in theological issues, where he upheld traditional Baptist views on the incarnation and literal resurrection while defining himself as a theistic evolutionist for his entire career and avowing pacifism for much of his adult life. However, when the United States plunged into two world wars, he dropped his pacifism in convenient fashion. In the interwar years, he originally supported disarmament but moved to promote rearmament and support of the British and Chinese when he recognized the threats of Nazism and Japanese militarism. He opposed dancing, jazz music, and the legalization of professional boxing and supported a ban on movies shown on Sundays. He opposed the horrendous and racist convict leasing system but supported continued segregation. He often sided with labor instead of business and supported equality for women but recognized that socialism or communism would not work within a democracy. He never wrote a systematic theology, but, as this author's choice of a category to define him demonstrates, he probably contributed almost as much to the theology of Baptists, especially Alabama Baptists, as any Baptist theologian of the early twentieth century, even with all his complexity and seeming contradiction. As Wayne Flynt writes, Gwaltney "was a complex man." Gwaltney reminds the twenty-first century reader that Baptists, and indeed, Christians and human beings, are complex creatures and that even flawed creatures can accomplish much good.[14]

Suggested Reading

The Alabama Baptist with Elizabeth Wells and Grace Thornton, in *The Alabama Baptist: Celebrating 175 Years of Informing, Inspiring and Connecting Baptists* (Birmingham: The Alabama Baptist, 2017).

J. Wayne Flynt, *Alabama Baptists: Southern Baptists in the Heart of Dixie* (Tuscaloosa: University of Alabama Press, 1998).

Michael E. Williams, Sr., and Walter B. Shurden, *Turning Points in Baptist*

[14] Ibid., 319–59. For greater detail on Gwaltney's pacifism, see Michael E. (Mike) Williams, Sr., "Leslie Lee Gwaltney: Editor of *The Alabama Baptist*, Peacemaker, and the Dilemma of Two World Wars," in *Baptist History & Heritage* 55, no. 1 (Spring 2020): 38–51.

History: A Festschrift in Honor of Harry Leon McBeth (Macon, GA: Mercer University Press, 2008).

Michael E. Williams, Sr., "Leslie Lee Gwaltney: Editor of The Alabama Baptist, Peacemaker, and the Dilemma of Two World Wars," *Baptist History & Heritage* 50, no. 1 (Spring 2020): 38–51.

Clarence Leonard Jordan (1912–1969), "Ex-Baptist," "Saint in Overalls," and "Prophet in Blue Jeans"[1]

Social Justice

Mandy McMichael

Thirteen years before Civil Rights protestors launched the Montgomery Bus Boycott to integrate buses in Montgomery, Alabama, Clarence Jordan and Martin England launched an interracial Christian farming community in Sumter County, Georgia. Like their justice-seeking counterparts more than a decade later, Jordan and England undertook practices that were met, at times, with hatred, disgust, and violence. Shortly after arriving at the farm, they hired a former sharecropper to help them. They worked together and ate together. Word of this breach of common custom made its way around the town, prompting a visit from some of their "neighbors."

One man said to Jordan, "We're from the Ku Klux Klan, and we're here to tell you we don't allow the sun to set on anybody who eats with n ----s." Noticing that the sun was about to set, Jordan reached out his hand to shake the man's hand and responded, "Why, I'm a Baptist preacher and I just graduated from the Southern Baptist Seminary. I've heard about people who had power over the sun, but I never hoped to meet one." As the story goes, they shared a laugh as the man admitted to being the son of a Baptist preacher, the sun set, and the situation was diffused.[2] This was not the only run-in with the Klan that Jordan would face. Nor would every encounter be so easily diffused.

Still, Jordan's quick wit served him well. Coupled with his knowledge and understanding of Southern culture, his theological training, and his conviction that God intended Christians to live out the teachings of Jesus,

---

[1] Henlee H. Barnette, *Clarence Jordan: Turning Dreams into Deeds* (Macon, GA: Smyth & Helwys, 1992), 2 and 22.

[2] Clarence Jordan and Joyce Hollyday, *Essential Writings* (Maryknoll, NY: Orbis Books, 2003), 20–21.

Jordan became known to some as a "saint in overalls" or a "prophet in blue jeans." Others, of course, viewed him as a troublemaker and an agitator. A son of the Southern Baptist Church, he embraced the Baptist beliefs of the Lordship of Christ, the sole authority of the Bible, and the priesthood of the believer, which resulted in a life committed to the Baptist principle of social justice. His prophetic vision mimicked that of early Baptists determined to return to the teachings and practices of the New Testament church. Like the "Rebel Jesus" he followed, Jordan was a radical dissenter whose countercultural witness disrupted the lives of good religious folk and demanded sacrifice. His legacy as a Baptist witness continues through his many writings, including his Cotton Patch version of the Gospel, but it lives and breathes in the ongoing work of Koinonia Farm.

Clarence Leonard Jordan was born on July 29, 1912, in Talbotton, Georgia, to J. W. and Maude Josey Jordan. From his parents, especially his mother, he learned to treat others with kindness and respect regardless of race. He also inherited his deep Christian faith from his family. Yet even as a child Jordan was struck by the seeming incompatibility between the teachings of Jesus and the reality of Southern culture. Growing up in a house that sat near a "chain-gang camp," Jordan often visited the prisoners, most of whom were Black, on his way to and from school. One story he recounted often was of witnessing the warden of the jail, Mr. MacDonald, singing "Love Lifted Me" in the church choir only to be awoken that night to the sounds of a prisoner being beaten and realizing that the perpetrator of that violence was Mr. MacDonald. Jordan struggled to reconcile these two images, citing this incident as one that influenced his life's trajectory to unite belief and practice.[3]

Jordan enrolled in the University of Georgia to pursue a degree in agriculture in hopes that such a degree would equip him to help poor Black sharecroppers and begin to address some of the economic inequities of the region. He graduated in 1933, but his experiences during university, including a deep encounter with Jesus' Sermon on the Mount, changed his charted course. While completing an ROTC exercise, he was confronted with the incompatibility of Jesus' command to love your enemies and the military training he was receiving.[4] He resigned his commission and left

[3] Frederick L. Downing, *Clarence Jordan: A Radical Pilgrimage in Scorn of Consequences* (Macon, GA: Mercer University Press, 2017), 23–27.

[4] Ibid., 90–92.

Georgia to pursue a ministry degree at Southern Baptist Theological Seminary (SBTS) in Louisville, Kentucky.

During his time there, his faith continued to take a radical turn as he dove headfirst into the study of Scripture, earning a master's degree in 1936 and a PhD in New Testament Greek in 1939. Edward A. McDowell, a professor of New Testament and Greek at Southern, had a particularly profound influence on Jordan. McDowell not only taught Jordan how to read the Bible in dialogue with culture but also took Jordan to a conference on race. Both experiences deepened Jordan's commitment to serving among the poor and disenfranchised in defiance of Southern cultural mores, something he put in practice throughout his time in Louisville and beyond.[5] The study of Scripture was not merely an academic exercise for Jordan; in the Bible he "found more than forms and syntax; he found the example and teaching of Jesus."[6] It was those examples that compelled him to live a radically different life.

In addition to being equipped for his life's work during seminary, Jordan also found a life partner in the person of Florence Kroeger, who served as a librarian's assistant at the seminary. The two married shortly after Jordan graduated from SBTS on July 21, 1936. Together they had four children and embraced a mission that was anything but boring. Jordan had the academic, oratorical, and interpersonal gifts to become a golden boy of the Southern Baptist Convention, but he sensed even before he married that God had other plans for him, famously telling Florence, "If you want to be the wife of a pastor of the First Baptist church someplace, you don't want to marry me, because I'll never be pastor of a First Baptist church, or any church maybe."[7]

This is not to suggest that Jordan neglected to serve his denomination but merely that he refused to shirk his convictions and bow to cultural expectations in order to do so. During his time at SBTS and in his years in Louisville following graduation, he acted as pastor or supply preacher at many Kentucky Baptist churches. He was also well known in the Baptist student groups, embracing opportunities to speak at Ridgecrest Camp in North Carolina as well as on several Baptist university campuses. Most formative, however, was the time he spent working in the inner city as

[5] Ibid., 106.

[6] Frank Stagg, quoted in Barnette, *Clarence Jordan*, 103.

[7] Downing, *Radical Pilgrimage*, 104.

director of the Sunshine Center mission and later as the director of missions for the Long Run Baptist Association that oversaw the Union Gospel Mission in the Haymarket District.[8] This role deepened his understanding of the consequences of racial inequality and poverty.

In 1941, during his time working with the mission, Jordan met an American Baptist missionary named Martin England. They discovered a mutual love of Scripture and a belief that the Sermon on the Mount articulated a way of life meant to be practiced, not merely discussed. Together they began dreaming about the possibility of founding a Christian community dedicated to the principles laid out in Jesus' teachings, one that privileged racial equality, nonviolence, and a shared common life. They felt God calling them to this work and began the task of finding an appropriate location, eventually settling on 400-acre farm in Sumter County, Georgia, and relocating there in November 1942. Compelled to live out their faith on this "demonstration plot for the Kingdom of God," they named the place Koinonia Farm and commenced with the work of reconciliation to which they felt called.[9] The word *koinonia* is the Greek word used to describe the shared communion and fellowship enjoyed by the early church. This was not the first time that Jordan had attempted to establish such a Christian community, but it would be the most successful and long-lasting.

A decade later, the group had grown to nineteen adults and twenty-two children living and working together. The journey to sustainability was not an easy one, however. In fact, it remained costly. Threats of violence came almost immediately with actual violence following later. The radical lifestyle of those at Koinonia simply did not make sense to the surrounding community. What seemed so obviously biblical to Jordan appeared dangerous to the good church people of Sumter County, and, at times, attempting to explain simply made matters worse. Over time, Jordan and the inhabitants of Koinonia Farm found themselves banned from fellowship at Rehoboth Baptist Church, endured an economic boycott by

---

[8] Ibid., 110, and Barnette, *Clarence Jordan*, 2–3. According to Barnette, "Before the advent of the auto and the supermarket, the Haymarket was the place where farmers brought and sold their produce in a semi-open place that covered a city block. The canopied sidewalks of Jefferson Street were still there in the early 1940s where other merchants hawked their wares from small stalls. Both wealthy and poor people purchased vegetables and fruits from this community" (3). It was also the home of some of Louisville's poorest residents, many of whom were unchurched.

[9] Jordan and Hollyday, *Essential Writings*, 16.

the town, had their roadside market blown up, had KKK crosses burned on their property, and lived in fear of gunfire attacks. Both the FBI and the GBI investigated Jordan, some labeled him a communist, and he had ammunition fired into his house.

It was the bullying of his daughter Jan at school, however, that Jordan recounted as the moment he came closest to breaking his commitment to nonviolence. Knowing of the pain she withstood daily at the hands of Bob Speck and the principal's subsequent refusal to do anything about it, Jordan confessed his strong desire to "beat the hell out of Bob Speck." In the end it was his daughter who figured out a creative way to avoid violence. In recalling this event in a lecture at Southern Baptist Theological Seminary, Jordan noted that "young kids maybe can think of creative ways of dealing with evil that an older Christian can't. And I think this is what we got to do....Maybe we need to turn loose our kids with some creativity in this thing to find new ways and new methods of dealing with evil."[10] The attacks endured by those living and working at Koinonia Farm provided them plenty of opportunities to manufacture—and test—creative solutions.

Jordan's prophetic teachings spread beyond the acreage of Koinonia Farm as he was invited often to speak and teach around the nation. Koinonia also hosted a number of guests, including Dorothy Day (co-founder of the Catholic Worker Movement), Will Campbell (Baptist pastor), A. C. Miller (director of the Christian Life Commission of the Southern Baptist Convention), and Millard Fuller (attorney and businessman). At times, Koinonia Farm also held a summer camp for inner-city children from several states.[11] Such visits allowed individuals to experience life at Koinonia, including the threat of violence and feelings of isolation and fear. Visitors learned more about the convictions of the residents, worked alongside them, and joined in their fellowship. Visits varied in length, but some visitors, such as Millard Fuller and his wife Linda, eventually joined the community.

Jordan's writings and sermons also helped promote the vision and work of Koinonia. In a sermon on the "Substance of Faith," he recorded his oft-quoted definition of faith as "not belief in spite of the evidence but a life in scorn of the consequences."[12] And in one on "The Mind of Christ

---

[10] Barnette, *Clarence Jordan*, 32–34.
[11] Jordan and Hollyday, *Essential Writings*, 24, 28.
[12] Ibid., 143.

in the Racial Conflict," he determined, "it is not difficult to discover the mind of Christ. I find it difficult to implement the mind of Christ."[13] Both speak to the challenge of living a godly life, something with which Jordan was intimately familiar. Perhaps his most influential teachings are found in his writings on the Sermon on the Mount. For Jordan, the Sermon on the Mount was the "Platform of the God Movement," calling Christians to live a life of discipleship. Jordan never shied away from pointing out how modern churches had acquiesced to culture. In recalling the persecution of the early church, he mused, "One wonders why Christians today get off so easily. Is it because unchristian Americans are that much better than unchristian Romans, or is our light so dim that the tormentor can't see it? What are the things we do that are worth persecuting?" He concluded, "Either the world has been completely converted to Christ and his Way, or the Church has watered down and compromised its original heritage. In the latter position, the church, due to its weakness, loses its influence and is discarded."[14] Persecution, according to Jordan, meant you were doing something right. Comfort and luxury were dangerous temptations.

Another of Jordan's enduring legacies is his homespun translations of the New Testament, commonly referred to as the Cotton Patch version. These interpretations attempted to bridge the gap between ancient Scripture and modern culture by retelling the narratives of Scripture in the Southern vernacular. Gone were the ancient cities, with Tallahassee, Atlanta, and Chattanooga taking their place. The fig tree in Matthew 21 became a peach tree, the crucifixion a lynching, and the Good Samaritan a Black man. So powerful were Jordan's renditions that his paraphrase of Matthew was turned into an off-Broadway musical known as *The Cotton Patch Gospel.*

Koinonia Farm became Koinonia Partners in 1968 as Jordan and Fuller began work on a new project involving affordable housing that built and sold homes at cost. Jordan never got to see this part of the vision fully realized because he suffered a heart attack and died on October 29, 1969, at the age of fifty-seven. Since the coroner would not come to Koinonia to issue the death certificate, Fuller drove Jordan's body into Americus in a station wagon. A simple funeral service was held the next day, and Jordan, wearing his blue jeans, was buried in a cedar crate in an unmarked grave

---

[13] Ibid., 151.

[14] Ibid., 120.

on the farm. Clarence Jordan's legacy lives on in Koinonia Farm, which remains a community committed to peace, justice, and reconciliation as evidence of their faith as followers of Christ. It stands as a testament to what is possible when one man says yes to God.

For some, mostly progressive Baptists, Jordan looms large in their collective consciousness. For others, he offers a cautionary tale of the dangers that befall those outside of institutional Baptist life. Perhaps for the majority, however, this "prophet in blue jeans" and "saint in overalls" remains largely unknown. And yet Baptists have much to learn from the witness of this self-proclaimed "ex-Baptist." Jordan's determination and courage to live out the principles of Jesus Christ when they challenged cultural Christianity drip with Baptist DNA, a denomination founded by dissenters who valued both the freedom of individual conscience and the beauty of beloved community. His high view of Scripture that led him to read and offer culturally relevant and appropriate interpretations, his submission to the Lord above man or institution, and his refusal to bend his conscience to that of Rehoboth Baptist Church offer further proof of his Baptist identity. In other words, Jordan's Baptist witness committed to social justice stands over against a capitalistic society that privileges profit over people. As a Jesus follower, Jordan preached and modeled a different way, one of radical discipleship that sought to demonstrate—as far as was possible—the Kingdom of God in which all are equal and equally loved.

From Jordan, as from other famous Baptist "saints" like Lottie Moon, Martin Luther King, Jr., and Walter Rauschenbusch, Baptists learn the power of personal conviction that demands a countercultural response. Jordan understood that being a Christian required sacrifice; it was costly. It did not end with an admiration of Jesus but with a willingness to follow Jesus even unto the cross.

Suggested Reading

Henlee H. Barnette, *Clarence Jordan: Turning Dreams into Deeds* (Macon, GA: Smyth & Helwys, 1992).

Frederick L. Downing, *Clarence Jordan: A Radical Pilgrimage in Scorn of Consequences* (Macon, GA: Mercer University Press, 2017).

Clarence Jordan and Jimmy Carter, *Cotton Patch Gospel: The Complete Collection* (Macon, GA: Smyth & Helwys, 2012).

Clarence Jordan and Joyce Hollyday, *Essential Writings* (Maryknoll, NY: Orbis Books, 2003).

Clarence Jordan, *Sermon on the Mount* (rev. ed.; Valley Forge, PA: Judson Press, 1971).

Clarence Jordan, *The Substance of Faith and Other Cotton Patch Sermons*, ed. Dallas Lee (Eugene, OR: Wipf & Stock, 2005).

Dallas Lee, *The Cotton Patch Evidence: The Story of Clarence Jordan and the Koinonia Farm (1942–1970)* (3rd ed.; Eugene, OR: Wipf & Stock, 2011).

Charles Marsh, "In the Fields of the Lord: The God Movement in South Georgia," in *The Beloved Community: How Faith Shapes Social Justice from the Civil Rights Movement to Today* (New York: Basic Books, 2004), 51–86.

James Wm. McClendon, Jr., "The Theory Tested: Clarence Leonard Jordan—Radical in Community," in *Biography as Theology: How Life Stories Can Remake Today's Theology* (Eugene, OR: Wipf & Stock, 2002).

Joseph Martin Dawson (1879–1973), Defender of Separation of Church and State

Religious Liberty

Jack Goodyear

Following the death of Joseph Martin (J. M.) Dawson in 1973, one colleague praised Dawson's contribution to Baptist life with these words: "More than any other person in his day he influenced his own denomination toward a recommitment to religious liberty and the separation of church and state."[1] This well-earned description is quite the accomplishment for someone who was the firstborn of an impoverished young couple, struggling to survive on a cotton field while living in a one-room log cabin. From these beginnings, Dawson rose to influence his community, state, country, and ultimately the global community of Baptists. J. M. Dawson's life contributed greatly to the Baptist heritage and witness.

Born June 21, 1879, in central Texas near Waco, Dawson grew up in a farming family that valued hard work and discipline, understanding that for their family, "there was no cash except in cotton."[2] However, physically and economically, the farming life took its toll, prompting a moment of crisis for Dawson at age fourteen. With poverty gripping the family and his father injured and unable to work temporarily, Dawson recalled "a sense of encircling doom," which led him to question God's goodness: "I seethed in anger that a wise God would permit so many children, fiercely rebelled at grinding poverty and the persistent, abominable irritation in the home." However, the steadfast spirits of his mother and father and their continued faith in God to walk through the storm with their family kept him grounded. It was a vulnerable time for Dawson, who admitted, "A finger's weight of pressure toward a wrong tilt could have made me a

[1] James E. Wood, "The Legacy of Joseph Martin Dawson (1879–1973)," *Journal of Church and State* 15 (1973): 363–66.

[2] Joseph Martin Dawson, *A Thousand Months to Remember* (Waco: Baylor University Press, 1964), 27.

malicious delinquent. I shudder today to contemplate what might have happened."[3]

Dawson embraced his opportunity for education, finding a passion in writing that led him to dream of becoming a journalist. When he was eighteen and in full pursuit of a career in journalism, his pastor inquired about God's calling on Dawson's life, suggesting that full-time ministry might be in his future. However, Dawson wanted no part of this calling; he had endured poverty as a child and was certain that a career in ministry would lead to more of the same. As he sought the Lord in prayer, he felt a prompting of the Spirit telling him, "You are called to preach...preach...preach."[4] In obedience, Dawson surrendered to the call, painfully giving up his desire to be a journalist, yet he also never regretted his decision because he realized that the love of writing would serve him well as a preacher.

While at Baylor University, where he graduated in 1904 as valedictorian, Dawson helped found the student newspaper and served as editor of the school annual. Surrendering to the call to ministry, Dawson went on to pastor three central Texas churches: First Baptist Church of Hillsboro, First Baptist Church of Temple, and most notably First Baptist Church of Waco, where he served for thirty-one years from 1915 to 1946. During his first pastorate, he married Willie Turner of Dallas in 1908. Together, until her death in 1963, they faithfully raised five children. Willie supported Dawson's ministry and became a sought-after speaker herself, recognized as the "ideal wife, Christian mother and grandmother, denominational leader, speaker with spiritual charm, lady of compassion and consecration, of intellect and integrity, a soul-winner and a cherished friend."[5]

Perhaps it was his wife's influence on his life, his childhood growing up poor, or his admiration for such thinkers as Walter Rauschenbusch that developed Dawson's passions in ministry as a combination of personal evangelism and social justice. A beloved pastor and talented author, Dawson led denominationally in the Baptist faith while committing himself as a civil libertarian politically. Whether it was as a pastor or as the first Executive Director of the Baptist Joint Committee on Public Affairs, Dawson's ministry and service influenced Baptist thought and the broader Christian thought throughout his entire adult life. At a time when some

---

[3] Ibid.

[4] Ibid., 44.

[5] Ibid., 250.

saw a commitment to Baptist principles of religious liberty and separation of church and state waning, Dawson undergirded the denominational commitment through his writings and actions.

Throughout his ministry, Dawson emphasized human dignity through the teachings of Jesus, which led him to champion education and social action. Dawson believed that Baptists needed to recommit to religious liberty and the separation of church and state. Roger Williams and Walter Rauschenbusch were two towering figures who most directly impacted his views.[6] His personal study and commitment to lifelong learning through reading led Dawson to a continual openness to inquiry. He criticized some in the Baptist tradition, such as J. Frank Norris, fundamentalist and longtime pastor of the First Baptist Church of Fort Worth, Texas, for their anti-intellectualism, claiming that Christian faith and humanity's freedom required one to continually embrace education and intellectual thought. The high rate of illiteracy he found most commonly within heavily Baptist communities discouraged Dawson, and he called for these communities to repent for their "sin of omission in neglecting their cardinal, historic concern for education."[7]

As pastor and denominational leader, Dawson displayed his commitment to the dignity of humanity by emphasizing social justice, civil rights, peace, morality, and religious liberty. His ecumenical spirit allowed him to build social cohesion in communities to influence the consciences of the people in order to demonstrate compassion through the influence of the love of Christ. As Dawson wrote, "Jesus came preaching liberation, His message centered in the dignity, worth and competency of the individual, emphasized the power to choose and promised deliverance from fear and death and anxiety over life's problems."[8] In other words, Dawson described Jesus as the Great Emancipator and believed the church should strive for impacting the society for Christ. When churches were more concerned with themselves than with the communities, Dawson criticized them as a "sadly impaired religion" and a "sham," lamenting that "a religion that dreams of a home in heaven but is not concerned about making safe and wholesome homes on earth misses the mark as tragically as the worst sin."[9]

---

[6] Wood, "Legacy of Joseph Martin Dawson," 366.

[7] Dawson, *A Thousand Months*, 165–66.

[8] Joseph Martin Dawson, "The Church and Religious Liberty," *The Review and Expositor* (1963): 148.

[9] Joseph Martin Dawson, *Christ and Social Change* (Philadelphia: The Judson Press, 1937), 35, 54.

For Dawson, churches could ill afford to remain cloistered in their sanctuaries and instead needed to go outward and minister to the society in tangible ways, including but not limited to meeting the needs of the poor as well as remaining conscientious objectors in a time of war and standing for social justice. Avoiding these responsibilities led to corporate sin, which Dawson considered just as evil as individual sin. This corporate sin expressed itself economically, compelling Dawson to criticize capitalism and materialism in the United States, describing it as a "pagan" system that pursues "profit" over service. He wrote, "The profit motive tends to render men predatory, with unmistakable selfishness, greed and inconsiderateness. Its quest is money, not service. Yet service, according to Lord Christ, was the principle of his life and is to be the rule of our lives." Further, Dawson criticized the profit drive of an economy for leading to exploitation, division, class warfare, crime, and poverty. Instead, Dawson promoted a cooperative world economically that would emphasize the individual less and the community more, ushering in a "Beloved Community."[10]

In his idea of a "Beloved Community," Dawson addressed racism and prejudice, advocating for civil rights well before the movement in the United States began. Although members of his church at FBC Waco were part of the Ku Klux Klan, Dawson publicly denounced the Klan and their actions, including forcefully condemning lynching. Finding himself often to be the lone voice among pastors on this issue, Dawson wrote, "I swore then on the altar of God I would henceforth forever fight lynching, if every Baptist church in the South kept silent."[11] He called on his congregations to engage the world as the Good Samaritan—crossing barriers of race and class through the love of Christ. Likewise, he also advocated for the proper treatment of German immigrants during World War II, and he denounced the internment of Japanese Americans on the West Coast. Additionally, his compassion for all humanity caused him to speak out against war and most notably against the "immoral" bombing of Nagasaki and Hiroshima.[12]

Dawson envisioned a world governed by persuasion rather than force, believing that valuing global humanity was more in keeping with the teachings of Jesus than advocating for a nation's military victory. The

---

[10] Ibid., 83, 215.

[11] Dawson, *A Thousand Months*, 165.

[12] Ibid., 164.

global social order he desired could only happen through the influence of Christianity. Dawson believed Christianity could influence society in numerous ways, such as advancing healthcare access, valuing the dignity of children, fostering increased educational opportunities, and embracing human rights.[13] However, even though Dawson believed religion plays a large role in a society, he did not desire a violation of the separation of church and state.

Dawson contributed most significantly to Baptist life through his work with the Baptist Joint Commission on Public Affairs and his emphasis on religious liberty and maintaining the wall of separation, preaching and writing that separation of church and state was best for both the church and the state. Dawson strove for religious liberty for all people, regardless of faith identification, and defined religious liberty as "the right and security of every person and group for freedom of conscience, belief and practice, together with free association and unrestricted propagation of faith."[14] Dawson found his inspiration for championing religious liberty in his studies of Roger Williams and Thomas Jefferson, whom he credited for exalting the importance of religious liberty in the United States. Dawson held on to the principle and importance of separation of church and state by reminding others that Christianity's existence and influence did not depend on any certain type of government, writing that "Christianity has existed under all political and economic systems—tribalism, feudalism, fascism, socialism and capitalism."[15]

Therefore, Dawson encouraged Baptists to continue to advocate for separation of church and state, resisting the temptation of political power and selfish gains, a temptation that he warned gave rise to Hitler in Germany as the church succumbed to his political clout. To guard against this in the future, Dawson emphasized to his audience not to fear pluralism or secularism but rather to protect the country from sectarianism gaining governmental influence. He also pled with Baptists to remember their heritage and to pass down religious liberty principles to the coming generations, working ecumenically to strengthen religious freedom across denominations and faiths.[16]

---

[13] Dawson, *Christ and Social Change*, 219.

[14] Dawson, "The Church and Religious Liberty," 147.

[15] Dawson, *Christ and Social Change*, 78.

[16] Dawson, "The Church and Religious Liberty," 152–53.

Dawson recognized and encouraged the contributions that the church makes to society, including transforming individuals and changing attitudes toward fellow humanity. While he advocated for separation, he opposed the silencing of the church, believing that the church must speak out on societal injustices and take proper social action. This allowed the church and state to remain separate from each other but also to cooperate in improving society: the church through spiritual and moral persuasion and the state through civil relationships and force when needed.[17] Dawson differentiated between church and state as existing in two spheres—the state functioning within a constitutionally bound use of legislative force and the church functioning within divine authority and depending on persuasion, love, and reason.[18] As a result, the only responsibility a state has to religion is to "guarantee its free exercise, so that government is forbidden to establish one church, all churches or any particular religion."[19]

Although Dawson advocated for religious liberty and civil rights, his prejudice toward one group, Roman Catholics, was notable. Dawson considered Catholics a threat to religious liberty, believing that Catholicism's views on church and state would be damaging for religious liberty in the United States. Mainly, he accused Catholicism of reinterpreting the First Amendment to allow for governmental funding toward Catholic institutions, stating, "If they succeed in their purpose, they will sound the death knell of religious liberty in the United States."[20] While anti-Catholicism was common in the United States during Dawson's lifetime, he denied that he carried personal prejudice toward Catholics. Instead, as Executive Director of the Baptist Joint Committee on Public Affairs, he cited what he considered four specific violations of Roman Catholicism concerning church-state and religious liberty in the United States: federal aid to parochial schools, religious instruction in public schools, President Truman's appointment of an ambassador from the US to the Vatican, and federal aid to religious charities.[21] While one could label these views as anti-Catholic, the objections to each of these practices were consistent with Dawson's overall philosophy on church-state separation. Toward the end of his

---

[17] Travis Summerlin, "Church-State Relations and the Thought of Joseph Martin Dawson," (PhD diss., Baylor University, 1984), 124.

[18] Joseph Martin Dawson, *America's Way in Church, State, and Society* (New York: MacMillan Company, 1953), 21.

[19] Dawson, "The Church and Religious Liberty," 158.

[20] Dawson, as quoted in Summerlin, "Church-State Relations," 135.

[21] Summerlin, "Church-State Relations," 139.

life, Dawson wrote *Jose Antonio Navarro: Co-Creator of Texas* (1969), which covers the life of a leader in Texas "who was an ardent Roman Catholic defender of religious liberty."[22]

Regardless of denomination, Dawson opposed any governmental funding given to religious institutions, including parochial schools, noting, "The effect of state-supported church schools would spell the end of our public school system.... Next to the constitution itself, our public school system has been our strongest bulwark against the development of religious intolerance in our political life." Likewise, he opposed all religious instruction in public school classrooms, regardless of denomination. Further, he fully supported the Supreme Court's decision to consider compulsory school prayer as unconstitutional, claiming that as a result of the decision, the court upheld "true prayer," which was private prayer rather than forced public prayer. Through his career-long advocacy for religious liberty, Dawson sought to maintain the commitment to separation of church and state found in the US Constitution: "Unless we shake off the pressures which are being applied for alteration of the American Constitution with its guarantee of full religious freedom for all and its bulwark against union of Church and State, we shall revert to old world abuses which have impeded the progress of mankind."[23]

Dawson's contributions and significance to Baptist life are extensive. Countless articles, booklets, and pamphlets written for such organizations as *The Dallas Morning News*, *The Baptist Standard*, and *Christianity Today* as well as the numerous books he wrote carried his words and convictions to fellow Christians throughout the world. He impacted Baptist life through his involvement with multiple organizations, such as beginning the student newspaper at Baylor University while an undergraduate student, serving as a trustee at Baylor University following his days as a student, being a founder of Hillcrest Baptist Hospital in Waco, Texas, serving on the Editorial Council for the *Journal of Church and State*, and becoming the first Executive Director of the Baptist Joint Committee on Public Affairs. His influence was local, national, and international, covering a majority of the twentieth century. However, the greatest honor for him came when Baylor University named the church-state academic program in his honor: the J. M. Dawson Institute of Church-State Studies. This institute's purpose seeks to carry on Dawson's legacy and desire—"to

---

[22] Wood, "Legacy of Joseph Martin Dawson," 364.

[23] Dawson, *A Thousand Months*, 200, 258, 261.

stimulate intellectual interest and encourage research and publication in the broad area of church-state relations."[24]

From a child born into a poor farming family to an international scholar and denominational leader, J. M. Dawson lived a full life of influence and significance. Perhaps he said it best in the words he first spoke in 1926 and admittedly repeated again and again to himself throughout his life: "I accept Jesus's word that life is not a quest but a surrender."[25]

Suggested Reading

J. M. Dawson, *Christ and Social Change* (Philadelphia: The Judson Press, 1937).

J. M. Dawson, *A Thousand Days to Remember* (Waco, TX: Baylor University Press, 1963).

James E. Wood, Jr., "The Legacy of Joseph Martin Dawson (1879–1973)," *The Journal of Church and State* 15 (1973): 363–66.

---

[24] Wood, "Legacy of Joseph Martin Dawson," 365.

[25] Dawson, *A Thousand Months*, 45.

Fannie Lou Hamer (1917–1977), Standard-bearer for Freedom

Social Justice

Michelle L. Henry

In the mid-twentieth century, America found itself embroiled in an age-old, bitter battle for its soul. The long, arduous struggle for freedom, racial equality, social justice, and full citizenship defined life for African Americans, especially in the South. Racial hatred and the discrimination and oppression that so ubiquitously flowed from it had deep roots. This racial hatred had fashioned an institution of slavery so vile and heinous that it would demand a contemptuous and costly Civil War to subdue, if not permanently defeat, its aims to promote White supremacy and ensure that any bid for political parity, economic equity, or social equality be met with fierce brutality and systematic resistance and retribution. In short, the animus that shaped American life and culture before the Civil War resurged to end any hopes of progress that the Reconstruction Era, at times, seemed to signal. The avenues for more egalitarian participation by African Americans in the political processes that would ultimately define their futures were virtually closed.

Emboldened by failed efforts to reconstruct the South into a more democratic environment within which newly freed Blacks could fashion a new existence, a recalcitrant South devised and promulgated a set of laws and ordinances known as "Jim Crow" to stem the tide of the modest gains achieved. Under the watchful gaze of Jim Crow, "almost every aspect of" Black life was restricted as the "codified system of racial apartheid" authorized the "segregation of schools, parks, libraries, drinking fountains, restrooms, buses, trains, and restaurants. 'Whites Only' and 'Colored' signs were constant reminders of the enforced racial order."[1] African Americans were not only subjected to separate accommodations but also forced to

[1] "Jim Crow Laws," *American Experience*, https://www.pbs.org/wgbh/american-experience/features/freedom-riders-jim-crow-laws.

dwell in and patronize ones that were inferior to those reserved for Whites. A racialized social order governed the movements of African Americans and hemmed them into their own communities, and it simultaneously and "systematically denied [them] the right to vote in most of the rural South through the selective application of literacy tests and other racially motivated criteria."[2] Political disenfranchisement would ensure Blacks stayed in their prescribed place, and limited opportunities to earn a decent wage or accumulate wealth would guarantee not only their immediate economic ruin but also their total and perpetual dependence on the White power structure for sustenance and their very existence. It is within this context that Fannie Lou Hamer,[3] a poor sharecropper who embodied the plight of African Americans in the rural South, "rose from humble beginnings in the Mississippi Delta to become one of the most important, passionate, and powerful voices of the civil and voting rights movements."[4] Unapologetically and courageously, Fannie Lou Hamer came forward to question America's commitment to its foundational creed and to hold it to account concerning its identity, its imperatives, and its impulses. With guiding principles deeply rooted in Black liberation theology and Christ's commitment to the oppressed, an inspiriting rhetorical power intimately drawn from Scripture, and an enduring faith lovingly sustained through her connection with the Black Baptist Church, Fannie Lou Hamer, providentially and prophetically, stood in the gap between America's promise and its unprincipled practices, and, as a standard-bearer for freedom, she demanded equity and social justice.

The youngest of twenty children, Fannie Lou Townsend was born on October 6, 1917, in Montgomery County, Mississippi. Her parents, James Lee and Lou Ella Townsend, were sharecroppers who devoted themselves to providing, as much as it was in their power to do so, a secure, religious, and caring environment for their family. The challenges the Townsend family faced were many and varied yet wholly representative of the predicaments of most African Americans in the rural South. The Townsends,

---

[2] Ibid.

[3] Throughout the analysis, the primary subject, Fannie Lou Hamer, is referred to by her married name. Born Fannie Lou Townsend, she married Perry Hamer in 1944. Her subsequent national prominence occurred during the span of their marriage.

[4] Debra Michals, "Fannie Lou Hamer, 1917–1977," National Women's History Museum, 2017, www.womenshistory.org/education-resources/biographies/fannie-lou-hamer.

like so many others, depended on sharecropping for a meager existence. Forced to commit their days to arduous labor to supplement the family's income, the Townsend children were unable to attend school regularly. With little to no formal education, substandard resources, and no access to political or economic remedies, the family had few prospects for a viable future. Constant threats of White violence and the oppressive tentacles of White supremacy worked in concert to preclude African American advancement in any respect.

Fannie Lou Hamer's upbringing produced within her a transformative and abiding faith that would prove essential to her physical survival, to her spiritual sustenance, and to the overall development of her ideas about race relations, the need for social justice, and the possibilities for a better future. Her parents, particularly her mother, shaped her religious views and love of Scripture; her brief time in school sparked a love for reading and a desire to learn more about the world around her; and the church planted within her a gift of song and gave her spiritual vitality.[5] Lou Ella Townsend's faith helped to establish her daughter's beliefs and values; she not only pulled the young child back from the brink of an emerging disdain for those who oppressed them but also from the verge of self-loathing. An observant and precocious child, Fannie Lou questioned why Blacks toiled so much for so little gain while their White counterparts flourished with little to no effort, it seemed, and had plenty. She resented the difference as she surmised their "color made something wrong" with them.[6] Graciously, Lou Ella counseled and consoled her daughter and imparted wisdom that would strengthen Hamer later in her life as she confronted Whites who sought to malign her Blackness and use it as a justification for their brutality against her. She would also use this wisdom to reprimand classist, formally educated Black men and women who thought she, an unlettered woman, should defer to their leadership. Hamer vehemently contested any effort to marginalize her within the movement and diminish her efficacy, for her mother had taught her that she should not ever negate or devalue any aspect of her identity. She commanded, "You respect yourself as a little child, a little black child. And as you grow older,

---

[5] According to Kay Mills, in *This Little Light of Mine: The Life of Fannie Lou Hamer* (UP of Kentucky, 2007), 17, Hamer "joined the Strangers Home Baptist Church at age 12 and was baptized in the Quiver River."

[6] Quoted in Mills, *This Little Light of Mine*, 21.

respect yourself as a black woman. Then one day, other people will respect you."[7]

Moreover, Hamer learned from her mother one of the most important "religious principles" for those who claim to love God. Hamer "was taught that hating made one as weak as those filled with hatred."[8] Hatred is born of fear and insecurity. To withstand the vicissitudes of life, Hamer would have to love others from conviction without regard for convenience or circumstance. Because of her mother's teaching, Hamer understood the significance of religious devotion and obedience to God's commandments. To love one's enemies was not a suggestion; it was a sacred charge. From her devotion and deeply held principles, Hamer cultivated an abiding faith characterized by love and mercy. "As Hamer envisioned it, love between the races was the only antidote to the sickness bred by hatred."[9] These lessons would be essential in the development and fulfillment of Hamer's political and spiritual aims to "repair" a nation wrought by divisiveness, to awaken both Blacks and Whites to their "intertwined destinies," and to advocate for racial conciliation and collaboration for the benefit of the nation.[10]

Hamer's family life and faith served as catalysts for action. Hamer's witness of her parent's constant struggles to outwit starvation, stave off injury and illness, and create conditions in which their children might thrive shaped her understanding of the plight of African Americans in the Mississippi Delta and other rural areas like it. Living in substandard housing and working in the grueling cotton fields while White families grew healthy and wealthy from the gains for which they had labored crystallized the fact that there would be no real economic opportunity for Blacks without social justice. The "anger…[she felt] about her lack of control over her own life" motivated her when she discovered she "was sterilized in 1961" during a surgical procedure for the removal of a benign uterine tumor, without "her knowledge or permission."[11] Yet, most importantly, it was her faith that told her she deserved more and that change was possible. Hamer "longed for the time when African Americans would stand up and

[7] Ibid., 11.

[8] Ibid., 17.

[9] Maegan Parker Brooks, "Oppositional Ethos: Fannie Lou Hamer and the Vernacular Persona," *Rhetoric and Public Affairs* 14, no. 3 (2011): 536.

[10] Ibid.

[11] Mills, *This Little Light of Mine*, 21.

be respected as humans."[12] She "was a person in search of a movement."[13] So in the summer of 1962, when Hamer attended a mass meeting organized by James Forman of the Student Non-Violent Coordinating Committee (SNCC) and James Bevel of the Southern Christian Leadership Conference (SCLC) at a local church near her home in Ruleville, she was perfectly poised to hear about the winds of change blowing in Mississippi.[14] There she learned for the first time that she had rights and that there was indeed a way to resist and overcome the debilitating oppression that had so overwhelmed her. As Brooks notes, "The idea that through the vote black Mississippians had the power to transform the exploitative conditions surrounding them [deeply] resonated with her."[15] Hamer "was more than ready to answer their call" for activists to register to vote and change the political and social atmosphere of the most intractable state in the South.[16] Ultimately, "Hamer's aim [would] not [be] mere inclusion in the political process but also freedom. She would settle for nothing less than liberation."[17]

Hamer's faith demanded revolutionary action. Her faith required her to challenge White supremacy, as it was a stronghold that ran counter to the liberating gospel of Christ. So, after that initial mass meeting, Hamer went to work. Without concern for the "virtual certainty of white reprisal," Hamer agreed to go the Indianola courthouse to attempt to register to vote.[18] Once there, Hamer was subjected to a literacy test and "instructed…to write out and interpret Section Sixteen of the Mississippi constitution." She was able to write the section competently, but she was not able to "interpret" it and failed as a result.[19] Even though she was not allowed to register, there were immediate consequences for Hamer's subversive act. For eighteen years, Fannie Lou and her husband, Perry, affectionately known as "Pap," worked and lived on a plantation just outside Ruleville owned by W. D. Marlow. There "[she] earned less than four

---

[12] Janice D. Hamlet, "Fannie Lou Hamer: The Unquenchable Spirit of the Civil Rights Movement," *Journal of Black Studies* 26, no. 5 (May 1996): 563.

[13] Mills, *This Little Light of Mine*, 41.

[14] Lynne Olson, *Freedom's Daughters: The Unsung Heroines of the Civil Rights Movement from 1830 to 1970* (New York: Touchstone, 2001), 253.

[15] Brooks, "Oppositional Ethos," 517.

[16] Olson, *Freedom's Daughters*, 253.

[17] Hamlet, "Fannie Lou Hamer," 563.

[18] Olson, *Freedom's Daughters*, 254.

[19] Ibid.

dollars a day in the cotton fields, lived in a small, unpainted frame shack...with no running water and a privy out back."[20] Though Hamer had proven to be quite invaluable to Marlow as a timekeeper, her efficiency and effectiveness were rewarded with an instant backlash for her attempt to step outside the boundaries set for her. On the same day Hamer tried to register to vote, Marlow contemptuously presented her with an ultimatum. Hamer was expected to either withdraw her application to register or she would be forced to leave the plantation. Unwaveringly, Hamer stood her ground and asserted to Mr. Marlow, "I didn't go down there to register for you. I went down there to register for myself."[21] Though Pap would be obligated to work through the harvest, both were summarily left "without jobs or a place to live."[22] Marlow's firing and dislocation of the Hamers was only the first set of consequences the couple would face. Not only did Marlow "[confiscate] much of their property"; they were also repaid with violence from the White community at large.[23] When the Hamers found refuge in the home of a friend, "[a] carload of white nightriders" shot "into the bedroom where [they] slept."[24] Though no one was injured in that incident, later that same evening, another home was rifled with bullets, and "two young women from Jackson State University, who had come to Sunflower County to help with the registration drive," were "seriously wounded."[25]

Despite constant threats and harassment by local officials, after a brief stint in Tallahatchie County, Fannie Lou Hamer returned to Ruleville and became a field worker for SNCC to avoid further endangering her friends. She devoted herself completely to educating African Americans about how voting would change the nature of their daily lives and imbue them with the integrity White supremacy tried to strip from them. By this time, Hamer had taken the literacy test again in December 1962, and she was informed in January 1963 that she had passed, and she subsequently "signed [the] voter rolls in Ruleville."[26]

Hamer quickly became an asset to SNCC not only because she was bold, forthright, and courageous but also because she exemplified what an

[20] Olson, *Freedom's Daughters*, 253.
[21] Quoted in Olson, *Freedom's Daughters*, 254.
[22] Olson, *Freedom's Daughters*, 253.
[23] Michals, "Fannie Lou Hamer, 1917–1977."
[24] Olson, *Freedom's Daughters*, 254.
[25] Ibid., 254.
[26] Mills, *This Little Light of Mine*, 316–17.

ordinary individual could do even though her circumstances were challenging and her material resources were limited. Her experiences demonstrated her direct link with the people she dared to represent, and her sacrifices on behalf of their collective progress gave her both authority and credibility. According to biographer Kay Mills, "Fannie Lou Hamer had a presence," and "[she] was smart."[27] Hamer often "[crafted] messages that were based on African American culture and Christian principles."[28] Her ability to weave a narrative about the need for and the power of genuine "freedom and justice" from the nexus between her "personal testimonies and hard truths about the state of America" helped African Americans to see that their hardships and trials were not the result of their collective unworthiness.[29] Instead, the tapestry Hamer so painstakingly knit together revealed that America's refusal to recognize their humanity and their contributions had left the nation, as a whole, weak and frayed. The power of Hamer's message may be attributed to her desire "to bring America face to face with its hypocrisy and bring to the forefront the notion that no one group is truly free unless everyone is free."[30]

Hamer's faith not only drove her to challenge the domineering White power structure but also compelled her to confront the learned hopelessness of African Americans, even though their silence and reluctance to resist oppression were often the products of fear and despair. Hamer inspired her audiences, activists and laypeople alike, with her plain but fervent speeches that drew parallels between the African American experience and those of God's chosen people, and she called her listeners to revolutionary action with her own testimonies of personal sacrifice and suffering for a greater, nobler cause. Hamer's ability to remain not only "stoic" but also loving and kind "in the face of death threats and the unrelenting verbal and physical abuse from whites" demonstrated the strength and resilience "of her spirit and character."[31] One of the most harrowing incidents Hamer experienced as an activist came on the heels of her attendance at a voter registration workshop in June 1963 in Charleston, South Carolina. As they were traveling home to Ruleville, "Hamer and several other black women were arrested for sitting in a 'whites-only' bus

---

[27] Ibid., 41.

[28] Hamlet, "Fannie Lou Hamer," 566.

[29] Ibid.

[30] Hamlet, "Fannie Lou Hamer," 570.

[31] Earnest N. Bracey, *Fannie Lou Hamer: The Life of a Civil Rights Icon* (Jefferson, NC: McFarland & Co., Inc., Publishers, 2011), 8.

station restaurant in Charleston, South Carolina."[32] Taken to jail in Winona, Mississippi, "they were brutally beaten."[33] Law enforcement kicked, cursed, and berated them, and they "forced two black inmates to deliver the beating to Hamer, which seemed to give the policemen a perverted, voyeuristic thrill."[34] Though "Hamer's beating left her with a permanent kidney injury and a blood clot in the artery of her left eye," she remained undeterred from her mission.[35] Hamer's recounting of the savage beating she endured highlighted the fact that the state of Mississippi, largely governed and policed by White supremacists, had absolutely no regard for the value and sanctity of Black life. Her story also underscored the extent to which those in power would go to maintain their dominance.[36] Furthermore, Hamer's testimony ignited righteous indignation as her audiences recognized elements of her brutal story in their own. African Americans could no longer afford to wait for those in power to decide to share their power. They could no longer preserve their lives by acquiescing to fear because their lives were in danger whether or not they capitulated to demands for obedience and subservience.

No matter how rousing the speech and no matter how stirring the calls for immediate action proved to be, the road to social justice was winding and seemingly without end. When the travails of the movement exacted a high toll and the vitriolic resistance of embittered Whites threatened, at every turn, to reverse every gain made in the march toward equality, the possibility of failure became all too real. The physical and psychological wounds suffered from the battles of constantly organizing around, outwitting, and outlasting the opponent often placed the civil and voting right movements on life support. In these times, Hamer turned to one sure remedy. She always had a song. Her earthy, strong "contralto" calmed her fears and those of others, "[inspired] action," and strengthened the resolve of those on the verge of giving up.[37] Encapsulated in her song

---

[32] Michals, "Fannie Lou Hamer, 1917–1977."

[33] Ibid.

[34] Beverly E. Mitchell, "The Vocation of Fannie Lou Hamer, Civil Rights Activist," *American Baptist Quarterly* 23, pt. 2 (2004): 185.

[35] Hamlet, "Fannie Lou Hamer," 565.

[36] It is important to note that Fannie Lou Hamer's jailing and subsequent beating in Winona occurred around the same time that Medgar Evers, a civil rights activist and the state field secretary of the NAACP in Mississippi, was assassinated outside his home in Jackson on June 12, 1963.

[37] Mills, *This Little Light of Mine*, 19.

was her mission and the power that drove it.[38] That spiritual vitality, which had been shaped by her mother and the religious conviction sealed by her baptism, breathed new life into the movement and renewed the people's collective sense of purpose. Hamer's tenacity was a concrete manifestation of the deeply abiding faith that continually saved, strengthened, and sustained her, and it was from this wellspring that "she gave hope to those who had no hope."[39]

Fannie Lou Hamer became a force within the civil and voting rights movements in Mississippi because of her integrity, ingenuity, and intrepidity. She recognized the importance of inspiring and empowering individuals to arm themselves with the vote and to pursue liberty and justice. Yet she and other grassroots organizers understood that their efforts, no matter how faithfully executed, would have limited impact if nothing was done to increase the national awareness of the plight of Mississippians and if there was no formal political organization to end systematic voter intimidation and suppression practices and to provide electable leaders who would challenge the status quo and represent them at the state and national levels. In response to those challenges, SNCC had to develop a strategy by which they could shine the light on and draw the nation's attention to the pervasive structural and racial inequalities in Mississippi. The organization had long resisted integrating the movement with aid from Whites in the North. By this point, though, they had not only stretched and exhausted their local resources but also needed to confront the reality that unless Whites, at great risk to their personal safety, made a stance alongside them, their pleas for equality would remain unheard. Though the reasons for refusing to integrate the movement were varied and complex, and not altogether without merit, the moment called for a reexamination of their mission and goals. At a meeting to discuss the Freedom Summer project,[40] Hamer "pointed out the contradiction inherent in

---

[38] Ibid.

[39] Bracey, *Fannie Lou Hamer*, 163.

[40] According to the Martin Luther King, Jr. Research and Education Institute at Stanford University, the "1964 Freedom Summer Project was designed to draw the nation's attention to the violent oppression experienced by Mississippi blacks who attempted to exercise their constitutional rights, and to develop a grassroots freedom movement that could be sustained after student activists left Mississippi." See "Freedom Summer," Martin Luther King, Jr. Research and Education Institute, Stanford University, https://kinginstitute.stanford.edu/encyclopedia/freedom-summer.

the organizer's opposition to whites."[41] She admonished that they would not "break down the barriers of segregation" if they were going to "segregate [themselves]."[42] Consistent with her faith and practice, Hamer underscored the fact that it would be a collaborative effort and a unified front that would ensure the gains they sought. She not only helped organize Freedom Summer but also assisted with the training of young White activists who would venture into rural Mississippi "to register black voters and teach literacy and civics at Freedom Schools."[43] Ultimately, Freedom Summer was successful in that it "pried open" the "closed society" of Mississippi that had been "imposed by white supremacists since Reconstruction."[44]

Freedom Summer activists also furthered the aims of what would become the Mississippi Freedom Democratic Party (MFDP). On April 26, 1964, the MFDP was established with the central goals of challenging "the militantly segregationist state Democratic party," which had consistently "denied [African Americans] the right to participate in the political and electoral processes of their state,"[45] and "unseating the all-white Mississippi delegation of the regular Democratic Party at the 1964 convention."[46] Hamer, as co-founder of the MFDP and deputy chair of the delegation, along with other members of the party, went to the Democratic National Convention in August to "[argue for the right] to be recognized as the official delegation."[47] Hamer's riveting speech before the Credentials Committee about the pervasive "racial prejudice" and injustice "in the South"[48] and her incredible account of the beating she had endured at the hands of police in 1963 prompted President Lyndon Johnson to attempt to block the televised coverage of the proceedings so as to minimize its impact and protect the Southern vote he needed for his election bid.[49] Though his impromptu press conference and behind-the-scenes political maneuvers ultimately squashed the immediate efforts of the MFDP to seat its full delegation, he did not foresee the national attention that would

---

[41] Olson, *Freedom's Daughters*, 294.
[42] Quoted in Olson, *Freedom's Daughters*, 294–95.
[43] "Freedom Summer."
[44] Olson, *Freedom's Daughters*, 326.
[45] Ibid., 314.
[46] Mills, *This Little Light of Mine*, 105.
[47] Michals, "Fannie Lou Hamer, 1917–1977."
[48] Ibid.
[49] Mitchell, "Vocation of Fannie Lou Hamer," 187.

result from the airing of Hamer's full testimony during evening news coverage, nor did he realize the extent to which her call for "mandatory integrated state delegations" would impact every other election cycle to follow.[50] Because of her tenacity and determination, in the long run, the national Democratic party was forced to redefine its commitments, change its complexion, and be more open to and representative of men and women from various walks of life.

Hamer's leadership in the MFDP and her commitment to the broader Civil Rights Movement led her to participate in party conventions and seek political offices; though unsuccessful in those bids, she paved the way for the increased engagement of women in the political process as a founder of the National Women's Political Caucus, which was established in 1971. When Hamer had expended her political currency, she returned to grass-roots activism, which then "ranged from schooling to health care to ending hunger."[51] She worked tirelessly, through pain and sickness, to bring about racial equality via economic strategies and educational reforms. She boycotted stores, "launched the Freedom Farm Cooperative," which "[bought] up land that blacks could own and farm collectively," and initiated school desegregation laws.[52] On March 14, 1977, at the age of fifty-nine, Fannie Lou Hamer died of heart failure due to complications with cancer, diabetes, and hypertension.[53]

As an activist for voting and women's rights and a civil rights leader, Fannie Lou Hamer presented to Baptists and to the world a shining example of faith-filled servant leadership and a progressive vision of what America could be. In the end, Hamer's faith was a redeeming one in that, as a standard-bearer for freedom, she sought to reclaim America's promise and to remind us of the link between faith and social justice. Hamer "was a missionary of the gospel of reconciliation of the races as an outgrowth of her faith in Christ."[54] Hamer's life remains a testament of how believers should translate faith into action and pair principle with performance in the pursuit of justice.

---

[50] Michals, "Fannie Lou Hamer, 1917–1977."

[51] Olson, *Freedom's Daughters*, 393.

[52] Michals, "Fannie Lou Hamer, 1917–1977."

[53] Mills, *This Little Light of Mine*, 320.

[54] Mitchell, "Vocation of Fannie Lou Hamer," 179.

Suggested Reading

Earnest N. Bracey, *Fannie Lou Hamer: The Life of a Civil Rights Icon* (Jefferson, NC; London: McFarland & Company, Inc., Publishers, 2011).

Maegan Parker Brooks, *Fannie Lou Hamer: America's Freedom Fighting Woman* (Rowman and Littlefield Publishers, 2020).

Maegan Parker Brooks, *A Voice That Could Stir an Army: Fannie Lou Hamer and the Rhetoric of the Black Freedom Movement* (Jackson: UP of Mississippi, 2014).

Kay Mills, *This Little Light of Mine: The Life of Fannie Lou Hamer* (UP of Kentucky, 2007).

Eric Charles Rust (1910–1991), Baptist Philosopher of History and Science

Education

Philip Irving Mitchell

British American Baptist Eric Charles Rust lived a scholar's life. In a teaching career of over thirty years, Rust influenced the lives of hundreds of theology and philosophy of religion students. The author of seventeen books and pamphlets, as well as numerous articles, essays, and reviews, Rust repeatedly put into print his intellectual and spiritual convictions about faith, nature, history, and salvation. At times criticized for his conclusions, Rust nevertheless remained a committed and orthodox Baptist believer. The life of a professor is an outwardly quiet one, yet inwardly it can be marked by great energy and passion. Rust spent his career on the importance of ideas, for he consistently sought to engage the larger academic world from the perspective of a biblical worldview. As a result, he is often remembered as someone who sought to grasp the big picture. Philosopher Richard Cunningham noted that he owed his "greatest intellectual debt" to Rust's wide-ranging teaching.[1] E. Glenn Hinson called Rust an "apostle to an age of science and technology,"[2] while Bob E. Patterson named him the "great reconciler" because of his gift of bringing together philosophy and science with Christian doctrine and the Scriptures.[3] For similar reasons, Larry Gregg called Rust "the Great Synthesizer" and "the

[1] Richard B. Cunningham, *C. S. Lewis, Defender of the Faith* (Philadelphia: Westminster Press, 1967), 12.

[2] Glenn E. Hinson, "Eric Charles Rust: Apostle to an Age of Science and Technology," in *Science, Faith, and Revelation: An Approach to Christian Philosophy*, ed. Bob E. Patterson (Nashville: Broadman Press, 1979), 13–25.

[3] Bob E. Patterson, "Eric Rust," in *Baptist Theologians*, ed. Timothy George and David S. Dockery (Nashville: Broadman Press, 1990), 469. For a brief assessment, cf. James Leo Garrett, Jr., *Baptist Theology: A Four-Century Study* (Macon, GA: Mercer University Press, 2009), 360–63.

Great Introducer."[4] Rust had the ability to help students enter a culture-wide, even civilization-wide debate.

Eric Rust was born June 6, 1910, in Gravesend, England, to Charles Henry Rust and Ruth Wiles. Charles was a bridge builder who was transferred to Sheerness during World War I to build small naval vessels for the Admiralty. Eric's parents were faithful members of the Sittingbourne Baptist Church, where his grandfather served as an elder and his father as a lay preacher. Rust himself was converted and baptized at age fourteen. He was a student at Borden Grammar School, and at eighteen he began preparing for a career as a mathematician and scientist. He studied both chemistry and physics and earned the bachelor's and master's degrees (along with the Diploma of the Imperial College) in science from the Royal College of Science in 1930 and 1932, then took a position as an instructor of mathematics while beginning research in atomic theory. At the same time, Rust regularly served in the London Baptist Preachers Association.[5] His scientific studies, however, began to create a dilemma for him: how was he to approach Scripture in light of the findings of modern science? Unfortunately, the Baptist churches had not prepared Rust for working through this conflict, and the general distrust of science among the parishioners left him confused and yet hungry to find a way forward. He feared intellectual dishonesty and yet felt called to be "a bridge builder between faith and science."[6] With such aspirations in mind, he switched to the academic study of theology.

Rust undertook his career change as an answer to his own intellectual doubts, and he spent his life helping others with high-level questions not only to retain their faith but also to bring it to bear on the modern world. Between 1932 and 1935, Rust studied theology at Regent's Park College, Oxford, under H. Wheeler Robinson, R. H. Lightfoot, and T. W. Manson, as well as history and philosophy under R. G. Collingwood. During this time, he was exposed to a holistic theology of salvation history that sought to take seriously modern critical studies of the Bible. Under Collingwood, Rust also began to think deeply about the meaning of history and the nature of historiography. Rust received from Oxford the BA in

[4] Bob E. Patterson, "Introduction," *Perspectives in Religious Studies* 22, no. 4 (1995): 346.

[5] Patterson, "Eric Rust," 466.

[6] William L. Hardee, "The Christian Philosophy of Eric Charles Rust: A Critical Evaluation" (PhD diss., Southwestern Baptist Theological Seminary, 1985), 3–4.

1935, the MA in 1938, and the BD in 1946. In 1936, he married fellow Baptist Helen Mitchell Kenn, and together they had three children, Margaret, Christine, and David Charles. Rust was recognized for his Bachelor of Divinity with his book, *The Christian Understanding of History*, a volume that he mostly drafted in his young family's backyard bunker during the Nazi bombing raids.[7] In many ways, this first of his books predicted his two great subjects of study, history and nature. During World War II, he served in three pastorates in the UK: at Bath (Hay Hill Baptist, 1935–1939), at Birmingham (Oxford Road Baptist 1940–1942), and at Huddersfield (New Road Baptist 1942–1946), as well as serving as chaplain to the Royal Signal Corps. In the post-war years, he spent six years (1946–1952) as a senior tutor at Rawdon Baptist College, University of Leeds, where he taught courses in philosophy of religion, world religions, and systematic theology. After failing to secure the principalship at Rawdon, Rust came to the United States in 1952 and 1953 as a visiting professor at Crozer Theological Seminary, Chester, Pennsylvania. While there, he published his next book, *Nature and Man in Biblical Thought*. He also gave to great acclaim[8] the 1952 Norton Lectures at the Southern Baptist Seminary, Louisville, Kentucky, on "Religion and Science" before accepting a full-time position at Southern the next year, where he served until retirement in 1979. While there, in addition to apologetics and later philosophy, Rust taught Old Testament theology. He also regularly served as a pulpiteer in local churches. After retirement, Rust was the Staley Distinguished Scholar Lecturer at Cumberland College (1982–1983) and in 1983 also gave the Page Lectures at Southeastern Baptist Theological Seminary.

Rust had a comprehensive mind and a proclivity for puzzle-solving. More than one colleague has recalled Rust's wide-ranging reading in general, as well as his love of British mystery novels.[9] He was concerned for his entire career with biblical categories of thought about the natural world, about human nature and its sinfulness, about history and its purpose, about salvation and the church, and about apocalypticism and the last things. He understood himself as Christian philosopher and apologist

[7] Patterson, "Introduction," 338.

[8] Wayne E. Ward, "Eric Rust as Colleague," *Perspectives in Religious Studies* 22, no. 4 (1995): 357.

[9] William F Ratliff, "Revelation as Disclosure Event," *Perspectives in Religious Studies* 22, no. 4 (1995): 441; Ward, "Eric Rust as Colleague," 355.

seeking to set forth Christian truth in a pluralistic world. While they overlap considerably, Rust's writings can be divided into two broad concerns: on the one hand, the meaning of history, both secular and sacred; and on the other, the nature of the natural world seen from a cosmic and evolutionary scale. In a sense, Rust's two great subjects were concerned with answering a single question: *what is the Triune God up to in the course of things?* Rust's characteristic answer was that there can be no understanding of history unless one affirms by faith that Christ is at its center.

Early in Rust's time at Southern, he came under criticism. In 1958, James M. Bulman in his periodical *The Faith and Free Press* criticized Rust's scholarly usage of terms such as "historical myth" to describe biblical events, in particular the virgin birth and Christ's resurrection. At the 1959 annual meeting of the Southern Baptist Convention, Bulman sought to read into the record passages from Rust's writings that he thought supported this criticism, but instead Duke McCall, president of Southern Seminary, to great applause[10] read passages from Rust that affirmed that the "Virgin Birth is not myth" and that the "Resurrection cannot be dismissed as the creation of faith; rather it is the historical actuality which vindicates the Cross and creates faith." Rust himself was not present. He was in the process of becoming a naturalized US citizen.[11] The debate over Rust occurred in the wake of McCall's forcing out of twelve professors at Southern, who afterwards titled themselves the "Dirty Dozen." Arguably McCall's dispute with them concerned governance issues rather than their theology, as was commonly believed at the time.[12] The loss of so many professors led to faculty shifts at Southern. Rust moved from being professor of Christian Apologetics to professor of Christian Philosophy in order to replace William A. Mueller, who had shifted to the department of

---

[10] Ward, "Eric Rust as Colleague," 360.

[11] Cf. Baptist Press releases for 1959 Annual Meeting of the Southern Baptist Convention: May 21, 1959, release for basic background; "Information concerning Professor Eric Rust of Southern Baptist Theological Seminary" release for McCall's reading into the record. See http://media.sbhla.org.s3.amazonaws.com/832,14-Mar-1959.pdf. Also see D. Larry Gregg, "The Method of Correlation in the Theology of Eric Charles Rust" (PhD diss., The Southern Baptist Theological Seminary, 1991), 253–55.

[12] Gregory Willis, *Southern Baptist Seminary 1855–2009* (New York: Oxford University Press, 2010), 402–403.

Church History.[13] Despite Rust's exoneration in 1959, after the publication of Rust's *Salvation History* four years later, Bulman again attacked him in the pages of *The Faith and Free Press.* He accused Rust of simply switching the label "historical images" for "myth" but of not actually affirming the historicity of key biblical events.[14] He also complained that one could not tell if Rust actually believed in the physical resurrection of Christ or in his actual bodily ascension. Bulman ended by accusing Rust of the ancient heresy of Docetism, a denial of the physical resurrection of Christ.[15]

However, Rust was clearly no Docetist. He stressed, on more than one occasion, that the bodily resurrection and physical ascension of Jesus actually occurred. Christ, he wrote, is the "God-man who rose from the dead in his full humanity."[16] In *Salvation History*, he insisted, "we have defended the historicity of the empty tomb and the objective nature of our Lord's resurrection body."[17] In this truth Rust saw wide, cosmic implications. "The resurrected body of Christ carries within itself the meaning of all created existence," he insisted, for not only will God raise up every believer bodily to new life, but all of history will be fulfilled because the risen Lord is at the center of all things.[18] Rust wrote similar things about the Incarnation and Ascension of Christ, for he always saw that historically what had happened in Christ was the center and key to what all of history was and is. Bulman was also wrong on the details of Rust's position. Rust had been using the terms "myth" and "historical imagery" in earlier books, too. It is important to remember that in the scholarly and philosophical language of the day, "myth" was a highly debated matter. Theologian Paul Fiddes has noted that in the twentieth-century examination of "myth" and theology, no one used the word to mean a bold-faced lie. By "myth," they could mean ineffectual attempts to describe divine action; stories about God that humans project onto their own past; or real events in the past

---

[13] Marvin E. Tate, "Eric Rust as Biblical Theologian," *Perspectives in Religious Studies* 22, no. 4 (1995): 429–30.

[14] James M. Bulman, "From 'Myth' to 'Image,'" *The Faith and Free Press* 19, no. 1 (Jan–Mar 1963): 3.

[15] Ibid., 4–8.

[16] Eric C. Rust, *Towards a Theological Understanding of History* (New York: Oxford University Press, 1963). 202.

[17] Eric C. Rust, *Salvation History: A Biblical Interpretation* (Richmond, VA: John Knox Press, 1962), 219.

[18] Rust, *Towards a Theological Understanding of History*, 262.

that critical documentary history struggles to accept.[19] When it came to gospel accounts, Rust always had the latter position in mind. In addressing myth, Rust sought to account for how metaphysical and religious imagery shape all cultures, including the modern world. He thought, for example, that modern political life and contemporary science also had myths that structured their chief beliefs.[20] At the same time, Rust shared an important insight with C. S. Lewis, among others. In the history of Israel and especially in Christ, myth has become history. Images and symbols in salvation history "are bound to specific historical events and express the activity of the transcendent, living God."[21]

In seeking to understand the broad sweep of things, Rust was a man of his time. Two world wars and the rise of fascism and communism made the subject of history of vital concern for many. Between the 1930s and the early 1960s, hundreds of books and articles were written by philosophers, theologians, and literary critics on the topic. Rust wrote three important books on the matter, *The Christian Understanding of History* (1946), *Salvation History: A Biblical Interpretation* (1962), and his magnum opus, *Towards a Theological Understanding of History* (1963), which drew insights from the earlier two books in order to offer a political theology as well as an analysis of how God has sovereignly offered his love in history to all cultures.[22] Rust's method was always a deeply Baptist one. He stressed that "divine disclosure" should be at the center of any Christian answer to non-Christian thinkers and belief systems. The Bible could be trusted and interpreted upon a twin foundation, that of God's personal revelation of himself and that of his inspiration of the event's interpreters, that is the apostles and the prophets.

On the matter of history itself, Rust wrote within two wide intellectual conflicts: (1) the meaning of general history—where it is going, what

---

[19] Paul Fiddes, "C. S. Lewis the Mythmaker," in Andrew Walker and James Patrick, eds., *A Christian for All Christians: Essays in Honor of C. S. Lewis* (Washington: Regnery Gateway, 1992), 134.

[20] Rust, *Towards a Theological Understanding of History*, 88–90.

[21] Ibid., 96.

[22] This is not to say that Rust only wrote for scholarly audiences. He regularly published from 1957 to 1962 in the *Baptist Student*, and he wrote articles for the *Encyclopedia of Southern Baptists* (Gregg, "The Method of Correlation," 259). Rust also prepared a short study for the Faith-Learning Studies series released by the Sunday School Board of the Southern Baptist Convention, cf. Eric C. Rust, *History* (Nashville: The Sunday School Board, 1969).

it means, and how it is researched and written; and (2) the special meaning of biblical history—its unique worldview, its prophetic and theological methods, and its precise subject, centered in Jesus Christ. Rust understood his intellectual opponents as falling into four broad camps: naturalism, humanism, philosophical idealism, and interreligious anthropology. Rust carefully stressed how human sinfulness and even the demonic could better explicate the aspirations and failures of human cultures and societies than could theories that sought to explain history as being obedient to natural sociological and economic "laws." Likewise, he rejected those positions that thought history could be explained by a pantheistic, immanent divine force seeking to realize itself through human actions. As Rust insisted, in light of the mystery of God's actions and of human sinfulness, a Christian philosophy of history was not possible or necessary; instead, a Christian *understanding* of history was, and this was to be derived from God's own disclosure of himself and of salvation in Christ. Theological categories such as judgment and God's wrath could help explain why proud and imperialistic cultures eventually fall and even why cultures that set out to do good eventually, in growing proud, end ironically doing evil. At the same time, God's omnipotent action and his loving mercy are one because God is wholly consistent and wholly personal. This is how God has revealed himself, and he is not subject to any human attempt to control him otherwise.[23]

Rust's later books, especially *Science and Faith: Towards a Theological Understanding of Nature* (1967), *Evolutionary Philosophies and Contemporary Theology* (1969), and *Nature—Garden or Desert? An Essay in Environmental Theology* (1971), turned increasingly back towards the scientific questions, for these had always been part of his concern. Early on, Rust's *Nature and Man in Biblical Thought* had been the fruit of his own struggle to bring the biblical world picture into conversation with modern science. *Nature and Man* sought to take seriously the nature of history as a science, as well as the nature psychology, sociology, and biology as sciences. In all his work, Rust distinguished carefully the findings of modern research from the theories behind those findings. He insisted that the real conflict was not between science and theology; it was between the biblical metaphysic and naturalist explanations.[24] Rust's essay, "The Biblical Faith and

---

[23] Rust, *Towards a Theological Understanding of History*, 158–69.

[24] Eric C. Rust, *Nature and Man in Biblical Thought* (London: Lutterworth Press, 1953), 18.

Modern Science" (1974), is a good example of what he held about the relationship of the two. Rust argued that God's disclosure of himself took place in a Hebrew culture with different conceptions of the physical world and of human nature than those of the twentieth century. Their world picture included ideas that modern science would recognize, such as the mind-body unity of the human person, regularity in the physical world that can be observed, and a deeply moral commitment to care for nature. At the same time, the biblical understanding addressed matters about which natural science could say (or should say) nothing. For example, God's ordering of the universe is a personal expression of his ongoing love for people and the creation; the Trinity is involved at every stage of that care; and the Incarnation and Resurrection of Christ are the principal meaning of human existence. Rust also stressed that natural science was limited in what it could actually claim. In an Einsteinian world, scientific claims are statistical models rather than mechanical certainties, and because they, by definition, cannot speak to the metaphysical or the final purpose of life, scientific methods do not handle well the wholeness of life.[25]

Harold Lindell's rejoinder to Rust's essay in the same 1974 issue says much about how such views would be understood or perhaps misunderstood by some. Lindell, an inerrantist and founder of Fuller Seminary, admitted that he and Rust mostly agreed on the contents of Scripture and the limits of natural science, but he also argued that Rust held a weak position on what the Bible did say about the natural world, and he worried that Rust assigned too much trust to evolutionary theory and thus played into the hands of metaphysical atheists.[26] Rust did accept the findings of biological evolution but not necessarily the philosophies that employed those findings. Rust was willing to read Genesis 1–3 in an open, metaphoric manner. Yet he insisted that interpreters should be careful never to "divest it of chronological reference."[27] In this, Rust was more concerned about what the Genesis narrative taught theologically. God had freely created the world *ex nihilo*, and it was good. But human freedom and self-transcendence had led to human rebellion against this good gift. Of course,

---

[25] Eric C. Rust, "Biblical Faith and Modern Science," *Review & Expositor* 71 (Spring 1974): 229–42.

[26] Harold Lindsell, "Response to Eric C Rust, 'The Biblical Faith and Modern Science,'" *Review & Expositor* 71 (Spring 1974): 243–48.

[27] Rust, *Towards a Theological Understanding of History*, 120. Cf. his *Nature and Man in Biblical Thought*, 20–36, and *Salvation History*, 41–44.

for many this approach rendered him automatically suspect. Rust would write of the "primordial decision" against God rather than about original sin.[28] However, just as Rust in the problem of history was debating persons and ideas beyond the orbit of much of denominational life, so Rust's real conversation partners in the matters of physical and evolutionary history were process theologians, philosopher Alfred North Whitehead, French scientist and priest Pierre de Chardin, and the host of naturalists who refused any ultimate meaning to the course of the universe. In this sense, Lindell need not have worried about Rust. Despite his conciliatory approach, Rust always knew that any claims for the transcendent had to make their way among strongly resistant worldviews.

Evolutionary Philosophies and Contemporary Theology (1969) is a good example of Rust's approach. Rust spends most of the book offering a close examination of other positions, yet just as he had rejected theories of history that reduced God to an impersonal *Zeitgeist* or World Spirit, so, too, he rejected process philosophies that proposed a learning, evolving deity. Rust admitted, even admired, the notion of a dynamic, even evolving universe, but he continued to stress a personal and transcendent God who was other than his creation and who did not change in his character and understanding. The unchanging God presides over a developing universe, one still unfinished that will only reach completion in the *eschaton*. The levels of emergent organization the world has undergone are sweeping, even breathtaking: "The biological shows a transformation of the physical, just as the personal means a transformation of the biological."[29] And that human beings have developed the capacity to be free, social beings means that they are able to sense the exalted otherness of God and yet, by the gift of grace, are able to enter a relationship with him. For such reasons, Rust continued to stress that the personal was superior to the organic as a way of modeling human freedom and worth.

In the last decade of Rust's life, he continued to think and write. His second-to-last book, *Religion, Revelation and Reason* (1981), was in many ways his philosophical swan song. In it, Rust summed up his concerns with divine disclosure, religious symbolism and images, personal faith, evolution and a dynamic universe, human nature and destiny, and the problem of evil. He intended it to be a work of natural theology that made "sense

---

[28] Rust, *Towards a Theological Understanding of History*, 119.

[29] Eric C. Rust, *Evolutionary Philosophies and Contemporary Theology* (Philadelphia: Westminster Press, 1969), 214.

of the world from a theistic standpoint."[30] His last book, *The Word & Words Towards a Theology of Preaching* (1982), served as a bookend with one of his first published lectures, *Preaching in a Scientific Age* (1951). Rust's final essay, "The Dynamic Nature of Triune God," was written in 1987. In it, Rust continued to argue that the course of Christian history and the development of theology showed the hand of the Triune God, preparing his people in each generation to speak to the spirit of the age. The holy, loving, and personal God as Trinity is a social God, and thus, he constantly attends to a growing and developing creation. At every stage of human and natural history, God is at work.[31]

Rust died December 14, 1991, in Jefferson County, Kentucky. In the last year of his life, he still thought of himself as an English Baptist who had spent half his life among Southern Baptists.[32] Eric Rust continues to be a model of a Christian who took the big picture seriously and was not afraid to engage the larger intellectual culture. His theological and philosophical positions on the meaning of history and of science are still worth investigating. Rust always sought to mediate between a Baptist vision and those of other persuasions, and for that reason, if no other, he deserves to be read today. His basic trust in the grand biblical narrative and his continued emphasis that we encounter that narrative beginning in Christ point to a way of continuing to be the church even in a secular culture.

Suggested Reading

Bob E. Patterson, ed., "Essays in Honor of Eric Rust," special issue of *Perspectives in Religious Studies* 22, no. 4 (Winter 1995): 337–473.

Eric C. Rust, *Salvation History: A Biblical Interpretation* (Richmond, VA: John Knox Press, 1962).

Eric C. Rust, *Science and Faith: Towards a Theological Understanding of Nature.* New York NY: Oxford University Press, 1967.

Eric C. Rust, *Towards a Theological Understanding of History* (New York: Oxford University Press, 1963).

Eric. C. Rust, *Religion, Revelation and Reason* (Macon, GA: Mercer University Press, 1981).

---

[30] Hardee, "The Christian Philosophy of Eric Charles Rust," 23.

[31] Eric C. Rust, "The Dynamic Nature of the Triune God," in *Perspectives on Scripture and Tradition: Essays in Honor of Dale Moody*, ed. Robert L. Perkins (Macon, GA: Mercer University Press, 1987), 31–46.

[32] Gregg, "The Method of Correlation," 264.

Prathia Hall (1940–2002), Activist and Womanist Prophet

Social Justice

Courtney Pace

Rev. Dr. Prathia LauraAnn Hall was a civil rights activist, community organizer, scholar, and womanist preacher, affiliated with Progressive National and American Baptists. Raised in Philadelphia, Hall was deeply formed by social gospel ministry, race theory, and nonviolence. She served as a leader in the Student Nonviolent Coordinating Committee during the Civil Rights Movement, after which she pursued theological education (MDiv and PhD) at Princeton Theological Seminary. Hall was among the first Black women ordained by American Baptists (1977), was the first woman accepted into the Baptist Minister Conference of Philadelphia and Vicinity (1982), served the faculty of United Theological Seminary (UTS) in Dayton, Ohio, and Boston University School of Theology, and became a well-respected professor of Christian ethics, womanist theology, and African American religious history. She served as Associate Dean of Spiritual and Community Life, Director of the Harriett L. Miller Women's Center, and Dean of African American Ministries at United Theological Seminary in Dayton, Ohio (1989–1998), and held the Martin Luther King, Jr. Chair in Social Ethics at Boston University School of Theology (2000–2002). In 1997, *Ebony* magazine named her first in its list of "15 Greatest Black Women Preachers," and she was the only woman considered for its list of "10 Greatest Black Preachers," ultimately placing eleventh. In 1999, the International Theological Center in Atlanta awarded her its annual Womanist Scholar Award. She received numerous awards for her preaching and was a highly sought preacher and speaker, denominational consultant, and ministry mentor.[1]

---

[1] Prathia Hall, Curriculum Vitae, Prathia Hall Papers, archived at Princeton Theological Seminary, Princeton, NJ, but not currently accessible to the public (hereafter PHP). Hall won a number of awards including the following:

- Womanist Scholar Award, International Theological Center, 1999–2000

Though raised to recognize and oppose systemic racism, when Hall expressed interest in attending college at Tuskegee, her father, scared for her safety, forbade her to go. She instead attended Temple University, where she studied political science. During college, she was involved with Fellowship House, an ecumenical social justice organization in Philadelphia, where she learned nonviolence philosophy and direct-action demonstrations. After her father's 1960 death, Hall felt the freedom to go South. Upon graduation from Temple in 1962, Hall joined the Student Nonviolent Coordinating Committee (SNCC). Within a few days of her arrival in Atlanta, Charles Sherrod recruited her to join him in Albany, Georgia.

Hall was one of few female SNCC field workers. Because of the immense danger of door-to-door voter registration, women typically worked as educators to prepare potential voters for registration tests, or they assisted with clerical tasks. Hall, however, was second-in-command of SNCC's Southwest Georgia Project in Albany. With family roots in the South but raised in the North in a predominantly Black neighborhood while attending primarily White schools, Hall understood how to code-switch for survival and helped new SNCC workers understand how to safely navigate the racism of the rural South. While SNCC workers had important information about voter registration and political rights, Hall understood that the people in the counties where SNCC worked had the

---

• First among "15 Greatest Black Women Preachers" and the only woman considered for its "10 Greatest Black Preachers," ultimately placing eleventh, *Ebony Magazine*, 1997

• Davis-Putter Scholarship Fund, 1995

• Ebony African American Achievement Award, Honorable Mention, 1994

• American Baptist Churches, USA Ellen Cushing Scholar Award, 1985 and 1986

• Black Doctoral Scholarship, Fund for Theological Education, 1983, 1984, 1993

• Hawkins Memorial Award for Scholastic Excellence, Princeton Theological Seminary, 1982

• Blizzard Memorial Award for Social Ministry, Princeton Theological Seminary, 1982

• Jasow Preaching Award, Princeton Theological Seminary, 1981

• Benjamin E. Mays Fellowship, Fund for Theological Education, 1981

• Roosevelt Board of Education Service Award, 1976

• International Theological Center Womanist Scholar Award and Visiting Professorship, 1999–2000 "wisdom of the ages"—the inherited freedom faith that empowered them to survive enslavement, Jim Crow, and systemic oppression of every kind.

When Martin Luther King, Jr., visited Albany, Sherrod frequently chose Hall as the primary mass meeting speaker. During a 1962 visit, after the burning of four Black churches affiliated with the movement, Hall used the phrase "I have a dream" in a prayer service that King attended. In her SNCC memoir, Hall confirmed her origination of the phrase "I have a dream," though she modestly denied influence for what King did with the phrase. She deeply respected King and did not want to undermine his reputation or significance in any way. He so admired her preaching that he described her as "the one platform speaker I would prefer not to follow." She and he spoke at an event in Chicago the night before the March on Washington, which she watched from the hotel television because she could not get to DC for the event. Hall became one of SNCC's top speakers, spending the last part of 1962 and early 1963 touring the North to raise financial and other support for SNCC's work in the South.

Hall later became the leader of SNCC's Selma, Alabama, voter registration project in 1963, organizing voter registration drives and freedom schools. Later that year, SNCC leader Jim Forman called her to Atlanta to run civil rights collaboration between six organizations to desegregate Atlanta. Hall confronted Atlanta mayor Ivan Allen on multiple occasions and was arrested in a Toddle House sit-in during the 1963 US visit by Kenyan leader Oginga Odinga. Her case became a showdown between local and federal courts, making national headlines when she was released in March 1964.

Hall resigned from SNCC in 1966 when the organization transitioned away from nonviolence and its commitment to working interracially. Hall described her time in the movement as the best education she ever received. She continued raising money for civil rights work in the South and expanded her activism to include education, women's job placement, and community resources.

Hall married Ralph Wynn almost immediately after returning from SNCC, and the couple had two children: Simone Denise Wynn and Ralph DuBois Wynn. Hall joined the Civil Rights Movement, in part, to run from her calling to preach, but her experiences in the movement confirmed her call. Ralph was reticently supportive, and upon her decision to pursue advanced theological studies, the marriage became unsustainable. Hall filed for divorce, moved with her children to New Jersey, and faced significant financial and health challenges, no doubt exacerbated by the divorce.

Hall pastored Mt. Sharon Baptist, her father's church, commuting to Philadelphia weekly.

One of the most enduring legacies of Hall's pastoral career was her prophetic womanist ministry. Before the term "womanist" existed, Hall was modeling womanist preaching. She centered women's narratives in the text, used a Christocentric hermeneutic, and highlighted Jesus as a liberator, working against oppression over anyone. She rejected patriarchy in the text, instead using the text to demonstrate equality, justice, and the necessity of Christian commitment to liberation.

By combining the best of the Black preaching tradition with an unwavering call to womanist liberation, Hall demonstrated that salvation is not merely the deliverance from sin (personal salvation) but also living in opposition to systemic oppression so that all may be delivered (social justice). Hall's preaching bridged personal faith and social justice seamlessly, rooted in her belief that the gospel demands both. She was one of the first voices in Baptist life, White or Black, to advocate for the full equality of all people, arguing that unless preaching addressed personal salvation *and* social justice, the church had failed to proclaim the gospel: "For whatever it is that we who mount the sacred desk do when we come to the pulpit, if it is not good news to the poor, if it is not deliverance to the captives, if it is not sight to the blind, if it is not freedom to the oppressed, it may be sweet, it may be eloquent, it may even be deep, but it ain't preaching."[2]

A lifelong Baptist, Hall blamed Baptist denominations and their leaders for historically and systemically oppressing those on the margins, particularly women, and insisted that any denomination that perpetrated such injustices had turned its back on its people and the global community of faith. Explaining her conscious decision to remain Baptist as an insider prophet, Hall told a reporter in 1997, "The Baptist church is going to have

[2] Prathia Hall, quoted in Donna Allen, "Toward a Womanist Homiletic: Katie Cannon, Alice Walker, and Emancipatory Proclamations," PhD diss., Vanderbilt University, 2005; Prathia Hall, "Between the Wilderness and a Cliff," undated, Prathia Hall Papers. Hall's sermon "Between the Wilderness and a Cliff" was transcribed by Hall's graduate student LaGretta Bjorn sometime in the late 1990s or early 2000s. This sermon can also be found as Prathia Hall, "Between the Wilderness and a Cliff," in *Preaching with Sacred Fire: An Anthology of African American Sermons, 1750 to the Present*, ed. Martha Simmons and Frank A. Thomas (New York: W.W. Norton & Company, 2010), 687–95.

to deal with me. Some of us have to remain in the recalcitrant church. Everything we know about God is that the living God is not a bigot."[3]

Anything that worked against the liberation of all people was, as Hall described, "bondage doctrine." Anything that undermined liberation for anyone kept them enslaved to patriarchal dominance, inclusive of racism, sexism, classism, ableism, ageism, heterosexism, etc.[4] Hall's understanding also resembled what Kimberlé Crenshaw would later dub "intersectionality," or the compounding impact of multiple forms of oppression, in particular that Black women didn't merely face racism *and* sexism but faced racism *times* sexism *times* classism.[5]

For Hall, the epitome of the gospel was freedom faith: God wants everyone to be free and equips and empowers those who work for liberation and justice. Hall inherited freedom faith from her father's mentorship, but she contextualized her understanding of freedom faith as Christian orthopraxy through her experiences in the Civil Rights Movement, theological education, and pastoral leadership. Freedom faith is therefore a deeply Baptist concept, rooted in personal religious experience and the defense of freedom of conscience for all people. Baptists have historically insisted on individual freedom and responsibility for religious agency. Anything that denies someone basic human freedoms, then, and therefore their ability to relate directly to God—bondage doctrine and its practices—is anti-gospel. The work of the Baptist church becomes uprooting these chains so that people can respond to God freely.

In her preaching and ministry, Hall insisted that God's call was open to whomsoever God may call and that any biological limitations were bigotry imposed by humans and blamed on God. For churches to mediate the struggles of the people for freedom and liberation, these churches must

---

3 Ron Goldwyn, "Pastor Earns Acclaim as Lady of the House," *Philadelphia Daily News*, December 9, 1997; Ron Goldwyn, "Big Churches Hear but Don't Hire Popular Black Female Preacher," *Fort Worth Star-Telegram*, December 13, 1997.

4 Bell Hooks, *Feminism Is for Everybody: Passionate Politics*, 2nd ed. (New York: Routledge, 2014).

5 Kimberlé Crenshaw, "Demarginalizing the Intersection of Race and Sex: A Black Feminist Critique of Antidiscrimination Doctrine, Feminist Theory and Antiracist Politics," *University of Chicago Legal Forum*, 1989, issue 1, article 8; Prathia Hall, "The Religious and Social Consciousness of African American Baptist Women" (PhD diss., Princeton Theological Seminary, 1997), vii–viii; untitled and undated notes, PHP 1.066.

accept the women proclaimers God has called *and* eagerly hear their prophetic challenges. Hall knew too well that women in ministry fought for every inch of influence they dared to claim *and* that the church lost much in its rejection of women's preaching. Even Jesus' disciples ignored the first proclamation of the gospel because it came from women.

Tired of empty promises of eventual progress, Hall advocated for the immediate full inclusion of women in ministry. In order to be faithful witnesses to the liberating gospel of Jesus Christ, the church must be inclusive. When Baptists perpetuated patriarchal dominance, they traded the gospel for power and taught women to limit their spiritual imagination for how God might use them. What Hall later called pathologized oppression, this voluntary self-dehumanization morphed into an internalized self-hatred, wherein women learned to oppress themselves.[6] She told a reporter, "Ministers have a responsibility to stand against racism, sexism, ageism—all the '-isms' that put people down. It's not a ministry if it doesn't liberate us."[7]

Hall also believed that denominational leaders—Baptists and beyond—might allege that congregations were not ready for women in ministry when those leaders were actually the ones not ready. She insisted that pulpit committee advisors, Baptist association and conference leaders, and denominational leaders needed to be intentional about helping qualified women find pulpits. Hall compared "the scandal of sexism" to "racism and classism as another idolatry." Referring to the Civil Rights Movement, Hall said, "In the 1970s the church woke up and confessed its sin of racism. There has to be a similar confession from males—Black and white, Asian, Hispanic and Native American—about the sins of sex idolatry." When asked pointedly whether Baptist men were bigots, Hall answered, "I have to call it what it is. This gender-based exclusion is bigotry, and they blame it on God and say God ordained it. That is outrageous. The church has to be purged of that oppression."[8]

---

[6] Prathia Hall, "The Challenge of True Kinship," in *What Does It Mean to Be Black and Christian? Pulpit, Pew, and Academy in Dialogue*, ed. Forrest E. Harris Sr. (Nashville: Townsend Press, 1995), 111–24.

[7] Ervin Dyer, "Heeding the Call of a Divine Mother," *Pittsburgh Post-Gazette*, undated.

[8] Prathia Wynn, "Accepting the Call to Leadership," *American Baptist* (July/August 1987): 22.

Hall claimed that Baptist churches "defy God and curse Christ" in their sexism because they positioned themselves as mediators of God, interrupting individuals' freedom to respond to God. She was unambiguous about her urgency: "Sexism in the Church represents a theological scandal.... Gender-based oppression isn't a trivial inconvenience. It's human devastation."[9] Just like "the racist lie," sexism "distorts the humanity of victims and perpetrator alike."[10] Hall claimed, "the most bodacious lie that this demon tells is the lie that it tells on God. For you see we lift this reasoning to the level of a theology and claim that God said it, that God ordained it, and I feel tonight God's fist in my back saying, 'Preacher, I'm tired of folk lying on me!' The living God is not a bigot."[11]

Just as Baptist theology favored individual conscience over imposed theology, so the Bible, Hall argued, had overturned sexism. This new relationship must be at the center of churches' ministry to families and understanding of human identity "if we are to equip our families and our young people in particular to face together the challenges of the struggle for the survival and liberation of our people."[12] Hull agreed in his statement that Baptists must "use every means of dissent at their disposal to protest these infringements of basic human rights."[13]

Hall's research on the Women's Convention Auxiliary (WC) of the National Baptist Convention, USA, Inc. (NBC) explored ways that Black Baptist women created agency for themselves within patriarchal institutional structures. As did many women throughout Christian history, Baptist women faced moral crossroads, torn between obedience to God and obedience to church. They sacrificed their own voices to bolster racial advancement and peace within their churches because disobedience was

[9] Prathia Hall, co-author, "A Call to a National Dialogue: The Challenge of a Black Theology to the African American Church," Kelly Miller Smith Institute on African American Church Studies (Nashville, TN, 1992), 14–16; Ray Waddle, "Black churches harbor sexism, minister charges," *St. Petersburg Times*, 24 October 1992.

[10] Prathia Hall, title illegible, undated, though likely in preparation for KMSI document, PHP 1:304.

[11] Prathia Hall, "Beyond Eden," 1989, PHP.

[12] Prathia Hall Wynn, "Theological/Educational Foundations for the Black Church's Ministry to Families," 7 December 1984, p. 17, PHP 1:923.

[13] William E. Hull, *The Meaning of the Baptist Experience* (Brentwood, TN: The Baptist History and Heritage Society, 2007), 12.

costly.[14] This self-sacrifice for organizational loyalty compromised the integrity of the entire church.[15] Ignoring the moral crisis of gender compromised Baptists' ability to faithfully fulfill their historical mission.[16] By silencing the women, the NBC had no credibility as a church.[17]

While Hall affirmed the separation of church and state, she insisted that Christians had the freedom, and the responsibility, to speak within their contexts with prophetic witness in activism and advocacy for the full liberation of all people.[18] Recognizing systemic oppression that inhibited people's freedom necessitated prophetic proclamation, not as a violation of the separation of church and state but as a practice of the historic Baptist advocacy for freedom. Just as Baptists had historically been subversive for freedom's sake, the Baptist future must unashamedly oppose anything denying full religious freedom to anyone, and, as William Hull stated, "root out the last vestiges of discrimination that embarrass our most basic convictions."[19] Just as Baptists had to organize politically in search of government solutions to limited freedoms in Baptist beginnings, Baptists will need throughout history to organize politically to advocate for full liberation of all people.

Hall's preaching brilliance made her womanist message accessible, including recovering lost narratives of biblical and historical women and expanding the realm of acceptable topics for preaching to include women's health, family systems, and social issues. Her provocative womanist hermeneutics "demonstrate[d] that just as Scripture has been used to oppress women, Scripture can be used to liberate women."[20] Rather than eisegetically imposing a justice agenda into the text, Hall's preaching exegetically

---

[14] Hall, "Dilemma," undated, PHP 1:045.

[15] Prathia Hall, "Womanist Moral Leadership and Ecclesial Integrity, or The Silencing of Women and the Crisis of Morality in the Church," Womanist Consultation of the Womanist Approaches to Religion and Social Group at the American Academy of Religion, 21 November 1997.

[16] Prathia Hall, "The Church at the Crossroad," 4 March 2000, PHP.

[17] Prathia Hall, "Womanist Moral Leadership and Ecclesial Integrity, or The Silencing of Women and the Crisis of Morality in the Church," Womanist Consultation of the Womanist Approaches to Religion and Social Group at the American Academy of Religion, November 21, 1997.

[18] Hall's word here would align with Walter Shurden's paradigm of Baptist identity as the pairing of four fragile freedoms and responsibilities. See Walter B. Shurden, *The Baptist Identity: Four Fragile Freedoms* (Macon, GA: Smyth & Helwys, 2013).

[19] Hull, *Meaning of the Baptist Experience*, 10, 20–21.

[20] Allen, "Towards a Womanist Homiletic," 67.

exposed Jesus as a justice activist who engaged engaged oppressive political and ecclesial systems in his context. She questioned whether the text reflected God's will or human actions done in the name of God. Good preaching should interrogate the text in conversation with the Holy Spirit.[21]

Such engagement with the text is at the foundation of Baptist identity, affirming full and direct access of every individual to God and the ability and responsibility of all believers to interpret the biblical text, free from bondage to traditions and culture. Hall let the biblical text guide her understanding of Christian orthopraxy in her context, even as she depended on Black Baptist heritage. She modeled the correlation between Baptist faith in the text and faith in a living God who continues to reveal new meanings of the text to believers in their time. Hall drew from the biblical text to reform the church caught in bondage doctrine without filtering her exegesis through the lenses of church status quo, calling it instead to the vibrant witness of freedom faith.

True freedom faith required the complete elimination of any extant oppression within the church. Hall labeled this process "chain removal," avowing the absolute incompatibility of oppression (injustice) with the liberating gospel of Christ. Exegesis, for Hall, must include consideration of whether the text was authored in a context of racism, sexism, or classism and the historic use of the text to propagate oppression. Liberating preaching speaks "closely, specifically to the dying," by naming the chains that bind, even those within the church: "race, sex, class, even homophobia."[22] The church must take up the mantle of the liberating gospel to remove the chains of oppression within itself and in the world. Freedom faith means working together for the liberation and freedom of all people.

Hall's womanist hermeneutic found liberation and freedom in Christ: "We have a hope more powerful than death. We have hope—and that hope is Christ, the liberator, Christ the fellow sufferer, Christ who is grace in the wilderness and the Fire that extinguishes the Powers of Death.... Build, sisters and brothers, build! Build on your heritage and stand on your hope."[23]

---

[21] Hall, interview by Allen, in Allen, "Towards a Womanist Homiletic," 58–59.

[22] Prathia Hall, "Preaching a Liberating Word to a Dying World," *Urban Outreach*, October 3, 1996, PHP 14:95–118.

[23] Prathia Hall, "Building Between Heritage and Hope," undated, PHP box 23.

Hall pastored Mt. Sharon for nearly a quarter century. Despite her homiletical brilliance and multiple invitations to apply for prestigious pulpits, she never received an offer. As professor and preacher, Hall mentored over two hundred aspiring Black clergy women. Hall remained active in the Progressive National Baptist Convention, the American Baptist Churches USA, the New York Board of Education, the Association of Black Seminarians, the Children's Defense Fund, and domestic and international advocacy for liberation and equality of men and women of all ethnicities.

After a long battle with cancer, Hall died in Boston in 2002. Throughout her battle with cancer, she advocated for Black people to join the Bone Marrow Registry so that more Black people could have access to life-saving transplants. While she never found a match for herself, her condition is now considered treatable, largely because of her advocacy for more donors. Hall was survived by her mother, Ruby; two sisters, Teresa and Betty; her son, DuBois; and two grandchildren, Michael and Siana.

Hall's freedom faith inspired her to pursue justice from a young age through education, civil rights activism, community organizing, and ministry. Her preaching insisted that anyone who claimed the gospel must join in the work of liberation for all people regardless of race, gender, or class. Hall's womanist proclamation worked to dismantle oppressive hermeneutics, exposed the "bondage doctrine" of systemic oppression as anti-gospel, and maintained such as a critical aspect of Baptist identity and a necessary aspect of the Baptist future. Personal salvation (conversion) and social justice (transformation) are two sides of the same coin because the gospel demands both. May it be so.

Suggested Readings

Edward Crowther and Keith Harper, eds., *Between Fetters and Freedom: African American Baptists Since Emancipation* (Macon, GA: Mercer University Press, 2015).

Wilda Gafney, *Womanist Midrash: A Reintroduction to the Women of the Torah and the Throne* (Louisville, KY: Westminster John Knox, 2017).

Bell Hooks, *Feminism Is for Everybody: Passionate Politics*, 2nd ed. (New York: Routledge, 2014).

Courtney Pace, *"Freedom Faith": The Womanist Vision of Prathia Hall* (Athens: University of Georgia Press, 2019).

Rosetta Ross, *Witnessing and Testifying: Black Women, Religion, and Civil Rights* (Minneapolis, MN: Fortress Press, 2003).

Cora Anne Davis (1937–2006), *Pioneer in Church Social Work*

Ministry

T. Laine Scales

Cora Anne Davis left a tremendous mark on Baptist social ministry by integrating graduate-level social work education with ministry contexts. Leading the establishment of Carver School of Church Social Work in the 1980s, Davis had a passion to harness the knowledge, skills, and social justice values of professional social work to galvanize Southern Baptist agencies and churches for ministry. She articulated a biblical basis for helping and a reminder that every Christian is called to minister to other human beings. She believed that the best leaders for the church's social ministry efforts would be professional social workers equipped with a combination of the accredited Master of Social Work degree and theological study. In 1984, Davis became the first woman dean appointed to any seminary of the Southern Baptist Convention (SBC).

An additional area of influence for Davis was the support and mentoring of Baptist women ministers. Reaching her professional maturity in the late 1970s and 1980s, Davis supported a younger generation of would-be ministers, helping to establish a national organization to support women seeking ministry careers. A skilled preacher herself, Davis affirmed women answering the call to all ministry roles, including preaching ministry.

A lifelong Baptist, she has a body of work that includes lectures, sermons, articles, and books with theological reflections on what the Scriptures say about helping relationships. After her retirement and the controversial closing of the Carver School in the mid-1990s, Davis continued working for another decade with laypersons, ministers, and church social workers to address social justice concerns with professional skills.

Baptist Roots

Born in rural Virginia in 1937, Anne Davis was surrounded by a large extended family with more than forty relatives living near her. These family ties shaped her understanding of relationships, particularly helping relationships. Davis and her siblings contributed to the family's livelihood by working on the farm, and her agricultural experiences provided a setting for many of her favorite stories and sermons as an adult. Her extended family made up the majority of Ebenezer Baptist Church, a church that cooperated with the local Methodist church in a way that Davis describes as "very ecumenical."[1] Early experiences of sharing resources and cooperating with neighbors would shape Davis's understanding of churches cooperating for community social services.

Ebenezer Baptist Church placed a high value on employing a preacher who was seminary educated, instilling in Davis an appreciation for masters-level ministry preparation. Cooperating with two other Baptist churches, they engaged a preacher who would come to Ebenezer every second Sunday morning and fourth Sunday night. This arrangement motivated church members to lead pastoral ministries throughout the week, a model that became a foundation of Davis's ecclesiology. The arrangement also opened the pulpit to lay preachers twice each month, creating opportunities for other church members, including Anne, to preach.[2]

The summer she was thirteen, Davis made a commitment to Christ and to vocational ministry, "and life was different from then on." She did not, however, have a clear picture of what type of ministry she would do. "At that point, all I knew a woman could do was be a missionary to China," she recalled.[3] As a young person, Davis understood one essential truth about herself that would pull her toward social work: she experienced God's love through relationships rather than through mystical religious encounters. "It did not fall my lot to have too many visions from God.... What I was going to know about God I had to find inside relationship with other people."[4]

---

[1] C. Anne Davis, interview by T. Laine Scales (recording), Carver School Project, 15 and March 23, 2005, Baylor University Oral History Institute, Waco, TX.

[2] Ibid.

[3] Ibid.

[4] C. Anne Davis, "The Church and Helping Ministries: Continuing Theological Education Conference," July 12, 1972, Southern Baptist Theological Seminary, Louisville, KY.

In her church, Davis had plenty of opportunities for leadership as a young person, and she was able to step out of traditional gender roles. In spring 1955, young Anne came home from college to preach her first sermon at Ebenezer on Easter Sunday. "They didn't care whether I was a man or a woman. In that part of the country, everybody had to work; everybody had a role."[5] Davis continued to preach throughout the rest of her life, even as Southern Baptists fought over women's roles in ministry, particularly preaching. Although a talented preacher, Anne Davis found her primary calling in another type of ministry: church social work.

Education for Social Work

At age seventeen, Davis went to Averett College in Danville, Virginia, supported by scholarships from the Woman's Missionary Union (WMU), a Southern Baptist auxiliary group promoting missions and education. She managed to retain her scholarships when she later transferred to Westhampton College in Richmond. In her junior year, Anne Davis found her life's work when she enrolled in an Introduction to Social Work course. "It was like somebody was singing my song; I just knew that was what I wanted to do."[6] She began volunteering with the Baptist Student Union (BSU) at various mission points in Richmond, including Fulton Street Baptist Center where she led a group of thirteen-year-old girls. She began to identify parallels between her social work courses and her volunteer ministry experiences in Baptist agencies. As graduation from Westhampton approached, Davis remembered her commitment to ministry and decided to complete further social work education in a Baptist seminary context. In fall 1958 she headed to Carver School of Missions and Social Work in Louisville, Kentucky, and was again supported by WMU scholarships.[7] Carver School, originally known as the Woman's Missionary Union Training School, had been in operation nearly fifty years when Anne Davis arrived. The purpose of the school was to train women as missionaries and social workers. It had been renamed in 1953 to honor W. O. Carver, legendary missions professor from the adjacent Southern Baptist Theological Seminary. Carver School women attended theological and biblical classes with seminary men and studied missions and social work in their own school and residence hall on the adjacent

---

[5] Davis, interview by Scales, 2005.

[6] Ibid.

[7] Ibid.

campus.[8] Davis chose to major in social group work and recalled, "I just loved social work so much and thought it was really the type of ministry Jesus would do and wanted us to do. So it fit me well."[9] These years of theological study and practical field work at Louisville's Portland Avenue Baptist Center provided opportunities for Davis to link her Christian faith with social work. For example, in a biblical studies class with Dr. Jerry Vardaman, Davis studied justice issues. "It just came naturally to me to put the two [theology and social work] together. I would look at a situation, and it would just make an inordinate amount of sense to me what they were saying—the whole thing about relationships, the whole thing about justice, what love really is."[10]

Dual Identity as Minister and Professional Social Worker

After graduating with the Masters of Religious Education (MRE) from the Carver School in 1960, Anne Davis began working for the Home Mission Board of the SBC. For the next six years she would serve as executive director of the Baptist Center in Lexington, Kentucky. The work involved partnerships with local churches, making this an important time for Davis to clarify her ideas about the nature of the church and its role in social ministry.[11] She came to understand Christian social ministries as the responsibility of every believer and the mandate of every church. Throughout her career, she would often repeat, "The church, to be the church, *must* be involved in social ministries."[12] In later years she reflected on three reasons that she gave her life to church social work: (1) she was imitating the life and model of Jesus, (2) she drew from Scripture a "justice mandate" and a "priestly mandate" that called Christians to serve other people, and (3) she understood social ministries to be "an integral part of the nature of the church: that Christians were to do what Jesus did until he comes again." She continued, "I want to do that with the best knowledge I can have with the best skills I can have. When I looked around for a profession that could teach me how to do church, social work seemed to be the one

---

[8] T. Laine Scales, *"All That Fits a Woman": Training Southern Baptist Women for Charity and Mission, 1907–1926* (Macon, GA: Mercer University Press), 252–53.

[9] Davis, interview by Scales, 2005.

[10] Ibid.

[11] Ibid.

[12] C. Anne Davis, address, National Consultation on Community Ministries, 22 April 1988, Carver School of Church Social Work, Southern Baptist Theological Seminary, Louisville.

that taught me best from a professional standpoint."[13] Identifying herself as both a "minister of the Gospel" and a social worker, Davis spoke of the first as her calling and the second as her profession.[14]

Anne Davis's experiences convinced her that social work knowledge and skills were the best resources for "doing" church and that church leaders needed to earn a Master of Social Work (MSW) degree, both to enhance their skills and to gain credibility in the community. Davis felt that her professional work had been hampered because she lacked the MSW.[15] In 1966, Davis moved to Louisville to establish residency and to work at Crescent Hill Baptist Church, and by 1970 she had earned her MSW from the Raymond A. Kent School of Social Work at University of Louisville. At Kent School, Davis continued reflecting on how to integrate her Christian tradition with what she was learning in social work. For example, Davis studied the social work value of self-determination, in which the worker must not assume to know what the client needs, but rather the client must express his or her wants and needs. "And my mind went back," recalled Davis, "to when the blind man approached Jesus and Jesus didn't assume that the man wanted to be healed of his blindness; do you remember what Jesus asked him? What do you want?"[16] As she continued with her own integration of biblical principles and social work values, she was preparing the soil for the next phase of her life's work: bringing professional social work education to the ministry of Baptist churches and agencies.

Teaching an Ethic of "Doing the Word"

In 1970, Davis's friend and colleague Walter Delamarter suggested that she apply for an open position as an assistant professor at Southern Baptist Theological Seminary. She was hired to lead in the steadily growing social work program he directed within the School of Religious Education. When Delamarter left in 1973 for a sabbatical and accepted another position, Davis was chosen to lead the program.[17]

---

[13] T. Laine Scales and Andrew Rawls, *Church Social Work in Rural America*, video recording, 1992, Southern Baptist Theological Seminary, Louisville, KY.

[14] Davis, address, National Consultation.

[15] Davis, interview by Scales, 2005.

[16] Ibid.

[17] C. Anne Davis, "A History of Christian Ethics, Church and Community, and Social Work at Southern Seminary," *Review and Expositor* 82, no. 1 (Winter 1985): 89–100.

For the following two decades, Davis would educate a new generation of Baptist church social workers. Her faculty position provided opportunities to articulate for Baptists her ideas about church and social work. Dismayed when she saw that some Baptists utilized social ministry projects as merely a vehicle for proselytizing, Davis emphasized that social ministries were for all people. She said, "I do not connect this kind of ministry solely with lost people, I believe there are many Christians who need social ministries; so I am talking not only about [social ministry] as an evangelistic effort but as a basic ministry effort."[18] In her lectures, workshops, and sermons, Davis emphasized helping others as part of the church's mission and said that social ministry leaders needed to have more than compassion, that is, they needed professional training. "Just as theology must be systematic, helping must be systematic," she argued. "People think anyone can do it, but there is a way of going about it."[19] Davis's own educational journey, in which she had to assemble independently her own systematic approach to integrating social work and theology, fueled her commitment to build an educational structure for church social work. Her vision was to prepare Baptists called to ministry to work in Baptist congregations and denominational agencies. Educating seminary students was one part of the job, but preparing congregations and agencies to put them to work was an equally daunting task; Anne Davis excelled at both. Elements of the curriculum she designed with her team still serve as a model for the dual degrees in social work and ministry offered by Baptist seminaries in the twenty-first century.[20]

A Model and Support for Baptist Women

While exploring theological questions concerning social ministries, Davis also made significant contributions to the ongoing dialogue in the SBC about the role of women in ministry. Beginning her career in 1960, Davis was in the first generation of Southern Baptist women that used the word "ministry" to describe their calling and work.[21] In 1976, she articulated for

---

[18] "Current Developments in the Field of Social Ministries," 2 May 1979, sound recording, Southern Baptist Theological Seminary.

[19] "The Director of Missions," 19 January 1982, 10:30 a.m. session, sound recording, Southern Baptist Theological Seminary.

[20] T. Laine Scales and Melody Maxwell, *"Doing the Word": Southern Baptists' Carver School of Church Social Work and Its Predecessors, 1907–1997* (Knoxville, TN: University of Tennessee Press), 171–85.

[21] Leon McBeth, *Women in Baptist Life* (Nashville: Broadman Press, 1979), 164.

SBC audiences the dilemma of the woman who is called and prepared to minister but cannot find ministry employment within the SBC. She described the "painful paradox" experienced by seminary women: "It is hard to handle the difference between the encouragement one received up to the point of seminary graduation and the mixed response she then received in her attempts to secure employment.[22]

A model and mentor for women in ministry, Davis paved the way for women and men to expand their views of ministry roles to include women. In the 1980s, as the SBC intensified conflicts that would ultimately split the denomination, Davis continued advocating for expanding women's leadership roles in the ministries of the church. Davis was among the original organizers of Women in Ministry, SBC, and in 1983 she convened the planning meeting that led to the formation of that women's group later in the year in Pittsburgh.[23]

Building Carver School of Church Social Work

As Davis continued teaching social work, she became concerned, partly due to her own experience, that graduates who earned an MRE degree with a major in social work would not have the professional credibility of an MSW graduate.[24] She also had been working to increase her own credibility as a seminary educator by earning a PhD in higher education, completing the degree in 1984 at the University of Louisville. Davis began to imagine the possibility of establishing an accredited MSW program at Southern Seminary, a project that Carver School had attempted in the 1950s but soon abandoned when the Council on Social Work Education (CSWE) would not grant accreditation. In 1979, Davis and her faculty team convinced Seminary Provost Roy L. Honeycutt and the seminary faculty that they could demonstrate the feasibility of creating an accredited MSW program. After conducting a thorough self-study, the faculty team proposed a plan in which the seminary would establish an independent school of social work.[25] Davis led the Carver School faculty to create a unique curriculum for denominational service. Southern Baptist church

---

[22] Anne Davis, "Women and Seminaries," *Contempo* (January 1976): 15.

[23] The organization changed its name in 1995 to Baptist Women in Ministry (Eileen Campbell-Reed, and Pamela R. Durso, "The State of Women in Baptist Life," 2007 report, https://bwim.info/state-of-women-in-baptist-life).

[24] Davis, interview by Scales, 2005.

[25] Davis, "A History of Christian Ethics," 97.

social workers, called to ministry and credentialed by their profession, would lead the social ministries of the denomination's local churches and social service agencies of the Home Mission Board such as children's homes, Baptist centers, weekday ministries, and homeless shelters. The church social worker would need one year of theological preparation coupled with two years of masters-level social work courses that were comparable to MSW courses in any accredited curriculum. The curriculum's distinct focus was on congregations and church-related agencies as a context for social work practice while also taking into account the minister's faith formation and calling.[26] In 1984, Southern Seminary opened the new Carver School of Church Social Work, naming Davis the founding dean. She and her faculty team immediately pursued accreditation from the CSWE.[27] The new Carver School had strong support from SBC affiliates, particularly the Home Mission Board and Woman's Missionary Union. In 1987, Carver School became the first and only MSW program in the world to be located in a seminary and accredited by CSWE.[28]

At the heart of the new program was the concept of church social work. While Davis shared credit with her faculty for reviving and shaping the concept of church social work, the term as promoted at Carver School clearly reflects Davis's strong influence in two areas: her own ecclesiology, shaped by her work experience with congregations, and her confidence that social work was the best degree for church leaders doing social ministry. The term "church social work" had been used in the Carver School of Social Work and Missions in the 1950s and again in the early 1970s under Delamarter.[29] Davis defined ministry as a role for all Christians who are called, rather than a title reserved for the ordained. She led students to embrace their callings to church social work, expressing her own dual identity of minister and social worker.[30]

[26] The Southern Baptist Theological Seminary, Self-Study Report for Candidacy for the Master of Social Work Degree, March 15, 1987, Louisville, KY.

[27] Scales and Maxwell, *"Doing the Word,"* 2019, 113–35.

[28] Ibid., 130.

[29] Davis, "A History of Christian Ethics," 97.

[30] Davis, address, National Consultation.

Church Social Work: Influencing Baptists and the Social Work Profession

After helping it achieve accreditation, Davis led the Carver School in a period of growth over the next decade. The Home Mission Board (HMB), leader of the SBC's social ministries, was one of the strongest supporters and partners. Davis had launched her career in 1960 with the HMB and had a strong reputation and excellent contacts at the agency. She secured student scholarships and internships while both students and faculty gave back to the HMB by providing manuals and models for practice. For example, in 1987, Davis joined Carver faculty member Patricia Bailey in contributing to a manual of operations for Baptist Centers called *Its OK to Care*, published by the HMB.[31] The strong relationship between Carver School and the HMB led directly to employment opportunities for Carver graduates.

At the same time the Carver School was making a significant impact on the denomination, it also was influencing the social work profession to view the church as a viable context for social work practice. This was no easy task; Carver faculty member, Diana Garland, remembered social work of the 1970s as "rather allergic to the church…lack[ing] any framework for considering a marriage between the profession and religious organizations."[32] Davis and her faculty worked to build the needed framework, and by 1995, the *Encyclopedia of Social Work* included church social work as an entry. Authored by Garland, the entry signaled the profession's acceptance of this specialized area of practice pioneered by Davis and the Carver School.[33]

Under Davis's leadership, the Carver School prospered for twelve years. However, as her retirement years were approaching, the Southern Baptist Convention (SBC) was embroiled in controversy as conservatives took over leadership of the denomination and attempted to turn the denomination to the right. Southern, the denomination's flagship seminary, became a battleground as conservatives gained control of its Board of

---

[31] Patricia Bailey et al., *It's OK to Care: Manual of Operations, Baptist Centers and Pastor Center Ministries* (Atlanta, GA: Home Mission Board, 1987).

[32] Diana Garland, "Tribute to C. Anne Davis," April 4, 2002, Baylor University, Waco, TX.

[33] See Diana Garland, "Church Social Work," *Encyclopedia of Social Work* (Washington, D.C.: NASW, 1995).

Trustees.[34] Davis announced her retirement as dean in 1993 and returned to the faculty to teach.[35] Roy L. Honeycutt, president of Southern Seminary, retired that same year, and by fall 1994 R. Albert Mohler had assumed the presidency. Davis rightly predicted that the new president's conservative theology would come into conflict with Carver School purposes and social ministry values. By 1995, Davis and other seminary faculty were weary of the battles, and she, along with twelve other faculty, retired completely in 1995.[36] Meanwhile, Diana Garland was appointed to follow Davis as Dean of the Carver School. In a storm of controversy in 1995, Mohler fired Garland from her position as Dean, accusing her of "a breach of personal and confidential communication" after she publicly raised objection to his institutional hiring policies that led to rejection of a faculty candidate.[37] In April 1995, seminary trustees appointed a subcommittee to study what should be done with the Carver School. Several months later, the trustees voted unanimously to close the Carver School, stating that the theological direction of the seminary and social work education were incongruent with one another. Classes continued so that students could complete their degrees with the final Carver School courses ending in May 1997.[38]

During her lifetime, Anne Davis had witnessed the closing of her beloved Carver School twice: once in 1963 when it was merged with the seminary and again in 1997. The first time, she was a former student grieving the loss of her alma mater. The second closing of the Carver school signified for Davis the SBC's abandoning of its commitment to social ministries, a commitment that Davis had seen flourish in the 1970s and 1980s and recede in the 1990s.

Supporting the Next Generation in Ministry

As Davis departed from Carver School, conservatives dismantled the denomination's social ministries programs with the HMB closing to form

[34] Bill Leonard, "Seminary Crackdown," *Christian Century*, May 10, 1995, pp. 500–501.

[35] Anne Davis, interview by Scales, March 2005.

[36] Ibid.

[37] Diana Garland, "When Professional Ethics and Religious Politics Conflict: A Case Study," *Social Work and Christianity* 26 (Fall 1999): 60–76; Scales, *"All That Fits a Woman,"* 254–55.

[38] Ibid.

the new North American Mission Board.[39] Still called to teach and preach, Davis found a receptive audience with the Woman's Missionary Union, which had supported her throughout her education and career. WMU hired her as a consultant to launch a series of Bible studies, which were published in 1997 as a collection called *Come Go with Me.* In 1998, she moved to Waco, Texas, where she worked part-time as Director of Operations for the Advocacy Center for Crime Victims and Children and as a consultant to Baylor University School of Social Work, designing a new MSW curriculum with her former colleague Diana Garland. Davis retired for a final time in 2003 but stayed in touch with her Baptist friends near and far until her death in 2006.

Cora Anne Davis left a remarkable legacy for Baptists concerned about social ministry. For Baptist women seeking ministry positions, she served as a model and a source of encouragement. Her theological reflections on helping relationships remind us that every Christian is called to minister in practical ways to other human beings, and that mandate is grounded in Scripture. In addition, Davis's sermons, lectures, and writings urge churches to take seriously their social responsibility in the world and their obligation to provide community leadership for important social and ethical issues. For anyone called to lead social ministries, Anne Davis provided a theological basis and an important model for integrating that calling with professional social work preparation.

Suggested Reading

C. Anne Davis, *Come Go with Me* (Birmingham, AL: Woman's Missionary Union, 1997).

C. Anne Davis, "History of the Carver School of Church Social Work," *Review and Expositor* (Spring 1988): 209–20.

C. Anne Davis, "Women at Seminaries," *Contempo*, January 1976, 14–16.

T. Laine Scales, *"All That Fits a Woman": Training Southern Baptist Women for Charity and Mission, 1907–1926* (Macon, GA: Mercer University Press, 2000).

T. Laine Scales and Melody Maxwell, *"Doing the Word": Southern Baptists' Carver School of Church Social Work and Its Predecessors, 1907–1997* (Knoxville: University of Tennessee Press, 2019).

[39] Martin King, "HMB job offers, terminations begin NAMB staffing process," *Baptist Press News*, April 3, 1997.

Addie Davis (1917–2005), Pioneer Baptist Woman Minister

Pastoral Ministry

Pamela R. Durso

On August 9, 1964, Addie Davis became the first ordained woman minister in Southern Baptist circles when Watts Street Baptist Church in Durham, North Carolina, set her apart for the gospel ministry. In the years since 1964, thousands of Baptist women called and gifted by God have been ordained, most of whom do not even know Addie's name even though they walk on the trail that she blazed. Addie's place in history makes her story an extraordinary one, but her own understanding of her life was that she was an ordinary person—one who sought to be faithful to God's call.

Addie's story began and ended in Covington, Virginia. She was born there on June 29, 1917, to a family of committed Baptists. Her paternal great-great-grandfather was an itinerant Baptist preacher in Amherst County near Lynchburg, Virginia,[1] and both Addie's maternal and paternal grandparents were faithful members of the Covington Baptist Church.[2] Addie's parents were active in the church and made sure that she and her two siblings "were always there when the church doors were open."[3]

Early in her life, Addie felt drawn to faith. In a 1985 interview, she recalled, "I was baptized between the ages of eight and nine. I have as long as I can remember had a very strong religious interest." As a child, Addie

---

[1] Portions of this chapter originally appeared in Keith E. Durso and Pamela R. Durso, "'Cherish the Dream God Has Given You': The Story of Addie Davis," in *Courage and Hope: The Stories of Ten Baptist Women Ministers* (Macon, GA: Mercer University Press, 2005), 18–30.

[2] Addie Davis, interview by Eljee Bentley, 9 June 1985, recording located in the Alma Hunt Library of the Woman's Missionary Union, Birmingham, AL.

[3] Cody Lowe, "Pastor says furor over her ordination didn't bother her," *The Roanoke Times*, August 28, 2004.

also began sensing a call to ministry but was uncertain about what to do with this calling: "As a child, I felt a call to preach, but women were not preachers so I never expressed this openly."[4] But even though she did not talk about this calling, she tried on the preacher role. In her playtime, Addie often pretended to be a preacher, and even then, as a little girl, she knew she liked preaching.[5]

Throughout her childhood and teenage years, Addie continued to be active in church, and she diligently sought to understand the calling that God had placed in her heart. She faithfully attended the Girls' Auxiliary and Young Women's Auxiliary and for a time considered that missions might be the vocation to which God was leading her. But her calling to be a preacher persisted, which must have been confusing for the teenage Addie given that she had no role models for pastoral ministry.

The other barrier that threatened Addie's calling was education. Neither of her parents had received much formal education. Her father had to leave school at the age of fourteen to help support his family after his own father's death. He worked hard, saved as much as he could, and finally had enough money to open a furniture store in Covington. His lack of educational opportunity fostered in him the determination that all three of his children would go to college,[6] and finally, at the age of twenty-one, the time had come for Addie to go to college.

In 1938, Addie enrolled in Meredith College, a Baptist women's school in Raleigh, North Carolina. She majored in psychology and minored in speech, and upon graduation in 1942 she found a position as education director at the 500-member First Baptist Church in Elkin, North Carolina, a town just west of Winston-Salem and about three hours south of her hometown of Covington. Addie served the church for four years, and while this position allowed her to live into God's calling, she knew in her heart that she had been called not to be a religious educator but to be a pastor.[7] She left Elkin in 1946 to take the position of dean of women at Alderson-Broadus College, a Baptist school in Philippi, West Virginia.

While at Alderson-Broadus, Addie recognized her need for theological education and strengthened her commitment to pursue her calling.

---

[4] Davis, interview by Bentley.

[5] Lowe, "Pastor says furor over her ordination didn't bother her."

[6] Ibid.

[7] Addie Davis, interview by Robin McKenzie (Hardison), October 25, 2001, in Durso's possession.

She applied to and was accepted by both Duke Divinity School and Yale Divinity School, but as she prepared to make this transition, a need in her family took precedence. Her father had died in 1944, and Addie's mother took over management of the furniture store. By the end of the 1940s, her mother needed help with the store, and thus, instead of heading off to divinity school, Addie returned home to Covington. For over ten years, she worked alongside her mother, selling furniture. But Addie never gave up on her call to ministry.

During her decade at home, Lone Star Baptist Church, a rural congregation just sixteen miles outside of Covington, called Addie to serve as their interim pastor. She served in this position for six months. The interim role provided Addie with opportunities to preach and gave her invaluable pastoral experience.[8] A personal health crisis created a turning point for Addie during those years in Covington. A bout with appendicitis and peritonitis became critical when the doctors failed to diagnosis her illness correctly. Addie's appendix burst during surgery, and her brush with death left her more determined to follow God's leadership.[9] During her recovery, Addie concluded, "If I was permitted to live, I will do what I've always felt in my heart I should do, which was to be a preacher."[10]

In 1960, Addie's mother retired, leaving her forty-three-year-old daughter free to pursue her dream of becoming a pastor. By this time, Southeastern Baptist Theological Seminary in Wake Forest, North Carolina, had begun allowing women to study for a Bachelor of Divinity degree, which is the equivalent to a current Master of Divinity degree, and Addie was among the first women to attend and graduate from the seminary. Her graduation program in 1963 lists the names of six women, including Addie's, among the 144 graduates that May.[11]

During her seminary years, Addie was an active member of Watts Street Baptist Church in Durham. There she met Warren Carr, pastor of

---

[8] Ibid. Addie did not remember the exact dates of her interim pastorate, only that it was sometime during the 1950s.

[9] Addie Davis, interview by Pamela R. Durso, December 8, 2004, in Durso's possession.

[10] Davis, interview by Bentley.

[11] Addie Davis, graduation program, May 1963, Southeastern Baptist Theological Seminary, Wake Forest, NC, Addie Davis Papers, Special Collections, Jack Tarver Library, Mercer University, Macon, GA. The six women graduates were Margaret Bloom, Addie Davis, Dorothy Deering, Laura Kendall, Judy McLamb, and Ida Marie Parker.

Watts Street. As she neared graduation, Addie knew that she needed to be licensed to preach. In early 1963, she talked with Carr about the possibility of the church's granting her a license. Both Carr and Watts Street "had achieved something of a reputation for their civil rights activism."[12] Most likely, the willingness of this church to take radical stands on racial issues made Addie comfortable in asking them to consider another radical stand—to endorse a woman preacher. Indeed, Carr and members of Watts Street, like many progressive Baptists in the 1960s, had begun to see "it as illogical to take stands on behalf of black liberation and refuse to do so on behalf of the freedom of women to choose the ways to direct their service to the same God whose teachings mandated freedom for oppressed blacks."[13]

In the minutes of the church's March 13, 1963, business meeting, the clerk recorded, "Recommended that Watts Street Church grant to Miss Addie E. Davis a license to preach. Miss Davis is a member of this church and will be graduated from Southeastern Baptist Theological Seminary in May, 1963."[14] The church presented Addie with her ministerial license that same evening following the vote.

In addition to working toward licensure, Addie spent those months before graduation looking for a church to pastor. Wanting to stay in the South, she contacted several state executives about placement. None of the executives knew "of any church that would consider a woman," she recalled, "and the truth is that they weren't willing to recommend a woman to any church. I had the feeling that most of them were a little bit afraid to be the first to make a suggestion like this."[15]

Addie's search for a pastorate continued for more than a year, and finally realizing that she would not find a Southern Baptist church open to her leadership, she contacted her college friend, Elizabeth Miller, who worked for the American Baptist Churches, USA. After college, Miller had been pastor of First Baptist Church in Readsboro, Vermont, and she knew that the church in 1964 was without a minister. Miller recommended Addie for the position. In spring 1964, following a year-long

---

[12] Elizabeth H. Flowers, *Into the Pulpit: Southern Baptist Women and Power Since World War II* (Chapel Hill: University of North Carolina Press, 2012), 28.

[13] David Stricklin, *A Genealogy of Dissent: Southern Baptist Protest in the Twentieth Century* (Lexington: University of Kentucky Press, 1990), 120.

[14] Church minutes, March 13, 1963, Watts Street Baptist Church, Durham, NC, Addie Davis Papers, Jack Tarver Library.

[15] Davis, interview by Bentley.

search by Addie, she finally found a church that would talk to her. In June, Addie traveled to Vermont, interviewed with the search committee, and, on Sunday, June 7, she preached to the congregation. The pulpit committee recommended forty-seven-year-old Addie Davis to be the church's pastor, and the congregation soon extended a call to her. With this invitation, Addie now needed to be ordained. She first approached her home church, Covington Baptist Church. She had grown up in that church, served there, and still had family connections in Covington. Addie was hopeful that the congregation would bless and affirm her new ministry, and she sent a letter requesting ordination. She soon discovered that the church's current pastor strongly opposed women ministers and that her ordination there would cause great controversy within her beloved home church, so she withdrew her request.[16]

Addie then contacted several churches in Raleigh about the possibility of their ordaining her. When those churches declined, she feared that she might never be ordained in a Southern Baptist church. Some of her friends told her that her quest was hopeless. Addie was aware that she could seek and be granted ordination by an American Baptist Church, but as a lifelong Southern Baptist, she very much wanted to be affirmed by the denomination that had birthed and nurtured her faith and with which she had now been affiliated for forty-seven years.[17] She held on to that hope and contacted the church that had licensed her the year before. The deacons at Watts Street reviewed her request for ordination, and Warren Carr sat with Addie to talk about her calling. In a 1979 interview, he recounted his conversation with her, noting that she was certain that God had called her "to be a preacher."[18]

Carr proceeded to select an ordination council to examine Addie, and all council members promised to evaluate her based on her calling and confession. On the day of the examination, she was one of two candidates for ordination. The council voted to recommend the other candidate, the chaplain to Baptist students at Duke University, despite what they believed to be the young man's unorthodox belief concerning the Virgin Birth. Addie's conservative theology posed no problems for the council, but two members confessed that despite their previous assurances they could not recommend a woman for ordination. After a heated discussion, one

[16] Ibid.

[17] Davis, interview by McKenzie.

[18] George Sheridan, "Tremors of Change," *Home Missions*, May 1972, 27.

supportive council member asked the two holdouts to explain their apprehension: "Brethren, you leave me confused. In the case of our first candidate, you were quite insistent that he believe that a Virgin bore the word. How is it that you are now so adamant that a virgin should not preach the word?"[19] The council ultimately voted unanimously to ordain Addie, with only one member abstaining.[20]

An ordination service at Watts Street Baptist Church was then scheduled for 3:00 p.m. on August 9, 1964. John Davis, associate pastor at Watts Street, opened the service with a call to worship followed by the prayer of invocation. Warren Carr preached the ordination sermon. Two of Addie's professors at Southeastern Seminary also participated. Luther Copeland, who taught Christian missions and world religions, offered the charge to the candidate. The second professor, R. C. Briggs, who taught New Testament at Southeastern, led the ordination prayer. All the ordained ministers in attendance were invited to be part of the laying on of hands. The service concluded with the chairman of the Watts Street's board, V. A. Parks, Jr., presenting the newly ordained minister with a Bible, and Addie speaking the words of benediction.[21]

Not everyone, of course, was supportive of the ordination. Carr received nearly fifty letters criticizing him and the church. Addie also was the target of criticism, which she had expected. A handful of men sent her scathing, hurtful letters. A Richmond, Virginia, man demanded, "Renounce your ordination!"[22] Another man told her to learn from her husband, an ironic demand given that Addie was unmarried.[23] Another labeled her "a child of the Devil."[24] Addie "never bothered to answer any of them." Instead, she determined to "just take it as a grain of salt and keep on."[25]

---

[19] Sheridan, "Tremors of Change," 27; "What Ever Happened to Addie Davis?" 1.

[20] Davis, interview by Bentley.

[21] Church bulletin, August 9, 1964, Watts Street Baptist Church, Durham, NC, Addie Davis Papers, Jack Tarver Library.

[22] Lowe, "Pastor says furor over her ordination didn't bother her."

[23] Laura Johnson and John Pierce, "'A Day to Remember': N.C. church marks 40th anniversary of first female Southern Baptist minister's ordination," *Baptists Today*, October 2004, 38.

[24] Addie Davis, "A Dream to Cherish," *Folio*, Autumn 1985, 1.

[25] Davis, interview by Bentley.

While Addie certainly encountered some opposition, historian Elizabeth H. Flowers concluded that the ordination did not "create a storm of controversy across the Southern Baptist Convention."[26] For most Southern Baptists, the event went entirely unnoticed. Only one story about the ordination appeared in Baptist Press, the SBC's official news service, and in that article, the writer offered the comment that "women graduates of Southern Baptist seminaries usually enter church vocations in education or music, become teachers or are appointed as unordained missionaries."[27] At the next gathering of the Southern Baptist Convention in June 1965, Addie's name was not mentioned nor was the topic of women's ordination addressed—at least not from the floor.[28]

In August 1964, Addie moved to Vermont, settled into a new home, and was in the pulpit on Sunday, August 30. That day's church bulletin included a note about her arrival: "We are very happy to have Rev. Addie Davis with us today as our supply minister. Rev. Davis will assume the ministry of this church the first of September." The bulletin also offered an invitation: "Sunday, September 13 at 7:00 p.m. there will be an Installation Service and Reception for Rev. Addie E. Davis, who arrived Monday from Covington, Virginia, to be the minister of this church. Plan to attend this service and meet your Pastor."[29]

Addie was the second woman to serve as the pastor of First Baptist, Readsboro, and in the earliest days of her tenure there, she discovered "little to no resistance to her" as a result of her gender. In 1964, the church at Readsboro had approximately 150 members. Because it was the only Protestant church in town, the congregation included many non-Baptist members.

During her years in Vermont, Addie was active in her community and among Baptists in the state. She participated in the Windham Baptist Association, serving on several committees. Because she was so active in the Vermont Baptist State Convention, the convention elected her as recorder in 1969. In 1971, the convention named her Vermont's pastor of the year,

[26] Flowers, *Into the Pulpit*, 28.

[27] "Church Ordains Woman to Pastoral Ministry," Baptist Press, August 12, 1964.

[28] Flowers, *Into the Pulpit*, 28.

[29] Church bulletin, 30 August 1964, First Baptist Church, Readsboro, VT, Addie Davis Papers, Jack Tarver Library.

an impressive accomplishment for someone who had just seven years earlier wondered if she would ever pastor a church.[30] On June 25, 1972, Addie submitted her resignation to First Baptist, having accepted the pastorate of Second Baptist Church of East Providence, Rhode Island.

Leaving Vermont must have been difficult, but Addie felt a strong call to her new church in Rhode Island. She began her pastorate at Second Baptist, a church of approximately 250 members, on September 17, 1972. Serving in "Roger Williams' territory," Addie continued to be a pioneer. She was the first woman pastor of this church. She also served as Rhode Island's first woman pastor, the first woman elected to the Providence Baptist Theological Circle, and the first woman vice president and then president of the East Providence Clergy Association.[31]

During her time at East Providence, Addie found that her gender did not impede her ministry. Although the congregation had taken a bit of time to adjust before they accepted her leadership, she discovered her new church to be warm and welcoming of her.[32] After many years of ministering in New England, Addie concluded that the people there, once they found a minister to be worthy and to have integrity, wholeheartedly supported the ministry of that person.[33]

In 1982, after ten years at East Providence, Davis resigned her position at Second Baptist Church and left New England to return to Covington, Virginia. Addie did not view this as a retirement from ministry but instead as a return home. With seventeen years of pastoral experience, Addie hoped to find a Baptist church near Covington to pastor. She was surprised by an even more conservative attitude toward women ministers among Southern Baptists: "I had expected to be able to pick up my work and take up another church.... But I am surprised by the ultra-conservative attitude which I have found since returning."[34] Not finding a Baptist church to pastor, however, did not end Addie's ministry. In 1983, she was invited to serve at Rich Patch Union Church, a rural ecumenical church in Alleghany County, where she served as co-pastor until her death.

[30] "What Ever Happened to Addie Davis?" 1; Davis, interview by McKenzie.

[31] "What Ever Happened to Addie Davis?" 4.

[32] Davis, interview by McKenzie.

[33] Ibid.

[34] Davis, interview by Bentley.

Addie Davis passed away on December 3, 2005, following a brief illness.[35] News of her death reminded moderate and progressive Baptists of the gift Addie had been. What made her so remarkable was not her place in history as the first woman to be ordained by a Southern Baptist church; it was her humility, her compassion, and her warm spirit. She faithfully followed God's calling, serving three churches as pastor or co-pastor. In those churches, she focused on "caring for the people and being with them in times of crisis."[36] Indeed, Addie was a remarkable human being, a persistent and compassionate woman, a gifted pastor, and a woman of great humility. Baptists could not have selected a better person to be "first."

Suggested Reading

Addie Davis, interview by Eljee Bentley, June 9, 1985, recorded interview located in the Alma Hunt Library of the Woman's Missionary Union, Birmingham, AL.

Keith E. Durso and Pamela R. Durso, "'Cherish the Dream God Has Given You': The Story of Addie Davis," in *Courage and Hope: The Stories of Ten Baptist Women Ministers*, ed. Keith E. Durso and Pamela R. Durso (Macon, GA: Mercer University Press, 2005), 18–30.

Pamela R. Durso, "Remembering Addie," in *The World Is Waiting for You: Celebrating the Fiftieth Ordination Anniversary of Addie Davis*, ed. Pamela R. Durso and LeAnn Gunter Johns (Macon, GA: Smyth and Helwys Publishers, 2014), 1–26.

Elizabeth H. Flowers, *Into the Pulpit: Southern Baptist Women and Power since World War II* (Chapel Hill: University of North Carolina Press, 2012).

[35] "Addie Davis, first woman ordained as Southern Baptist pastor, dies at 88," Associated Baptist Press, December 9, 2005.

[36] Ibid.

William J. Reynolds (1920–2009), *Church Music Leader*

Ministry

David W. Music

Baptists of the twenty-first century generally consider music to be a critical and important activity of the church. Vocal and instrumental ensembles; soloists; children's, youth, and senior adult musical activities; and congregational singing are key elements in the worship, evangelism, education, ministry, and fellowship of Baptist churches.

However, this high regard for music was not always the case among Baptists. While the denomination has long recognized the value of congregational singing, the concept of a music ministry that touches each member of a congregation at different points in their lives and in different contexts is a relatively recent development. Before World War II, church music among Baptists was often a haphazard affair, with untrained leaders, limited denominational leadership or support, and little recognition of its potential or effectiveness in worship services. Choirs were virtually nonexistent and congregational singing was restricted primarily to a single type, the gospel song.

In 1941, Baptists in the South began to address these needs by establishing a Church Music Department at the Baptist Sunday School Board in Nashville, Tennessee, to provide literature and training programs for the churches of the denomination. State Baptist conventions followed by organizing their own church music departments. After the conclusion of World War II, the leadership of the national and state church music departments and the seminaries increasingly promoted the value of a comprehensive, well-rounded music ministry for all ages. The result was spectacular growth in the number both of people involved in the music of Baptist churches and of leaders who were called into full-time music ministry. A large part of the credit for this expanded program was due to William J. Reynolds.

Born in Atlantic, Iowa, on April 2, 1920, the son of a revival music leader, William J. Reynolds grew up in Oklahoma and was converted at the age of five. He attended Oklahoma Baptist University for two years and graduated from Southwest Missouri State College (now Missouri State University). He then became a Master of Sacred Music student at Southwestern Baptist Theological Seminary. This was during World War II, and after a year and a half of study he interrupted his education to join the United States Maritime Service, serving on an oil tanker in the Atlantic Ocean. After his discharge, he returned to the seminary and graduated with his MSM, then enrolled as a Master of Music student at North Texas State College (now the University of North Texas), from which he graduated a year later. Reynolds was called as Minister of Music and Youth at the First Baptist Church of Ardmore, Oklahoma, but served that congregation for only four months before being called as Minister of Music for the First Baptist Church of Oklahoma City, the largest Baptist church in the state. At that time he served as only the second full-time music minister among Baptists in Oklahoma.[1]

In 1955, after Reynolds had served the Oklahoma City congregation for nine years, the Church Music Department of the Baptist Sunday School Board in Nashville called him as a part-time music editor. While in Nashville, he pursued a Doctor of Education in music at George Peabody College for Teachers. After finishing his course work, he became a full-time employee of the Church Music Department. He continued to serve as a music editor until he was named the secretary (i.e., director) of the department in 1971. In the meantime, George Peabody College awarded his EdD degree. Reynolds retired as director of the department after serving in that capacity for nine years, but Southwestern Baptist Theological Seminary immediately called him to serve on the faculty of the School of Church Music. There he taught introductory courses in church music for theology and religious education students and hymnology classes for church music majors.[2] He taught at Southwestern for eighteen years until his retirement from the faculty in 1998. He eventually moved back to Nashville, where he passed away on March 28, 2009.

---

[1] The first was R. Paul Green at Immanuel Baptist Church in Tulsa. "Full-time" in this context means that the position involved music only and was not a combination position with another ministry. For a study of Green's ministry see David W. Music, "R. Paul Green, Pioneer Minister of Music," *Baptist History and Heritage* 48: 3 (Fall 2013): 71–91.

[2] For details regarding the unfortunate circumstances of his retirement from the Baptist Sunday School Board see David W. Music, *William J. Reynolds: Church Musician* (Macon, GA: Smyth & Helwys, 2013), 75–77.

Reynolds made his greatest contributions to Baptists in three areas: (1) as an employee (and especially as director) of the Church Music Department of the Baptist Sunday School Board, (2) as the editor of the 1975 *Baptist Hymnal*, and (3) as a congregational song leader. Reynolds's many gifts and his long tenure in the Church Music Department led to his being recognized as one of the leading Southern Baptist musicians of his era; thus it was natural for him to be chosen to become the third director of the Church Music Department. As head of the department, he built on the foundations established by his predecessors B. B. McKinney and W. Hines Sims but brought his own distinctive abilities and viewpoints to the organization. He sought both to respect the history of Southern Baptists and to be forward-looking. Baptists had long based much of their musical repertory on the gospel song, and this style continued to be important to many churches. At the same time, church music ministries were growing and becoming more sophisticated, and they were increasingly capable of performing a greater variety of music. Reynolds and the department sought to meet the growing needs of the churches by providing educational materials, opportunities, personal examples, and new music to sing and play, but they did not abandon the heritage of church music that was already familiar and immediately meaningful. While attention was given to the large and medium-sized churches that could afford to hire full-time or combination music ministers, the needs of the smaller churches that made up the bulk of the Southern Baptist Convention were not neglected. Encouraged and supported by the Church Music Department, choral and handbell groups proliferated, ensemble and keyboard festivals and workshops were organized, and seminary music schools greatly increased in enrollment as scores of young people committed themselves to full-time church service through music ministry. Reynolds's role in this concentration of effort is aptly summed up by Terry W. York who writes,

> Bill Reynolds, as Secretary of the Church Music Department, like a magnet, had brought the center of Southern Baptist Church Music to the Church Music Department of the Baptist Sunday School Board in Nashville. No longer were church musicians looking first or foremost to seminary and college music deans for direction, no longer were they looking to evangelistic singers for identity, no longer were they looking to the music ministers of the largest churches first and foremost for inspiration, no longer were music missionaries the only saints among us; all that was now posited in

the department, the office, and the persona that was Dr. William J. Reynolds.[3]

During Reynolds's tenure as director of the department, the church music enterprise of Southern Baptists became widely recognized as one the most progressive and influential such programs in the United States.

The increasing growth and sophistication of Baptist music ministries is particularly evident in the hymnal that Reynolds edited. In 1956, the Baptist Sunday School Board had issued *Baptist Hymnal*, for which Reynolds had been a member of the committee. While this book represented a step forward from its predecessor, the *Broadman Hymnal* (1940), it was very much a nineteenth-century book, with little representation from the twentieth century except for the gospel songs of B. B. McKinney. Whole categories of historic hymnody, for example plainsong and African American spirituals, were mostly missing. Under Reynolds's leadership, the 1975 *Baptist Hymnal* gave attention to these and other types of song, including some of the first fruits of the British New English Renaissance of hymnody and the new youth-oriented music styles.[4] A particular emphasis of the book was on the inclusion of hymn texts and tunes by living or recently deceased Baptist authors and composers. As noted by a reviewer of the volume,

This is a hymnal for the people: it is not a selection of hymns and tunes that appeal only to the musically trained, nor for those to whom the nostalgia of the texts of the revival eras of their childhood constitute the limit of their only desire in hymnody. The compilers have skillfully selected the best of the gospel songs, and retained only texts and tunes that are meaningful and worshipful. To these still useful words and tunes for the worship of God, the compilers have added a group of relatively recent compositions (chosen from many hundreds written in this century) that will help congregations and individuals worship with understanding and mind and soul in situations that now confront them in a rapidly changing world.[5]

---

[3] Terry W. York, quoted in Music, *William J. Reynolds*, 74.

[4] The New English Renaissance was a renewal of hymn writing that began in England during the 1960s and emphasized the use of modern English with a strong focus on social aspects of the gospel. Youth-oriented music included songs from 1960s folk musicals such as *Good News* and individual songs like Ralph Carmichael's "He's Everything to Me."

[5] William Watkins Reid, review of *Baptist Hymnal*, *The Hymn* 27, 3 (July 1976): 92.

The reviewer went on to point out that this was "a young people's hymnbook," containing 181 texts and tunes from 118 authors and composers who had been born since 1880, "a figure we believe larger than in any other current congregational hymnal."[6] Essentially, *Baptist Hymnal* 1975 was a "catch-up" book, bringing Baptists into the mainstream of hymnody but also introducing new styles and individual hymns into the common repertory of congregational song for all English-speaking Christian groups in the United States. At the same time, as observed by the reviewer, gospel songs continued to fill an important place in the hymnal, including some, such as C. Austin Miles's popular "In the Garden," that were well known among Baptists but had not appeared in the two previous hymnals. The Sunday School Board distributed more than five and a half million copies of the hymnal, and while this was not quite as many as its predecessor, that probably had as much to do with the serious theological/political controversies that began to sweep through the Southern Baptist Convention shortly after its publication as with any aspect of the book.

Reynolds served for fifteen consecutive years as music director for annual meetings of the Southern Baptist Convention, by far the longest tenure to that point for anyone in that position.[7] This responsibility involved securing hymn leaders, instrumentalists, and special music for the various sessions, as well as his personally leading congregational singing. He also served as music leader for the large meetings of the Baptist World Alliance and Baptist Youth World Conferences, and he typically directed an evening of hymn singing (as well as the daily worship services) at the Baptist Church Music Conference weeks in Ridgecrest, North Carolina, and Glorieta, New Mexico, where hundreds of church musicians were present. During his years on the faculty at Southwestern Seminary he led annual chapel services of hymn and carol sings. He conducted dozens of hymn sings for local churches and other organizations, particularly after the publication of the 1975 *Baptist Hymnal.* Reynolds approached these events with a thorough understanding of the principles of effective congregational singing and leading that made a remarkable impact on those who attended these meetings. The confidence with which he led the singing and the creativity of technique he employed served as a model for many

---

[6] Ibid., 92–93.

[7] He had served a one-year appointment as convention music director earlier in his career, meaning that he held leadership of the convention's music for a total of sixteen years.

ministers of music, who often took the concepts, and even his specific methods, back to their home churches.

While the three activities mentioned above were probably the ones through which most Baptists encountered Reynolds and his work, several other areas of his work made a significant impact both within and outside the denomination. He had a lifelong interest in the study of hymnody, and this led to several important publications. He authored the first textbook designed specifically for use in hymnology classes, *A Survey of Christian Hymnody* (1963), which was widely used in colleges and seminaries of many denominations. A reviewer of the book called it "a unique publication prepared by a man who understands hymnic scholarship but also the mind and heart of the ordinary individual" and noted its "distinctive feature," an appendix of 160 hymns that served to illustrate the prose text.[8] Reynolds was personally involved in two more editions, coauthored with Milburn Price. The book reached a fifth edition in 2010, still following the basic format and much of the original content of its initial printing.

Reynolds also published the first hymnal handbook for Southern Baptists, *Hymns of Our Faith* (1964), a companion to the 1956 *Baptist Hymnal*.[9] After publication of the 1975 *Baptist Hymnal*, he wrote *Companion to Baptist Hymnal* (1976). To this point, he is the only person to have been the sole author of two commercially published hymnal companions. Another of his books, *Congregational Singing* (1975), was unique in dealing significantly with the performance of congregational song rather than only with its history or philosophy. He was also commissioned to write books on two prominent church music organizations, the School of Church Music at Southwestern Baptist Theological Seminary and the Church Music Department of the Baptist General Convention of Oklahoma.

Reynolds wrote dozens of articles on music among Baptists, dealing particularly with two prominent denominational musicians of the previous generation, B. B. McKinney and his own uncle, I. E. Reynolds, who had been the first director of the church music department at Southwestern Seminary. He was called upon frequently to address groups of church

---

[8] Deane Edwards, review of *A Survey of Christian Hymnody*, *The Hymn* 15, 3 (July 1963): 92.

[9] A hymnal handbook (or companion) typically describes the origins and first publications of each text and tune in a hymnal and provides biographies of the authors, translators, composers, and arrangers.

musicians or other denominational meetings on topics ranging from acoustics for church music to the future of congregational song. In addition to the writings that were aimed primarily at scholars and professional ministers, he wrote books that provided laypersons with a greater understanding of and appreciation for congregational song, including *Christ and the Carols* (1967) and *Songs of Glory: Stories of 300 Great Hymns and Gospel Songs* (1990). His work in hymnology helped stimulate a younger generation of Baptist musicians, who produced a steady stream of books, articles, and dissertations on the subject.[10] Perhaps the greatest tribute to the impact of Reynolds's scholarship came in the *Handbook to the Baptist Hymnal* (1992), a companion to *Baptist Hymnal* 1991. Whereas the two previous hymnal companions had been written by Reynolds alone, the 1992 book was the work of a team of nine Baptist scholars (including Reynolds), a mark of how hymnological study had grown among Baptists since Reynolds's pioneering work.

William J. Reynolds was also a prolific composer and arranger of music. As a music editor at the Baptist Sunday School Board, it was his responsibility to make sure that the magazines published by the board—especially *The Church Musician*—contained music that was both accessible and challenging.[11] Because *The Church Musician* was issued monthly, a large amount of music was needed. At the time Reynolds began his work at the Sunday School Board, there were few Southern Baptist composers who had the experience and insight to supply the desired materials. Because of this and the tight schedule of publication, it was frequently necessary for Reynolds to provide much of the music himself, which he often did under a pseudonym. He composed, arranged, or edited more than 150 choral anthems as well as more than 150 children's songs. He also

---

[10] For a summary of the hymnological work of Baptists in America to 1990 see Paul A. Richardson, "Baptist Contributions to Hymnody and Hymnology," *Review and Expositor* 87 (1990): 69–70. According to Richardson, it is in the realm of hymnology that Baptists have made their most distinctive contribution to congregational song (pp. 70–71).

[11] *The Church Musician*, founded in 1950, was the first magazine published by the Church Music Department; it was issued monthly and remained the department's only periodical for thirteen years. The periodical contained both articles and a pull-out section of music for choirs and children's music activities. It was joined in 1963 by *The Junior Musician*, the first of a series of age- or repertory-specific magazines issued by the department. *The Church Musician* remained its flagship publication until it was superseded by the quarterly *Church Musician Today* in 1997; *Church Musician Today* ceased publication in 2002.

composed three large choral works and wrote the words and/or music for numerous hymns, one of which, "Share His Love," became well known among Southern Baptists. In honor of his contributions to church music composition he received a lifetime achievement award from the American Society of Composers, Authors, and Publishers, one of the country's premier performing rights organizations.

Reynolds also received national and interdenominational recognition through his activities in the Hymn Society of America (in 1991 renamed the Hymn Society in the United States and Canada). He joined the society in the mid-1940s, became a member of the executive committee, and was one of the driving forces in a reorganization of the society that took place during the 1970s. After the reorganization, he served a two-year term as the society's second president in its new format and later filled a term as a member of the Editorial Advisory Board for the society's journal, *The Hymn*. He reviewed for the journal, led plenary sessions and hymn festivals at annual conferences, and was honored for his contributions to congregational song by being named a Fellow of the Hymn Society.

Reynolds also made important contributions to the heritage of shape-note singing, a tradition not as well known to the church music world at large. He enthusiastically participated in *Sacred Harp* singings during his time in Nashville, and during his years on the faculty at Southwestern Seminary he founded an annual *Sacred Harp* singing on the campus.[12] He also had a hand in editing and proofreading the 1971 and 1991 revisions of the book as well as supervising a facsimile reprinting of the 1859 edition.

Perhaps Reynolds's greatest contribution was his service as a role model for a generation of Baptist church musicians. Essentially, he became the face of Southern Baptist church music, and his influence on the denomination's music and musicians was enormous. He elevated the status of music and musicians among Baptists and brought a new emphasis on professionalism, scholarship, and creativity to the use of music in the denomination. Ministers of music, scholars, composers, and text writers emulated the example he set, leading to a remarkable period of growth and

---

[12] The *Sacred Harp* was a tune book that was published in 1844 by two Baptists in the South, B. F. White and E. J. King. The book used four-shape shape-note notation and contained primarily eighteenth-century compositions by New England composers and folk hymn melodies that were popular in the Southern states. The book has been in continuous use in revised editions since its first publication. The Southwestern Seminary singing was eventually named in Reynolds's honor.

maturity in Baptist church music. He also brought visibility and recognition of the contributions of Baptists to the larger world of church music. Reynolds's impact has been succinctly summed up in his published biography:

While no single person could have brought this about, a large amount of the credit for helping make Baptist church music the vigorous young Hercules it became belongs to him. Styles, emphases, and institutions have changed, but Reynolds's influence lives on in the music he composed, the books and articles he wrote, the hymnals he edited, and—above all—the lives he touched as song leader, teacher, administrator, minister of music, husband, father, friend, and follower of Jesus Christ.[13]

Suggested Reading

"An Interview with William J. Reynolds," *The Hymn* 44, no. 4 (October 1993): 15–19.

David W. Music, *William J. Reynolds: Church Musician* (Macon, GA: Smyth and Helwys, 2013).

David W. Music, "William Jensen Reynolds," in James Leo Garrett, Jr., ed., *The Legacy of Southwestern: Writings That Shaped a Tradition* (North Richland Hills, TX: Smithfield Press, 2002), 309–18.

Jeannie Reynolds, "William Jensen Reynolds: Showing the Love of God," *Tennessee Baptist History* 10 (Fall 2008): 45–56.

[13] Music, *William J. Reynolds*, 92.

Glen Harold Stassen (1936–2014),
A Pacesetting Baptist Peacemaker

Ethics

Larry C. Ashlock

Henri Nouwen once said, "We cannot love issues, but we can love people, and the love of people reveals to us the way to deal with issues."[1] If ever there was a person who incarnated the life of loving people as a way to deal with moral issues, then it was Glen Harold Stassen. He was a people person and a problem solver, and he understood that both people and problems were interwoven and often embedded in even deeper moral conflict. He took seriously the role of peacemaker as Christ had stated in the Sermon on the Mount, and he poured his life into bringing people together in order to resolve differences and problems. Stassen's name, in this sense, became synonymous with "peace" and "peacemaking." Peace as the virtue, along with the attendant just peacemaking ethical theory, became the life thesis by which he influenced the world.

Stassen's name was also synonymous with "Baptist," as he was a part of six different types of Baptist groups from childhood until his death. He, of course, was foremost a Christian, but he remained a member of Baptist churches throughout his lifetime.[2] Hallmark Baptist principles such as discipleship, religious liberty, human rights, and, of course, the pursuit of justice and peace permeated his personal and academic life.[3] His influence, as

---

[1] John Dear, ed., *Henri Nouwen: The Road to Peace* (Maryknoll, NY: Orbis Books, 1998), 46.

[2] David P. Gushee, "An Interpretation of the Christian Ethics of Glen Harold Stassen: Incarnational Discipleship for Apocalyptic Times," *Perspectives in Religious* Studies 40, 3 (Summer 2013): 191.

[3] Michael L. Westmoreland-White, "Glen Harold Stassen: Follower of a Thick Jesus," in *Ethics as if Jesus Mattered: Essays in Honor of Glen H. Stassen*, ed. Rick Axtell, Michelle Tooly, and Michael L. Westmoreland-White (Macon, GA: Smyth and Helwys Publishing, 2014), 11.

a result, extended well beyond his denominational attachments, which allowed him to spread peace wherever he traveled.

Peace at Home and Beyond

Glen Stassen's family roots provided him with the foundation that led to his later global impact. Glen was born into the home of Harold and Esther Stassen on leap day, February 29, 1936. His parents were North American Baptists living in Minnesota. His father had been elected as the youngest governor in Minnesota history and eventually served in the Eisenhower administration as a peace envoy. Harold helped to charter the United Nations and was a prominent member of the Republican Party who also ran nine times for United States president. Glen's mother was an artist who also was instrumental in her husband's political career. They had a loving Christian marriage, and their peaceable spirits provided a stable home for Glen and his sister.

Glen's father was away for part of Glen's childhood while he served in World War II. There was, in fact, a time when the family thought that Harold had been lost in the war. This event, the horrors of war itself, and the atomic bombs dropped on Hiroshima and Nagasaki left a lasting imprint on Glen's life and would later inspire his efforts at peacemaking. The abuses caused by nationalistic authoritarianism and tyranny helped to shape Glen's views on human rights.[4] The elder Stassen had indeed returned home from the war and also became an active voice for human rights for all, as Glen says, "including racial minorities."[5] The events also left a critical mark on Glen's mind. These external events helped to shape Glen's life in his formative years but also shaped his character in a way that prepared him for his later calling.

His roots were certainly not buried in political elitism or social activism; rather, they were embedded in a love for Christ and God's word that prompted him to address key practical moral concerns.[6] Minnesotan populism also helped him to identify with those who lacked political influence and who had grown up with deep needs. He, in fact, often told his students that his grandfather was a German-immigrant tomato farmer with a deep

---

[4] Gushee, "Interpretation of the Christian Ethics of Glen Harold Stassen," 185.

[5] Glen Stassen, *A Thicker Jesus: Incarnational Discipleship in a Secular Age* (Louisville, KY: Westminster John Knox Press, 2012), ix.

[6] Gushee, "Interpretation of the Christian Ethics of Glen Harold Stassen," 181.

commitment to integrity, itself being a hallmark of "just-ness."[7] All of his developmental experiences left a deep imprint on Glen's moral growth. He would mature and spend his life advocating for nonviolence, justice, and human rights.[8] Each of these various virtues and values were planted within Stassen's heart and would bear later the fruit of peacemaking. He, in fact, became the quintessential peacemaking Christian soul, and it showed in every aspect of his life.

Sewing Christ's Peace into a Tattered World

Scholars are rarely self-made, often being influenced and identified by their mentors. The well-orbed moral approach that characterized Stassen's ethics was not created in a theoretical vacuum. His theological and ethical training provided him with a critical foundation in Christian "realism" that he gained from several key influences in his life. Stassen's academic preparation became quite useful in his practical efforts at just peacemaking.

Academic influences. The foremost guidance was gained from the Protestant theological ethicist Reinhold Niebuhr. Stassen encountered Niebuhr's teachings on realism while he was a student at Union Theological Seminary. He would further shape Niebuhr's influential ethical method, then apply it throughout his academic and professional life to help solve challenging moral issues. He also was a serious student of Scripture, and the Old Testament professor James Muilenburg provided him with an understanding of "rhetorical criticism." Stassen's New Testament professor W. D. Davies's studies in the Jewish background to the New Testament and his work on the Sermon on the Mount proved to be catalytic for the young scholar. Both areas of biblical study contributed to Stassen's later research and writing on transforming initiatives in Jesus' sermon. Dietrich Bonhoeffer's life and writings were also a powerful shaping force in the formulation of his peace ethic.[9] Stassen's own German-immigrant family roots and his facility with the language were instrumental in

[7] Gushee writes that Stassen was quick to note that he was from "German-immigrant stock," not German stock. He was proud of his German roots, but they were understandably veiled for much of his life due to the later extremes of Nazism and the post-WWII reaction to Nazi atrocities. His family spoke German inside the home and English outside of it. He also traveled extensively in Germany and taught there on a number of occasions (ibid.).

[8] Joyong Lee and Laura Rector, "Glen Stassen: Incarnational Disciple of Jesus," *Christian Ethics Today* 22, no. 5 (Fall 2014): 5.

[9] Westmoreland-White, "Glen Harold Stassen," 10, in *Ethics as if Jesus Mattered.*

his interest and strong attachment to Bonhoeffer. He was impacted greatly by Bonhoeffer's resistance to Nazism since Glen's own family had immigrated to the United States because of their refusal to fall prey to Prussian authoritarianism and tyranny.[10]

Stassen eventually chose to pursue doctoral studies in the South so that he could participate simultaneously in the Civil Rights Movement.[11] Naturally, the life and writings of Martin Luther King, Jr., contributed to Stassen's moral development. He proudly attended the 1963 civil rights March on Washington, D.C., and was wonderfully surprised to see his father there. He was supervised by Waldo Beach and influenced by a friend and fellow Baptist, Lonnie Kliever, as well as the Lutheran historical theologian Hans J. Hillerbrand.[12] Hillerbrand prompted Stassen's lifelong fascination with Anabaptist theology and its influence on early Baptist identity.[13] Each of these influencers contributed threads of knowledge and relationship that were being sewn into a beautiful tapestry of peace.

Stassen never allowed himself to become in person what he often warned against in his teaching and writings. He cautioned against "evading Jesus," meaning that Christians all too often ignore or misinterpret the teachings and practices of Christ, for example, in the Sermon on the Mount.[14] He believed that the Christian life consisted of "obeying his [Christ's] teachings and practicing the way of life he taught and modeled."[15] It seems inevitable that Christ's call to peacemaking would impact him.

Peacemaking, as found in the Sermon on the Mount, was the seed from which much of Stassen's moral advocacy grew to bear global fruit. He recognized the significance of the peace motif in the New Testament and its implications for the Kingdom of God. His life grew to become a peacemaking beatitude and contributed to his desire not "...to root out,

---

[10] Gushee, "Interpretation of the Christian Ethics of Glen Harold Stassen," 181, 182.

[11] Stassen, *A Thicker Jesus*, Preface, x.

[12] Westmoreland-White, "Glen Harold Stassen," in *Ethics as if Jesus Mattered*, 10.

[13] Ibid., 11.

[14] Glen H. Stassen and David P. Gushee, *Kingdom Ethics: Following Jesus in Contemporary Context* (1st ed.; Grand Rapids, MI: Eerdmans, 2003), preface.

[15] Ibid.

exclude, or do violence against those in the Christian community, or outside it, who disagree with the gospel as I understand it."[16] He also knew and advocated the type of peacemaking that sought to welcome outsiders because Jesus was a "Redeemer" and not a "Separator."[17]

Teaching and writing. Stassen's academic career spanned more than five decades at five different institutions.[18] He adopted the Minnesotan culture in his lifestyle, refusing to "put on airs," which carried over into his teaching. His own close family upbringing extended into his teaching, and students often counted him as a father and friend. He valued "humility, and integrity," and these virtues shone through in his life and teaching. He also was a populist, believing in people, so he sought to write and teach so that people might understand whether they were in the classroom or in churches.[19] He admitted that some would critique his style as being unscholarly; however, he believed that what he wrote was a "sophisticated, scholarly, even, in a sense, scientific argument for method in Christian ethics…."[20] Nevertheless, both scholars and laypersons widely recognized his precision in writing and praised his work as highly readable.

Scholarly research. It has been written that "incarnation" would be a proper lens through which to view Stassen's scholarship.[21] Many ethicists will spend their academic lives developing and then disseminating their various methods for considering ethics. Early on, Stassen began to demonstrate a similar path, but his research led ultimately to a practical focus that enabled him to craft the signature ethical method of "just peacemaking." This gave him a much wider cultural engagement than would have been possible were it not for his great desire to spread peace.

Cultural engagement. Stassen developed the concept of just peacemaking early in his scholarly work, but he never reduced it to simply a theoretical topic or an academic exercise. He embodied the rubric at home, in his work, and in wider culture. He and his wife Dorothy (Dot) Lively Stassen were married in 1957, and they had three sons. One of his sons, Bill,

---

[16] Glen H. Stassen, *Living the Sermon on the Mount: A Practical Hope for Grace and Deliverance* (San Francisco, CA: Jossey-Bass, 2006), 58.

[17] Ibid.

[18] Lee and Rector, "Glen Stassen: Incarnational Disciple of Jesus," 5.

[19] Gushee, "Interpretation of the Christian Ethics of Glen Harold Stassen," 182.

[20] Stassen, *A Thicker Jesus*, x.

[21] Ibid. Stassen's all-too-soon death cut short his development of the incarnational discipleship theme. It would have become, perhaps, his crowning ethical achievement.

pointed out at his father's memorial service in Pasadena, California, that his father's love was "not finite." He "poured all the love and enthusiasm into his family that he poured into his teaching."[22] Stassen certainly understood the moral link between love, justice, and peacemaking initiatives, and he practiced them both at home and in his wider engagements.

He saw evidence of peacemaking in worship; feeding, clothing, and housing the poor and hungry; Gentiles and Jews becoming one in the early Christian community; conflict resolution between warring nations; the practice of nonviolent direct action; and the struggle for human rights. He simply rolled up his sleeves and became involved in the world for the sake of Christ.[23] Like another pioneering Baptist ethicist, T. B. Maston, who had spoken prophetically about the subject of race, Stassen spoke out and immersed himself in the 1960s Civil Rights Movement. Here again he showed that peacemaking should be practiced in a real world. One may well recognize that inserting himself as a peacemaker into complex moral issues would lead to conflict.

Peacemaking Spirit despite Conflict

Stassen was a progressive conservative, an oxymoron by today's standards. This position helped him make countless friends among those who held similar theologies and ethical methodologies, but also this position caused him to fall out of favor with the Southern Baptist Convention leadership and Southern Baptist Theological Seminary administration where he had served as a professor from 1976–1996. Stassen's departure from the Southern Baptist Theological Seminary is well chronicled and does not require exhaustive analysis. However, it should be noted how he handled the separation. The seminary underwent a radical change in its theological approach in the late 1980s while Stassen was on faculty. Many of the professors were obsessed with the circumstances, but Stassen directed his passion towards kingdom of God "praxis." He said, "I have had some really productive conversations with the conservative faction.... I'm convinced that, if we consistently employ the peacemaking principles of Jesus, there is still hope for reconciliation."[24]

[22] Lee and Rector, "Glen Stassen: Incarnational Disciple of Jesus," 5.

[23] Glen H. Stassen, ed., *Just Peacemaking: The New Paradigm for the Ethics of Peace and War* (Cleveland, OH: The Pilgrim Press, 2008), 35.

[24] Alan Bean, "In Memoriam: Glen Stassen," in Friends of Justice blog, https://friendsofjustice.blog/2014/05/01/in-memoriam-glen-stassen/.

Peaceable Response to Critique of His Methods

There were those who regarded Stassen's trust in the biblical "efficacy of kingdom principles" as "hopelessly naive." Some said, "Glen really believed the Jesus stuff."[25] Not many scholars pursued ethics from a biblical approach, which is characteristic of much contemporary social ethics. Stassen knew this fact, but rather than making him bitter and isolated, it seemed to fuel his buoyancy.

Stassen's fresh biblical analysis of the Sermon on the Mount, for example, led him to claim that the traditional antithetical analysis of Matthew 5:21–7:12 was truly a triadic approach. He published this model in an article in the *Journal of Biblical Literature*, which was quite a distinction for someone whose academic discipline lay outside of biblical studies. The response to his approach ranged from acceptance by Willard Swartley, who termed his study "insightful," to polite disregard. Of nineteen sources that have been published since Stassen's article appeared in the *Journal of Biblical Literature* (2003), only two books and two articles refer to it, all in footnotes. Two were appreciative and two were dismissive. Craig Blomberg, for example, provided a critique that not all of Stassen's fourteen triads are "equally convincing, especially not 7.6 as foil to 7.7-11."[26] It is noteworthy that Stassen, ever the man of peace, did not become defensive. He, in fact, was ebullient, writing, "The transforming initiatives structure…has been accepted by all the New Testament scholars I have heard from, and I know of no dissent."[27] One supposes that his optimism stemmed from the fact that his ethics was not merely theoretical; instead, it served as his testimony. It was inconceivable that he would shed his ethic like some outer layer of theoretical skin because his moral theology was a matter of the heart. It was his witness.

Embodying the Message and Hope of Peace

Stassen's ethical concerns arose from deep within his faith commitment. He inspired scholars, students, and laypersons to catch his enthusiasm for addressing moral issues in a realistic way. Whether it was acting on his passion for civil rights, seeking a resolution to the divide in the Southern

---

[25] Ibid.

[26] Blomberg quoted in Michael Willett Newheart, "Stassen on the Mount: The Ethicist as Exegete," in *Ethics as if Jesus Mattered*, 29.

[27] Stassen quoted in Newheart, "Stassen on the Mount," 29.

Baptist Convention, or putting an end to the threat of wars, he desired peace to permeate all that he believed and practiced. Whether one adheres to his ethical positions is hardly the point. He simply sought to have a seat at the peacemaking table and to contribute to moral discussions within the church and wider global community. This attitude enabled him to find his place among Baptist, and Christian, peace influencers and to help shape further peacemaking efforts in several key areas.

Shaping Influences in a Theology of Peace

Transforming initiatives. It is widely recognized that Stassen sought for his work on the Sermon on the Mount to break new ground on the sermon's interpretation and application. He claimed that the sermon's central section (5:21–7:12) contained carefully crafted triads that were consistent across each of fourteen pericopes. This view diverged from the traditional scholarly understanding that 5:21-48 presents a dyadic structure—antitheses. While this aim may not have made the impact that he believed it had made, it did call attention to the practical peacemaking relevance of the Lord's teaching in a wide variety of daily circumstances. If anything, Stassen's work holds profound implications for discipleship, a core Baptist value. Stassen challenged Christians to embody this role of disciple-peacemaker, or incarnational disciple, in what some believe to be his crowning achievement.

Incarnational discipleship. Stassen penned *A Thicker Jesus: Incarnational Discipleship in a Secular Age* (2012), which provided an ethical framework and path for a rapidly changing world. His trademark realism, in contrast to Platonic idealism, led him to advocate for a form of discipleship that was grounded in practical living. It became evident that his understanding of peacemaking was maturing into a fully developed ethic that called for a radical form of discipleship as demonstrated in the Sermon on the Mount. Stassen believed that a "thick" interpretation of Jesus would lead Christians not to apply lofty ideals to reality but to follow the Savior's example in addressing historical struggles. He sought to bring the Christian Scriptures to bear upon current social problems "on their own terms in the language of history, politics, economics, and sciences."[28]

---

[28] Sarah A. Neeley, "Reviewed Work: A Thicker Jesus: Incarnational Discipleship in a Secular Age," in *Journal of the Society of Christian Ethics* 33, (Fall/Winter 2013): 200–201.

Stassen's impact would be lost were it not for the fact that he had grounded his views in a clearly Christological theology. His strong biblical approach that drew from both Old Testament prophecy and New Testament teachings provided him with fertile ground to encourage suffering Christians in an evil world. Real peacemaking requires people to follow Christ's example and embody his peace in the midst of deeply divisive moral concerns.

Just peacemaking practices. Due to Stassen's untimely death, just peacemaking represents the furthest reach of his moral thought. It should come as no surprise that Stassen poured his energies into the nuclear war issue. He had majored in nuclear physics at the University of Virginia and worked in nuclear research as a military contractor after graduation in 1957. His early life experiences, study, and work helped him come to the conclusion that he needed to study how to keep the destructive power of nuclear weapons in check.

The genius of just peacemaking, however, lies in its approach. Just peacemaking seeks to answer a "different question" than traditional just war theory or pacifism. Those approaches focus on justification for war, whereas just peacemaking spotlights prevention. It comes as no real surprise that praxis-driven Stassen, and the wide range of scholars who collaborated with him on the work, focused not on ideals or principles but on "realistic, historically situated practices" that had been empirically proven to demonstrate effectiveness in preventing war.[29] His approach to this most vexing moral issue truly reflected the man and characterized his entire life.

Conclusion

Stassen's own pilgrimage as a Baptist peacemaker is reflected in the totality of his life. His efforts to bring about conflict resolution at Southern Seminary and among warring nations are reminiscent of the Anabaptists who were noted for the same, even when they held sharp disagreements with one another. His passionate pursuit of rights for all humankind, whether among African Americans in their longing for full civil rights or in his pursuit of a reduction in military spending, arms trading, and nuclear warheads, reflects his strong belief in core Baptist principles. Stassen recognized the destructiveness of racism as well as nuclear annihilation, so he

[29] Glen H. Stassen, "The Unity, Realism, and Obligatoriness of Just Peacemaking Theory," in *Journal of the Society of Christian Ethics* 23, no. 1 (2003): 171–94.

pursued justice and peace for all. Even though his life ended all too soon by human measurements, he planted the seeds for strong biblical discipleship in his last writings that called for believers to embody the teachings of the Savior whom he loved so deeply. Glen Stassen definitely bent the arc of the moral universe toward peace, and we are better for it.

Suggested Reading

Glen H. Stassen and David P. Gushee, *Kingdom Ethics: Following Jesus in Contemporary Context* (1st ed.; Grand Rapids, MI: Eerdmans, 2003).

Glen H. Stassen, ed., *Just Peacemaking: The New Paradigm for the Ethics of Peace and War.* (new ed.; Cleveland, OH: The Pilgrim Press, 2008).

Glen Harold Stassen, *A Thicker Jesus: Incarnational Discipleship in a Secular Age* (Louisville, KY: Westminster John Knox Press, 2012).

Index